365 GREAT BARBECUE & GRILLING RECIPES

LONNIE GANDARA
WITH PEGGY FALLON

A JOHN BOSWELL ASSOCIATES BOOK

HarperPaperbacks
A Division of HarperCollins*Publishers*

HarperPaperbacks   *A Division of* HarperCollins*Publishers*
10 East 53rd Street, New York, N.Y. 10022

A hardcover edition of this book was published in 1990 by HarperCollins*Publishers*.

Cover design and illustration by Rich Rossiter
Text design by Nigel Rollings
Index by Maro Riofrancos

First HarperPaperbacks printing: June 1993

Printed in the United States of America

HarperPaperbacks and colophon are trademarks of HarperCollins*Publishers*

20 19 18 17 16 15

Acknowledgments

The title page may read "with Peggy Fallon," but there would not be a book without Peggy—my right arm and left brain. I could never have done it without her.

Thanks to Kass Kaspiac, who is always there when I need her. Thanks also to Annette Boyer and Dee Villaflor for their timely efforts.

Contents

Great Grilling

Barbecuing over an open fire is probably the oldest cooking technique in the world, and it's still everyone's favorite. Whether your equipment is a humble hibachi, a Cadillac of kettle grills, or a high-tech gas model, the results are always exciting.

This book has given me an opportunity to share my favorite barbecue and grilling recipes. Some may surprise you; all, I hope, will delight you. They are extremely easy and represent my firm belief that barbecuing is a great way to relieve pressure on the busiest cook.

To make sure that every meal you grill is great, here is a brief summary of all the information you'll need to become king (or queen) of the coals.

THE BASICS

CHOICE OF FUEL

Lump Charcoal

Advantage: Burns hot and slow. No chemical additives. You need to use only half as much as other types.
Disadvantage: Comes in irregular chunks. Must be broken into more uniform pieces before use. Throws sparks.

Standard Briquets

Advantage: Much easier and safer to use than lump charcoal.
Disadvantage: Chemical base must be burned off, which takes 15 to 20 minutes.

Instant Lighting Briquets

Advantage: Start quickly. Convenient to use.
Disadvantage: Cost much more than other fuels.

Aromatic Wood Chips and Chunks

Advantage: Give a unique smoked flavor to foods.
Disadvantage: Must soak in water for at least 30 minutes before placing over lighted charcoal.

Propane Gas

Advantage: Extremely convenient and inexpensive. Provides instant heat.

Disadvantage: Provides less smoky flavor, though any differences are virtually undetectable in quick-cooking foods.

FUEL TIPS

- All types of charcoal should be stored in a tightly covered container because they will absorb moisture from the air, making them slower to start.

- A strong-scented wood, such as mesquite, hickory, maple, or oak, actually flavors the food; milder types add a general smoky quality.

- Use a tasteless vegetable oil in place of lighter fluid to avoid chemical fumes.

HOW TO START A FIRE

Charcoal Chimney Starter: Place crumbled newspaper on bottom and fill with briquets. No starter fluid needed.

Electric Starter: This simple metal loop needs an outdoor outlet nearby. Use as directed by manufacturer.

Charcoal Lighter Fluid: Let soak into coals for a few minutes before lighting. Be sure to allow at least 20 minutes for all fluid to burn off before placing any food on grill.

Wood or Paraffin Blocks: Allow extra time for the fire to get going.

HOW MUCH CHARCOAL?

Most serious grilling requires a bed of charcoal about 2 inches deep (that's a double layer of briquets) and about 2 inches larger around than the food you're going to grill.

For small amounts of quick-cooking foods, a single layer of briquets will suffice.

HOW HOT?

Gas grills have their own temperature controls, which makes heat regulation easy. Simply turn to the setting for hot, medium-hot, medium, or low. Most models recommend allowing 15 minutes to preheat the lava rocks.

Note: *Distance from the heat is preset on gas grills. Directions in the recipes for distance from the coals apply to charcoal grills only.*

For charcoal grills, allow 25 to 35 minutes for coals to reach temperature for a hot fire. Ironically, unless you use an existing fire that has burned down, it takes longer to obtain a lower heat. For foil cooking which requires medium heat, allow 45 minutes. For low heat, use an existing fire.

Distance from the heat, opening of vents, and whether grill is covered or not will also affect heat. In general, the wider the vents, the hotter the fire. Covered grills will cook about 20 percent faster than uncovered. When in doubt, refer to manufacturer's instructions.

HOW CAN YOU TELL?

In daylight, a hot fire will be covered by gray ash. At night it will glow red.

To test, hold the palm over your hand about 5 inches from the coals. If you cannot hold it there longer than

2 to 3 seconds—the fire is hot
3 to 4 seconds—the fire is medium-hot
4 to 6 seconds—the fire is medium
7 to 9 seconds—the fire is low

HOT TIPS FOR COOL GRILLERS

- If you don't have a chimney starter, place charcoal in a pyramid to light. It allows air to circulate, resulting in a faster-starting fire.
- To clean grill rack, simply place over hot coals, heat for about 5 minutes, and brush with a stiff wire brush to loosen any charred bits.
- Always heat the grill rack and brush with oil before placing food on it. This reduces sticking and helps produce those distinctive grill marks you see in restaurants.
- Food to be grilled should be cool but not cold. Bring large cuts of meat to room temperature before grilling to shorten cooking time and help food cook more evenly.
- Try not to pierce meat unnecessarily, as juices will be lost. Use tongs for turning.
- If fire burns too hot, spread out the charcoal and, with a kettle grill, close vents halfway.

- If fire burns too low, tap ash from briquets and push them closer together. Then add more briquets to the outer edges of the fire.
- Always soak bamboo skewers for at least 30 minutes to prevent burning.
- Never use gasoline or other highly volatile fluids to ignite charcoal. Likewise, never add starter fluid to an existing fire.
- Always use tools with long handles and fireproof mitts to protect hands.
- Dress for the occasion. Don't wear clothing that has loose, flowing sleeves.

Now, let's get grilling!

Chapter 1

Hot Beginnings

Get the party started on a warm note with appetizers and hors d'oeuvres hot off the grill. Be sure to have plenty of napkins on hand because this is food for fingers, slim bamboo skewers, or toothpicks if you like—no forks and knives required.

Party Ginger Beef Bites, Charcoal-Grilled Pizza, and Cajun Firesticks with Fire and Ice Dipping Sauce are just a few of the tempting tidbits you'll find in this chapter.

So start the fire and use it right away. Then add more coals to lead on into the main course.

1 PEPPERED LEMON SHRIMP IN THE SHELL
Prep: 25 minutes   Marinate: 2 hours   Cook: 5 to 10 minutes
Serves: 10 to 12

2 pounds extra-large shrimp, in their shells	2 large garlic cloves, minced
½ cup lemon juice	½ to 1 teaspoon cayenne, to taste
½ cup olive oil	½ teaspoon paprika
2 tablespoons coarsely ground black pepper	Lemon wedges

1. Rinse and drain shrimp. If you wish to devein them, cut a slit down back of each with a small sharp knife and remove dark vein.

2. In a large bowl, combine lemon juice, olive oil, black pepper, garlic, cayenne, and paprika. Add shrimp and toss to coat. Cover and marinate, tossing occasionally, 2 hours at room temperature, or up to 8 hours refrigerated.

3. Prepare a hot fire. Grill shrimp, turning and basting with marinade frequently, until they turn pink and are opaque throughout, about 5 to 10 minutes. Serve warm or at room temperature, with lemon wedges.

2 CAJUN FIRESTICKS WITH FIRE AND ICE DIPPING SAUCE

Prep: 15 minutes   Marinate: 1 hour   Cook: 8 to 10 minutes
Serves: 8

4 skinless, boneless chicken
   breast halves (about 1
   pound)
2 tablespoons Cajun Spice
   Blend (page 185), or less
   for the faint-hearted

1 tablespoon fresh lime juice
1 tablespoon olive oil
   Fire and Ice Dipping Sauce
   (recipe follows)

1. Rinse chicken with cold water and pat dry. Slice each breast in half lengthwise and then crosswise in quarters to make a total of 8 pieces per breast half.

2. In a medium bowl, combine chicken pieces with Cajun Spice Blend, lime juice, and olive oil. Toss to coat well. Cover and marinate 1 to 2 hours at room temperature, or up to 24 hours refrigerated. Soak 16 bamboo skewers in water at least 30 minutes to prevent burning.

3. Prepare a hot fire. Thread 2 pieces of chicken onto each skewer and place on an oiled grill set 4 to 6 inches from coals. Grill, turning occasionally, until chicken is white throughout but still moist, about 8 to 10 minutes. Serve with Fire and Ice Dipping Sauce.

3 FIRE AND ICE DIPPING SAUCE

Prep: 15 minutes   Cook: none   Makes: 1 cup

This sauce also makes an excellent marinade for chicken or lamb.

½ cup plain yogurt
2 scallions, coarsely chopped
2 jalapeño peppers, seeded
   and coarsely chopped
¼ cup loosely packed fresh
   mint leaves, or 1 teaspoon
   dried

1 tablespoon brown sugar
1 tablespoon fresh lime juice
¾ cup loosely packed cilantro
   leaves or parsley
   Salt and freshly ground
   white pepper

Combine all ingredients in a food processor or blender. Purée until smooth. Season with salt and white pepper. Cover and refrigerate until serving time.

4   CHARCOAL-GRILLED PIZZA
Prep: 10 minutes   Cook: 15 to 20 minutes   Serves: 4 to 6

The trendiest restaurants now cook pizza in wood-burning ovens—so why not use your covered barbecue at home? It's easy with frozen bread dough, and just about any pizza topping can be used. Serve as the star attraction for lunch or supper, or cut into wedges for a hot hors d'oeuvre.

2 large ripe tomatoes, cut into ½-inch-thick slices
⅓ cup olive oil (or Garlic or Herb Oil, page 180)
1 pound frozen bread dough, thawed

1 tablespoon chopped fresh basil, or 1 teaspoon dried
½ teaspoon salt
⅛ teaspoon freshly ground pepper
½ cup grated Parmesan cheese

1. Prepare a medium fire. Brush tomato slices with oil and place on an oiled grill set 4 to 6 inches above coals. Cook, turning once with a wide spatula, until softened and cooked through but still intact, 4 to 6 minutes total. Transfer tomatoes to a dish and set aside while the coals cool a bit before cooking pizza. Let fire burn down to low or close vents to reduce temperature.

2. Divide bread dough in half and flatten into 2 6-inch rounds about ½ inch thick. Generously brush one side of each pizza with oil and place oiled side down on side of oiled grill set over low coals. Cook, covered, until browned and firm, about 5 to 7 minutes. (If crust becomes too dark at edges, move to a cooler part of grill.) Brush tops of dough with oil and turn pizzas over.

3. Distribute tomato slices over pizzas and top with basil, salt, and pepper. Grill, covered, for 5 to 7 minutes, repositioning pizzas if crust is getting too dark. Divide cheese over pizzas and grill, covered, until cheese melts, about 2 minutes. Let cool slightly before serving.

---

5   PIZZA PRONTO
Prep: 5 minutes   Cook: 3 to 5 minutes   Serves: 4

4 6-inch pita breads
2 tablespoons olive oil
½ cup bottled pizza sauce

½ pound feta cheese, crumbled
¼ cup chopped black olives

1. Prepare a medium-hot fire. Brush pita breads on both sides with olive oil. Spread pizza sauce on one side of each pita, then top with cheese and olives.

2. Place pita, topping side up, on an oiled grill set 4 to 6 inches from coals. Grill until topping is hot and crust is nicely browned, about 3 to 5 minutes. Cut into quarters to serve.

6 SMOKED SALMON PIZZA
Prep: 5 minutes   Cook: 10 to 14 minutes   Serves: 4 to 6

1 pound frozen bread dough, thawed
⅓ cup olive oil
1 cup sour cream
¼ pound thinly sliced smoked salmon

¼ cup chopped red onion
1 tablespoon chopped fresh dill, or 1 teaspoon dried
¼ teaspoon freshly ground pepper
Lemon wedges, for garnish

1. Prepare a low fire. Divide bread dough in half and flatten into 2 6-inch rounds about ½ inch thick. Generously brush one side of each pizza with oil and place oiled side down on side of oiled grill. Cook, covered, until browned and firm, about 5 to 7 minutes. (If crust becomes too dark at edges, move to a cooler part of grill.)

2. Brush tops of dough with oil and turn pizzas over. Grill, moving if crust is getting too dark, 5 to 7 minutes, or until nicely browned and crisp.

3. Remove pizzas from grill and spread sour cream on top of each. Arrange salmon slices over sour cream and top with red onion, dill and pepper. Serve with lemon wedges.

---

7 PIZZA AL PESTO
Prep: 5 minutes   Cook: 15 to 19 minutes   Serves: 4 to 6

¼ cup pine nuts (pignoli)
1 pound frozen bread dough, thawed

⅓ cup olive oil
1 cup Pesto (page 182)
¼ cup grated Parmesan cheese

1. Prepare a low fire. Wrap pine nuts in foil and place on grill. Toast, turning frequently, until lightly browned, about 5 minutes. Remove and set aside.

2. Divide bread dough in half and flatten into 2 6-inch rounds about ½ inch thick. Generously brush one side of each pizza with olive oil and place oiled side down on grill. Cook, covered, until browned and firm, about 5 to 7 minutes.

3. Brush tops of dough with oil and turn pizzas over. Grill, moving if crust is getting too dark, 5 to 7 minutes, or until nicely browned and crisp.

4. Remove pizzas from grill and spread pesto over top. Sprinkle toasted pine nuts over pizzas and top with Parmesan cheese. Return to grill and cook, covered, about 2 minutes, until cheese just begins to melt. Serve hot.

8 GRILLED QUESADILLAS
Prep: 10 minutes   Cook: 3 to 4 minutes   Serves: 2 to 4

4 flour tortillas, about 8 inches
   in diameter
2 tablespoons vegetable oil
   Salsa Fresca (page 161), or 1
   cup bottled salsa

6 ounces Monterey jack
   cheese, shredded (about
   1½ cups)
Sour Cream and sprigs of
   fresh cilantro or parsley

1. Brush one side of 2 of the tortillas with oil and place oiled side down on a baking sheet. Spread 2 tablespoons Salsa Fresca over each. Divide cheese between 2 tortillas, covering them to ¼ inch of edge.

2. Top with remaining tortillas and brush with remaining oil. (If made in advance, cover well with plastic wrap and refrigerate.)

3. Oil grill and place rack over ashen coals. (NOTE: If the rungs of your grilling rack are not spaced closely together, you may wish to top with a wire screen or a piece of heavy-duty foil, punctured several times with the tines of a fork.) Grill tortillas carefully over indirect heat, turning once or twice, until cheese has melted and tortillas begin to brown, about 3 to 4 minutes total. Transfer tortillas to a wooden cutting board and cut each into quarters. Serve immediately, garnished with additional salsa, sour cream, and fresh cilantro, if desired.

---

9 PARTY GINGER BEEF BITES
Prep: 35 minutes   Marinate: 1 hour   Cook: 4 to 5 minutes
Serves: 24

Halve this recipe if you wish to serve it to a smaller group, but be forewarned, they disappear quickly.

3 pounds top round or other
   lean beef
6 garlic cloves, crushed
½ cup coarsely chopped fresh
   ginger
¼ cup soy sauce

¼ cup dry sherry or vermouth
¼ cup rice wine vinegar
¼ cup peanut or vegetable oil
2 tablespoons Asian sesame
   oil

1. Trim beef of all fat and cut into ¾-inch cubes. In a medium bowl, combine garlic, ginger, soy sauce, sherry, vinegar, peanut oil, and sesame oil. Add meat and toss to coat. Cover with plastic wrap and marinate for 1 to 2 hours at room temperature, or up to 24 hours refrigerated.

2. Soak bamboo skewers in water for at least 30 minutes to prevent burning.

3. Prepare a hot fire. Drain meat, reserving marinade, and pat dry. Thread 2 or 3 chunks of meat onto each skewer. Grill over hot coals, turning once and brushing with reserved marinade, for about 4 to 5 minutes, until browned outside but still rosy and juicy inside.

10 GRILLED EGGPLANT SPREAD
Prep: 10 minutes   Cook: 50 minutes   Serves: 8 to 12

Serve this Middle Eastern specialty, *baba ghanoush*, with warm pita bread or crisp fresh vegetables for dipping. This can be stored, tightly covered, 3 to 4 days in the refrigerator.

2 1-pound eggplants
¼ cup extra-virgin olive oil
2 tablespoons fresh lemon
  juice
2 garlic cloves, minced
2 tablespoons salt

¼ teaspoon ground cumin
  Dash of cayenne
2 tablespoons chopped
  parsley
  Lemon wedges

1. Prepare a medium fire. Pierce eggplants 2 or 3 times with a sharp knife to allow steam to escape and prevent bursting. Place whole eggplant on an oiled grill and cook about 50 minutes, turning occasionally, until skin is charred and eggplant is puffed out and very tender through to center when pierced with a knife. When cool enough to handle, scoop eggplant pulp into a medium bowl, discarding skin. Pour off any liquid and remove any large clusters of seeds.

2. Gradually whisk olive oil into eggplant pulp. Stir in lemon juice, garlic, salt, cumin, and cayenne until well blended. Serve chilled, topped with chopped parsley and garnished with lemon wedges.

11 CORN KEBABS WITH SANTE FE BUTTER
Prep: 10 minutes   Cook: 7 to 8 minutes   Serves: 6

8 tablespoons (1 stick) butter,
  softened
1½ tablespoons minced cilantro
1½ tablespoons minced parsley
½ teaspoon ground cumin

1 jalapeño pepper, seeded and
  minced, or ¼ to ½
  teaspoon hot pepper
  sauce
1 garlic clove, crushed
6 ears fresh corn, husked
  Salt

1. In a food processor or blender, combine butter, cilantro, parsley, cumin, jalapeño, and garlic. Process until well blended. Or mix together by hand in a small bowl. Cover and refrigerate until serving time.

2. Prepare a hot fire. If using bamboo skewers, soak in water for at least 30 minutes to prevent burning. Melt Santa Fe Butter in a small saucepan on side of grill. Cut corn crosswise into 1½-inch rounds and thread through cob onto skewers.

3. Place corn kebabs on an oiled grill set 4 to 6 inches over coals. Grill, turning frequently and basting generously with the melted butter, until lightly browned all over, about 7 to 8 minutes. Season with salt.

12   DEVILED DIJON CHICKEN
Prep: 15 minutes   Marinate: 1 hour   Cook: 5 to 7 minutes
Serves: 6 to 8

5 skinless, boneless chicken
   breast halves (about 1½
   pounds total)
⅛ teaspoon cayenne
   Salt
¼ cup fresh lemon juice

¼ cup Dijon mustard
2 tablespoons chopped
   parsley
2 tablespoons minced shallots
1 cup fresh bread crumbs

1. Rinse chicken with cold water and pat dry. Cut each piece into ¾-inch chunks. Season with cayenne and salt.

2. In a medium bowl, whisk together lemon juice, mustard, parsley, and shallots. Add chicken and toss to coat. Cover with plastic wrap and marinate 1 to 2 hours at room temperataure, or up to 24 hours in refrigerator. Soak about 24 bamboo skewers in water for at least 30 minutes to prevent burning.

3. Prepare a hot fire. Remove chicken from marinade and dredge in bread crumbs to coat lightly. Thread 2 pieces of chicken onto each skewer and place on a well-oiled grill set 4 to 6 inches from coals. Grill, turning frequently, until chicken is just cooked through and crumbs are lightly browned, about 5 to 7 minutes.

13   CHICKEN DRUMMETTES VALENCIA
Prep: 15 minutes   Marinate: 2 hours   Cook: 15 to 20 minutes
Serves: 8 to 12

Drummettes are the meaty portions of chicken wings that resemble drumsticks.

3 pounds chicken drummettes
½ cup extra-virgin olive oil
   Juice of 2 oranges (½ cup)
¼ cup medium-dry or cream
   sherry
   Zest of 2 oranges, finely
   chopped

2 tablespoons fresh lemon
   juice
3 large garlic cloves, minced
2 teaspoons salt
½ teaspoon cayenne

1. Rinse chicken with cold water and pat dry. Arrange in a shallow nonreactive pan and cover with remaining ingredients. Marinate, turning occasionally, 2 hours at room temperature, or up to 48 hours refrigerated.

2. Prepare a hot fire. Grill chicken, turning occasionally and brushing with some of marinade, until cooked through, 15 to 20 minutes. Serve warm or at room temperature.

14 HONEY-THYME CHICKEN DIJONNAISE
Prep: 10 minutes   Marinate: 2 hours   Cook: 5 to 7 minutes
Serves: 4 to 6

5 skinless, boneless chicken
  breast halves (about 1½
  pounds)
  Salt and freshly ground
  pepper
¼ cup fresh lemon juice

Honey-Thyme Mustard
  (recipe follows)
3 tablespoons minced parsley
1 tablespoon chopped fresh
  thyme, or 1 teaspoon
  dried

1. Rinse chicken breasts with cold water and pat dry. Cut each piece of chicken into ¾-inch chunks and season with salt and pepper.

2. In a medium bowl, whisk together lemon juice, ¼ cup Honey-Thyme Mustard, and parsley until well blended. Add thyme and chicken pieces and toss to coat. Cover with plastic wrap and marinate in refrigerator 2 hours, or as long as overnight. Meanwhile, soak 25 bamboo skewers in water for at least 30 minutes to prevent burning.

3. Prepare a medium-hot fire. Remove chicken from refrigerator and thread 2 chunks onto each skewer. Place chicken on a well-oiled grill and cook, brushing with extra marinade, until just cooked through, about 5 to 7 minutes. Serve hot or warm, with remaining Honey-Thyme Mustard on the side for dipping.

HONEY-THYME MUSTARD

1 cup Dijon mustard
1 tablespoon minced fresh
  thyme, or 1 teaspoon
  dried

¼ cup honey
  Coarsely ground pepper

In a small bowl, combine mustard, thyme, and honey. Whisk to blend well. Season with pepper. Store in a tightly covered container in refrigerator for up to 1 month.

15 TARRAGON DIJON CHICKEN
Prep: 10 minutes   Marinate: 2 hours   Cook: 5 to 7 minutes
Serves: 4 to 6

5 skinless, boneless chicken
  breast halves (about 1½
  pounds)
  Salt and freshly ground
  pepper

¼ cup fresh lemon juice
  Tarragon Mustard (recipe
  follows)
3 tablespoons minced parsley

1. Rinse chicken breasts with cold water and pat dry. Slice each piece of chicken into ¾-inch chunks and season with salt and pepper.

2. In a medium bowl, combine lemon juice, ¼ cup Tarragon Mustard, and parsley. Whisk until well blended. Add chicken pieces and toss to coat. Cover with plastic wrap and marinate in the refrigerator 2 hours, or as long as overnight. Meanwhile, soak 25 bamboo skewers in water for at least 30 minutes to prevent burning.

3. Prepare a medium-hot fire. Remove chicken from refrigerator and thread 2 chunks onto each skewer. Place chicken on a well-oiled grill and cook, brushing with extra marinade, until just cooked through, about 5 to 7 minutes. Serve hot or warm, with remaining Tarragon Mustard on the side for dipping.

TARRAGON MUSTARD

1 cup Dijon mustard
1 tablespoon minced fresh tarragon, or 1 teaspoon dried, crumbled
1 large shallot, minced

2 teaspoons extra-virgin olive oil
1 teaspoon fresh lemon juice
Dash of cayenne

In a small bowl, combine all ingredients. Whisk to blend well. Store in a tightly covered container in refrigerator for up to 1 month.

---

16 DRUMMETTES ALLA DIAVOLA

Prep: 10 minutes   Marinate: 24 hours   Cook: 15 to 20 minutes
Serves: 8 to 12

A liberal dose of pepper is responsible for this recipe's Italian moniker, "hot as the devil."

3 pounds chicken drummettes
½ cup fresh lemon juice
2 teaspoons crushed hot red pepper flakes
2 teaspoons salt

2 teaspoons coarsely cracked pepper
2 large garlic cloves, minced
½ cup extra-virgin olive oil

1. Rinse chicken with cold water and pat dry. Arrange in a shallow nonreactive pan.

2. In a small bowl, combine lemon juice, hot pepper flakes, salt, pepper, and garlic. Whisk in olive oil and pour mixture over chicken. Cover and marinate, turning occasionally, 24 to 48 hours in refrigerator. (This long marinating time is essential for the balance of flavors.)

3. Prepare a hot fire. Grill chicken, turning occasionally and brushing with some of marinade, until cooked through, about 15 to 20 minutes. Serve warm or at room temperature.

17 CHICKEN SATAY WITH PEANUT SAUCE
Prep: 15 minutes   Marinate: 1 hour   Cook: 3 to 5 minutes
Serves: 6 to 8

These quickly grilled skewered chicken pieces, with a sauce cooked right on the grill, are ideal for outdoor entertaining.

4 skinless, boneless chicken breast halves (about 1¼ pounds)
⅓ cup soy sauce
2 teaspoons grated fresh ginger
2 garlic cloves, minced

2 tablespoons fresh lime juice
1 tablespoon peanut butter
1 tablespoon Asian sesame oil
½ teaspoon crushed hot red pepper flakes
Peanut Sauce (recipe follows)

1. Soak 30 long bamboo skewers in water at least 30 minutes to prevent burning. Rinse chicken and pat dry. Holding knife at an angle, slice chicken crosswise on the diagonal into wide, thin strips about ¾ × 2 inches. Thread chicken strips onto soaked skewers, leaving about 4 inches for a handle at one end. Place in a baking dish.

2. In a small bowl, mix together soy sauce, ginger, garlic, lime juice, peanut butter, sesame oil, and hot pepper. Pour over chicken and turn to coat. Cover and marinate, turning once or twice, 1 hour at room temperature, or 2 hours refrigerated.

3. Prepare a hot fire. Place satays on an oiled grill set 4 to 6 inches from coals. Grill, turning, until chicken is lightly browned and cooked through, about 3 to 5 minutes. Serve with Peanut Sauce for dipping.

18 PEANUT SAUCE
Prep: 15 minutes   Cook: 15 minutes   Makes: 2 cups

2 tablespoons peanut oil
½ cup finely chopped onion
2 garlic cloves, minced
1 tablespoon crushed hot red pepper flakes
1 teaspoon ground cumin
3 tablespoons lime juice

¼ cup soy sauce
1 cup peanut butter (smooth or chunky)
⅓ cup unsweetened coconut milk, canned or fresh
Optional: ¼ cup chopped fresh cilantro

1. In a small heavy saucepan, heat oil on side of grill away from direct heat. Add onion, garlic, hot pepper flakes, and cumin. Cook until onion and garlic are fragrant but not brown, about 10 minutes.

2. Stir in lime juice and soy sauce. Gradually stir in peanut butter and then coconut milk until smooth. Cook, stirring, until hot, about 5 minutes. Stir in cilantro just before serving.

19 BEEF SATAY

Prep: 10 minutes   Marinate: 4 hours   Cook: 4 to 6 minutes
Serves: 8

¼ cup fresh lime or lemon
    juice
¼ cup soy sauce
 3 tablespoons vegetable oil
 2 tablespoons honey
 3 garlic cloves, minced
1½ teaspoons ground coriander
    seeds

⅛ teaspoon cayenne
 2 pounds boneless beef
    sirloin or tenderloin, cut
    into 1-inch cubes
Peanut Sauce (page 14)

1. In a large bowl, mix together lime or lemon juice, soy sauce, oil, honey, garlic, coriander, and cayenne. Stir in beef cubes to coat well and marinate, covered, at room temperature for 4 hours, or overnight in refrigerator. If using bamboo skewers, soak in water for at least 30 minutes to prevent burning.

2. Prepare a medium-hot fire. Lift beef cubes from marinade and thread onto skewers. Grill on an oiled rack, turning frequently and basting with reserved marinade, until well browned outside and still pink and juicy inside, about 4 to 6 minutes. Serve with Peanut Sauce.

20 PORK SATAY

Prep: 10 minutes   Marinate: 4 hours   Cook: 7 to 9 minutes
Serves: 8

¼ cup creamy peanut butter
¼ cup soy sauce
¼ cup fresh lime or lemon
    juice
 2 tablespoons vegetable oil
 1 teaspoon ground cumin

 2 garlic cloves, minced
⅛ teaspoon cayenne
 2 pounds pork tenderloin,
    cut into 1-inch cubes
Peanut Sauce (page 14)

1. In a large bowl, mix together peanut butter, soy sauce, lime or lemon juice, oil, cumin, garlic, and cayenne. Stir in pork cubes to coat well and marinate, covered, at room temperature for 4 hours, or overnight in refrigerator. If using bamboo skewers, soak in water for at least 30 minutes to prevent burning.

2. Prepare a medium-hot fire. Lift pork cubes from marinade and thread onto skewers. Grill on an oiled rack, turning frequently and basting with reserved marinade, until well browned outside and just cooked through, about 7 to 9 minutes. Serve with Peanut Sauce.

21 SKEWERED DIJON CHICKEN

Prep: 10 minutes   Marinate: 1 hour   Cook: 5 to 7 minutes
Serves: 4 to 6

5 skinless, boneless chicken
    breast halves (about 1½
    pounds)
Salt and freshly ground
    pepper

¼ cup fresh lemon juice
¼ cup Dijon mustard

1. Rinse chicken with cold water and pat dry. Cut each piece into ¾-inch chunks and season with salt and pepper.

2. In a medium bowl, whisk together lemon juice and mustard until well blended. Add chicken and toss to coat. Cover with plastic wrap and marinate 1 to 2 hours at room temperature, or up to 24 hours refrigerated. Soak about 24 bamboo skewers in water for at least 30 minutes to prevent burning.

3. Prepare a hot fire. Thread 2 chunks of chicken onto each skewer; reserve any marinade in bowl. Place chicken on a well-oiled grill set 4 to 6 inches from coals. Grill, turning and brushing with marinade, until just white throughout but still moist, about 5 to 7 minutes.

22 SPIEDINI ALLA ROMANA

Prep: 20 minutes   Cook: 5 to 7 minutes   Serves: 6 to 8

Spiedini means "skewer," and these deliciously simple Italian kebabs can cook on the side of the grill while you finish the entrée. They require small plates and forks.

1 1-pound loaf day-old French
    or Italian bread, crusts
    removed
1 pound mozzarella cheese,
    preferably fresh

1 2-ounce tin flat anchovy
    fillets, packed in olive oil,
    oil reserved
1 cup Garlic Oil (page 180) or
    extra-virgin olive oil

1. Cut bread into 1-inch cubes. Cut cheese into ¾-inch cubes. Cut anchovy fillets into thirds. Combine anchovy oil with Garlic Oil or olive oil.

2. Dip bread cubes into flavored oil and place on 6 to 8 skewers, followed by a piece of anchovy, cheese, and more bread until all ingredients have been used. (Each skewer should begin and end with a bread cube.) If made in advance, cover and refrigerate.

3. Place skewers on an oiled grill over moderately hot coals and grill, turning, until bread is crisp and cheese is softened, about 5 to 7 minutes. Immediately scrape each skewer onto an individual serving plate.

23 ITALIAN GARLIC TOASTS
Prep: 10 minutes   Cook: 3 to 5 minutes   Makes: 12 slices

Enjoy this rustic garlic bread by itself, or topped with grilled vegetables (such as eggplant, zucchini, or peppers) and cheese.

12 1-inch-thick slices of day-old
   Italian or country-style
   bread
6 large garlic cloves, halved
	About ½ cup extra-virgin
	   olive oil
	Optional: Coarse (kosher)
	   salt

1. Toast bread slices over a hot fire until both sides are golden brown. Immediately rub one side of each toasted bread slice with a cut garlic clove half, pressing the garlic against rough surface of toast to distribute flavor.

2. Brush or drizzle olive oil over garlic toast and sprinkle with a dash of salt, if desired.

24 SOUTHWESTERN FRITTATA
Prep: 20 minutes   Cook: 45 minutes   Serves: 8 to 12

1 small red bell pepper
4 scallions, chopped
2 ears corn, husked
2 tablespoons corn oil
2 jalapeño peppers
6 eggs
	¼ pound Monterey Jack
	   cheese, shredded (about
	   1 cup)
	½ teaspoon salt
	⅛ teaspoon freshly ground
	   pepper
	Pinch of sugar

1. Prepare a hot fire. Set pepper directly on grill and cook, turning frequently, until skin is charred all over, 10 to 15 minutes. Seal in a plastic bag until cool enough to handle, 5 to 10 minutes.

2. While pepper is cooking, brush scallions and corn with oil and grill, turning frequently, until lightly browned and tender, about 3 to 5 minutes for scallions, 7 to 8 minutes for corn. At same time, grill jalapeño peppers, turning, until lightly charred all over, about 5 minutes.

3. Remove bell pepper from plastic bag, peel away charred skin under cold running water, and remove stem and seeds. Cut pepper into ¼-inch dice. Chop scallions. Cut kernels from corn cobs. Rub off most of charred skin from jalapeños, discard stems and seeds, and finely chop.

4. Preheat oven to 325°. In a large bowl, beat eggs until well blended. Stir in chopped grilled vegetables, cheese, salt, pepper, and sugar. Pour mixture into a buttered 8-inch square baking dish. Bake for 30 to 35 minutes, or until set. Let cool completely. Cut into 1-inch squares. Serve at room temperature or slightly chilled.

25 GRILLED WHEEL OF BRIE
Prep: 5 minutes Cook: 10 to 12 minutes Serves: 6 to 8

1 8-ounce wheel of Brie
   cheese, well chilled
2 tablespoons red pepper jelly

2 tablespoons chopped
   walnuts
   Unsalted crackers or water
   biscuits

1. Prepare a low fire or use embers from an existing fire. Using a long thin knife, cut cheese horizontally in half. Lift off top half of cheese and set aside. Spread jelly on lower half and top with walnuts. Replace top half of cheese, pressing down firmly.

2. Place cheese on a well-oiled grill and cook, using a wide spatula to turn once, until cheese is softened but still holds its shape, about 10 to 12 minutes. Transfer to a warm plate and serve with crackers.

26 RACLETTE ON THE GRILL
Prep: 5 minutes Cook: 10 to 14 minutes Serves: 4 to 6

This is a great appetizer to make while your fire is heating for the main course.

1 to 1½ pounds raclette,
   Jarlsberg, or Gruyère
   cheese
   Freshly ground pepper

Italian Garlic Toasts (page
17) or croutons of crusty
French bread

1. Use a fire that is just warming up or prepare a medium to medium-hot fire. Cut cheese into ½-inch-thick slices 1½ to 2 inches long. Arrange in a single layer in a heavy skillet with a heatproof handle, preferably cast iron.

2. Set skillet directly on grill and cook until cheese melts, 5 to 7 minutes. Scrape cheese onto individual plates, sprinkle with pepper, and eat while hot by spreading on Italian Garlic Toasts or croutons. Repeat with remaining cheese.

27 GRILLED GOAT CHEESE BUNDLES
Prep: 20 minutes Cook: 2½ to 4½ minutes Serves: 4 to 6

12 Swiss chard leaves
 5 ounces mild goat cheese in a
    log

1 to 2 tablespoons extra-virgin
   olive oil

1. Prepare a hot fire or use an existing fire. In a large pot of boiling water, boil Swiss chard leaves for about 30 seconds, until pliable. Drain and rinse under cold running water; drain well.

2. Cut goat cheese into 12 slices about ½ inch thick. Place each piece of cheese on a Swiss chard leaf. Fold up the bottom, fold in sides, and finally roll up to seal cheese inside. Brush bundles all over with olive oil.

3. Set goat cheese bundles on an oiled grill set 4 to 6 inches from heat. Grill, turning once, until chard is lightly browned and cheese is heated through, 1 to 2 minutes per side.

---

28 HOT AND SPICY NUTS
Prep: 5 minutes   Cook: 1 to 2 minutes   Makes: 2 cups

1 tablespoon light olive or
   peanut oil
1 garlic clove, minced
½ to ¾ teaspoon crushed hot
   red pepper flakes
½ teaspoon chili powder
¼ teaspoon ground cumin

⅛ to ¼ teaspoon cayenne
Grilled-Roasted Nuts
   (recipe follows), or
   ½ pound roasted nut
   of choice
Coarse (kosher) salt

1. Heat oil in a large skillet over moderate heat. Add garlic and hot pepper and cook, stirring, until garlic is softened and fragrant but not browned, about 30 seconds.

2. Add chili powder, cumin, cayenne, and nuts. Toss to coat nuts well with oil and seasonings. Pour into a bowl and season with coarse salt. Serve slightly warm or at room temperature. Store in an airtight container.

---

29 GRILLED-ROASTED NUTS
Prep: 2 minutes   Cook: 5 to 7 minutes   Makes: 2 cups

Toast nuts before your main course has cooked and use for Hot and Spicy Nuts (above) or later as a dessert topping.

½ pound shelled walnuts,
   almonds, peanuts,
   pecans, and/or cashews

2 teaspoons light olive or
   peanut oil

1. Prepare a medium fire or use an existing fire. Place nuts in center of an 18-inch square of heavy-duty aluminum foil. Drizzle on oil and toss to coat nuts. Fold up edges, pinching to make a secure packet.

2. Place packet on coolest part of grill away from direct heat of coals. Grill, turning and shaking packet several times, until nuts are toasted evenly, 5 to 7 minutes.

30   VEGETABLES UNDER WRAPS
Prep: 15 minutes   Cook: 10 to 15 minutes   Serves: 4 to 6

1 pound one or more of
   following vegetables:
   Zucchini, cut into 1-inch
      chunks
   Eggplant, cut into ¾-inch
      cubes and brushed lightly
      with oil
   Canned artichoke hearts or
      marinated artichoke
      hearts, well drained
   Pimiento-stuffed green
      olives

Jumbo pitted ripe olives
Plain mushroom caps,
   brushed lightly with oil,
   or marinated mushrooms,
   well drained
Canned water chestnuts,
   drained and marinated in
   soy sauce for 15 minutes
   before wrapping
Salt and freshly ground
   pepper
½ pound thinly sliced bacon

1. Prepare a hot fire. If using bamboo skewers, soak in water for at least 30 minutes to prevent burning. Season vegetables with salt and pepper.

2. Cut bacon slices crosswise into halves or thirds, just long enough to wrap once around vegetables, overlapping slightly. Thread on skewers and place on an oiled grill set over hot coals. Grill, turning and moving frequently to prevent burning or flare-ups, until bacon is browned and crisp and vegetables are crisp-tender, about 10 to 15 minutes. Drain on paper towels.

31   FISH UNDER WRAPS
Prep: 15 minutes   Cook: 10 to 15 minutes   Serves: 4 to 6

1 pound fish or shellfish, such
   as one or more of the
   following:
   Large raw shrimp, shelled
      and deveined
   Raw sea scallops
   Smoked or raw oysters

Chunks of firm-fleshed fish,
   such as shark or monkfish
2 tablespoons fresh lemon
   juice
Salt and freshly ground
   pepper
½ pound thinly sliced bacon

1. Prepare a hot fire. If using bamboo skewers, soak in water for at least 30 minutes to prevent burning. Toss fish in lemon juice and season with salt and pepper.

2. Cut bacon slices crosswise into halves or thirds, just long enough to wrap once around fish or shellfish, overlapping slightly. Thread onto skewers and place on an oiled grill set over hot coals. Grill, turning and moving frequently to prevent burning or flare-ups, until bacon is browned and crisp and fish or shellfish is opaque throughout, about 10 to 15 minutes. Drain on paper towels briefly before serving.

32 PINWHEELS UNDER WRAPS
Prep: 15 minutes   Cook: 10 to 15 minutes   Serves: 4 to 6

8 slices soft white bread
8 ounces cream cheese,
softened

2 tablespoons minced chives
½ pound thinly sliced bacon

1. Prepare a hot fire. If using bamboo skewers, soak in water for at least 30 minutes to prevent burning. Trim crusts from bread. Blend cream cheese and chives. Spread one side of each slice of bread with chive cream cheese and roll up, jelly-roll fashion. Cut into 1-inch pieces.

2. Cut bacon slices crosswise into halves or thirds, just long enough to wrap once around pinwheels, overlapping slightly. Thread onto skewers and place on an oiled grill set over hot coals. Grill, turning and moving frequently to prevent burning or flare-ups, until bacon is browned and crisp and bread is lightly toasted, about 10 to 15 minutes. Drain on paper towels before serving.

---

33 FRUIT UNDER WRAPS
Prep: 10 minutes   Cook: 10 to 15 minutes   Serves: 4 to 6

½ pound thinly sliced bacon
1 pound one or more of the
following fruits:
Fresh fig halves
Pineapple chunks
Pickled watermelon rind

Firm, 1-inch chunks of
banana, dipped in lemon
juice
Pitted prunes, plain, or
stuffed with an almond

1. Prepare a hot fire. If using bamboo skewers, soak in water for at least 30 minutes to prevent burning.

2. Cut bacon slices crosswise into halves or thirds, just long enough to wrap once around fruit, overlapping slightly. Thread onto skewers and place on an oiled grill set 4 to 6 inches from coals. Grill, turning and moving frequently to prevent burning or flare-ups, until bacon is browned and crisp, about 10 to 15 minutes. Drain on paper towels briefly before serving.

34 CURRANT-GLAZED COCKTAIL SAUSAGES
Prep: 5 minutes   Cook: 10 to 12 minutes   Serves: 4 to 6

Threading several cocktail sausages on each skewer makes grilling easier.

1 pound cocktail sausages	2 tablespoons orange juice
½ cup red currant jelly	Dash of cayenne

1. Prepare a hot fire. If using bamboo skewers, soak in water at least 30 minutes to prevent burning. Thread cocktail sausages onto skewers.

2. Combine currant jelly, orange juice, and cayenne in a small saucepan on edge of grill. Grill sausages, turning, until lightly browned, about 5 minutes. Then begin brushing with warm glaze and turning until well browned and sizzling, 5 to 7 minutes longer.

35 GRILLED RUMAKI
Prep: 20 minutes   Marinate: 15 minutes
Cook: 10 to 15 minutes   Serves: 4 to 6

1 pound chicken livers, trimmed	1 garlic clove, crushed
2 tablespoons soy sauce	1 teaspoon sugar
2 tablespoons dry sherry	⅛ teaspoon freshly ground pepper
½ teaspoon grated fresh ginger, or ¼ teaspoon powdered	1 bunch scallions
	½ pound thinly sliced center-cut bacon

1. Prepare a hot fire. Soak bamboo skewers in water for at least 30 minutes to prevent burning. Rinse livers and pat dry. Cut in half if larger than bite-size.

2. In a medium bowl, combine soy sauce, sherry, ginger, garlic, sugar, and pepper. Add chicken livers and toss to coat. Let marinate, tossing once or twice, 15 minutes.

3. Meanwhile, prepare a hot fire. Cut scallion greens into lengths long enough to wrap around livers, overlapping slightly. (Reserve white parts for another use.) Cut bacon strips the same length as scallions.

4. Wrap scallions and bacon around pieces of liver and thread onto skewers. Place on an oiled grill set 4 to 6 inches from coals. Grill, turning and moving frequently to prevent flare-ups and burning, until bacon is browned and crisp and livers are cooked through but still pink inside, about 10 to 15 minutes. Drain briefly on paper towels before serving.

Chapter 2

Barbecuing the Birds

Chicken is unbeatably popular these days, and barbecuing offers a whole new variety of ideas for preparing it. Grilling is an excellent way to cook all poultry, so besides a tempting assortment of easy-to-cook chicken recipes, we've included preparations for turkey, Cornish game hens, duck, and even quail.

These days turkey is packaged in many different cuts, and this chapter will show you ways to barbecue each of them beautifully. No matter which bird you grill, the basic rule of doneness is the same: Light meat should be white throughout, with no translucent pinkness, but still moist. Dark meat should run clear yellow when pricked near the joint.

Chicken breasts are extremely popular, both on the bone and already skinned and boned, sometimes called cutlets. They are usually a fairly uniform weight, and all the chicken breast recipes in this book are calculated for a 4- to 5-ounce skinless, boneless chicken breast half or a 7- to 8-ounce piece with skin and bone.

Grilling poultry with the bone in helps provide more even cooking at a slower rate, to keep the meat moist. It takes longer, however. Quick-cooking boneless cuts are extremely convenient. They should be grilled quickly over high heat and watched carefully to avoid overcooking for maximum juiciness.

When barbecuing chicken for a crowd, you can reduce the grill time by roasting the pieces in a 400° oven for 30 minutes beforehand to partially cook them. When guests arrive, finish the chicken on the grill, turning and basting with your favorite sauce or marinade for about 15 minutes.

36 GRILLED CHICKEN ITALIANO

Prep: 10 minutes   Marinate: 2 hours   Cook: 35 to 45 minutes
Serves: 4

1 3½-pound chicken, cut up	¼ cup dry white wine
1 cup bottled Italian salad dressing	2 garlic cloves, crushed

1. Rinse chicken with cold water and pat dry. Arrange chicken pieces in a glass baking dish.

2. In a medium bowl, combine salad dressing with wine and garlic and pour over chicken. Cover and marinate 2 to 4 hours at room temperature, or overnight refrigerated.

3. Prepare a hot fire. Remove chicken pieces from marinade and place on an oiled grill set 4 to 6 inches over coals. Grill chicken pieces, turning frequently and brushing with reserved marinade, until browned outside and cooked through, with no trace of pink near bone, about 35 to 40 minutes.

37 TANDOORI CHICKEN

Prep: 25 minutes   Marinate: 2 hours   Cook: 30 to 35 minutes
Serves: 4

This Indian marinade makes the chicken not only delicious, but also extremely tender.

1 3½-pound chicken, halved	1 to 1½ teaspoons cayenne
1 cup plain yogurt	1 teaspoon turmeric
½ cup fresh lemon juice	½ teaspoon ground cardamom
1 tablespoon paprika	1 teaspoon salt
1 tablespoon minced garlic	½ teaspoon freshly ground
1 tablespoon minced fresh ginger	pepper
1½ teaspoons ground cumin	2 tablespoons oil

1. Remove and discard chicken skin. Rinse chicken with cold water and pat dry. Using tip of a sharp knife, make diagonal slashes ½ inch deep and 1 inch apart in meat. Place in a large bowl or glass baking dish.

2. In a small bowl, combine yogurt, lemon juice, paprika, garlic, ginger, cumin, cayenne, turmeric, cardamom, salt, and pepper. Coat chicken all over with marinade, working it into slashes. Cover and marinate at least 2 hours at room temperature, or up to 24 hours refrigerated. If refrigerated, remove at least 1 hour before cooking to return to room temperature.

3. Prepare grill. Scrape away any marinade clinging to chicken and reserve for basting. Brush meat with oil and place meaty side down on an oiled rack. Grill over medium-hot coals until lightly browned on bottom, about 15 minutes. Turn, brush again with oil and reserved marinade, and continue cooking, turning and basting, until golden brown and cooked through, about 15 to 20 minutes longer.

38 LEMON CHICKEN ON THE ROTISSERIE
Prep: 15 minutes   Cook: 1 to 1½ hours   Serves: 4

If you have a large enough spit, you might want to roast two chickens and have one cold the next day; just be sure not to crowd them, so they'll cook evenly.

1 3½-pound chicken	½ teaspoon paprika
1 lemon	2 tablespoons softened butter
1 tablespoon olive oil	or olive oil
2 teaspoons salt	2 tablespoons lemon juice

1. Prepare a medium-hot fire. Remove giblets from cavity of chicken and reserve for another use. Rinse chicken with cold water and pat dry. Cut lemon into 4 wedges and place inside chicken cavity. Rub chicken with oil and season inside and out with salt. Dust lightly with paprika.

2. Pull the flap of neck skin to the back of chicken, securing with a skewer if necessary; tuck wing tips behind back. Moisten 2 10-inch pieces of cotton kitchen twine with water to prevent burning. Loop twine around wings in a figure-8 and tie a secure knot. Tie ends of drumsticks together; trim off any excess twine. Insert spit rod through cavity of chicken and secure with adjustable holding forks, taking care that chicken is balanced on rod.

3. Cook chicken on rotisserie placed 4 to 6 inches over coals until juices run clear and meat near thigh bone is no longer pink, about 1 to 1½ hours. (Meat should register 180 degrees on an instant-reading thermometer.) Melt butter with lemon juice and brush over chicken during last 15 minutes of cooking. Allow to rest 10 to 15 minutes before removing trussing twine and carving.

39 YANKEE DOODLE CHICKEN
Prep: 5 minutes   Cook: 35 to 45 minutes   Serves: 4

1 3-pound chicken, cut up	1 teaspoon salt
8 tablespoons (1 stick) butter	⅛ teaspoon cayenne
¼ cup cider vinegar	

1. Prepare a hot fire. Rinse chicken with cold water and pat dry. Combine butter, vinegar, salt, and cayenne in a small heavy saucepan. Warm on side of grill to melt butter.

2. Brush chicken pieces with butter mixture and place skin side down on an oiled grill over hot coals. Brown chicken quickly on both sides, then continue to grill, turning frequently and basting with butter mixture, until chicken is browned outside and cooked through with no trace of pink near bone, about 35 to 45 minutes total.

40 RED-WHITE-AND-BARBECUED CHICKEN
Prep: 5 minutes   Cook: 40 to 45 minutes   Serves: 6 to 8

Tomato-based barbecue sauces have a tendency to burn when exposed to direct heat for long periods of time. We prefer to partially grill the chicken before brushing on the sauce.

> 2 3-pound chickens, cut up
> 1½ cups barbecue sauce of
>   choice, homemade or
>   bottled

1. Rinse chicken with cold water and pat dry. Prepare a medium-hot fire.

2. When coals are white hot, place plain chicken pieces, skin side down, on an oiled grill set 4 to 6 inches from coals. Once chicken skin is browned, turn pieces over and grill for 30 minutes, checking occasionally for flare-ups. Then begin brushing with barbecue sauce, turning chicken pieces frequently to prevent burning. Grill until chicken is cooked through, with no trace of pink near bone, about 10 to 15 minutes longer.

41 MAPLE BARBECUED CHICKEN
Prep: 10 minutes   Marinate: 2 hours   Cook: 35 to 45 minutes
Serves: 4

A quick hunt through the kitchen cupboard will probably supply you with all the ingredients necessary for this recipe.

> 1 cup tomato sauce
> ¼ cup cider vinegar
> ¼ cup vegetable oil
> 2 tablespoons honey or maple
>   syrup
>
> 2 teaspoons chili powder
> ½ teaspoon salt
>   Dash of cayenne
> 1 3-pound chicken, cut up

1. In a small nonreactive saucepan, combine tomato sauce, vinegar, oil, honey, chili powder, salt, and cayenne. Bring to a boil over medium heat. Reduce heat to medium-low and simmer, stirring occasionally, until sauce is slightly thickened, about 10 minutes. Set aside and cool to room temperature.

2. Rinse chicken with cold water and pat dry. Arrange pieces in a glass baking dish and pour sauce over chicken; turn pieces to coat. Cover with plastic wrap and marinate 2 to 3 hours at room temperature, or up to 24 hours refrigerated.

3. Prepare a hot fire. Remove chicken from marinade and place skin side down on an oiled grill set about 6 inches from coals; reserve marinade. Grill until skin is browned on bottom, 10 to 15 minutes. Turn pieces over and grill for 10 to 15 minutes, checking occasionally for flare-ups. Brush with barbecue sauce and continue to grill, turning and basting frequently with sauce, until chicken is cooked through with no trace of pink near bone, about 15 minutes longer.

42 JUICY CHICKEN JUAREZ

Prep: 10 minutes   Marinate: 2 hours   Cook: 35 to 45 minutes
Serves: 4

1 3-pound chicken, cut up	¼ cup bottled taco sauce
¼ cup fresh lime juice	2 tablespoons chopped
¼ cup spicy tomato juice, such	cilantro or parsley
as Snappy Tom	

1. Rinse chicken under cold running water and pat dry; arrange pieces in a glass or ceramic baking dish. In a small bowl, mix together lime juice, tomato juice, taco sauce, and cilantro. Pour marinade over chicken; turn to coat. Cover with plastic wrap and marinate, turning occasionally, 2 to 3 hours at room temperature, or up to 24 hours refrigerated.

2. Prepare a hot fire. Remove chicken from marinade and place skin side down on an oiled grill set 4 to 6 inches from hot coals; reserve marinade. Grill, turning once, until chicken is browned on both sides, 10 to 15 minutes per side. Brush with marinade and continue to grill, turning and basting frequently, until chicken is cooked through with no trace of pink near bone, about 15 minutes longer.

43 POLYNESIAN CHICKEN

Prep: 10 minutes   Marinate: 2 hours   Cook: 45 minutes   Serves: 4

You'll want to pull out the Don Ho albums for this one!

1 3-pound chicken, cut up	⅓ cup brown sugar
¼ cup soy sauce	½ teaspoon powdered ginger
¼ cup pineapple juice	¼ cup vegetable oil

1. Rinse chicken with cold water and pat dry; arrange pieces in a glass or ceramic baking dish. In a small bowl, mix together soy sauce, pineapple juice, brown sugar, ginger, and oil. Pour over chicken; turn pieces to coat. Cover with plastic wrap and marinate, turning occasionally, 2 to 3 hours at room temperature, or up to 24 hours refrigerated.

2. Prepare a hot fire. Remove chicken from sauce and place skin side down on an oiled grill set 4 to 6 inches from coals; reserve sauce. Grill, turning once, until chicken is browned on both sides, about 15 minutes per side. Brush with sauce and continue to grill, turning and basting frequently with sauce, until chicken is cooked through with no trace of pink near bone, about 15 minutes longer.

44   GRILLED LEMON-LIME CHICKEN

Prep: 5 minutes   Marinate: 1 hour   Cook: 40 to 45 minutes
Serves: 4

1 3½-pound chicken,
   quartered
1 lemon
1 lime
3 tablespoons extra-virgin
   olive oil

1 garlic clove, crushed
1 teaspoon salt
½ teaspoon freshly ground
   pepper
⅛ teaspoon cayenne

1. Rinse chicken and pat dry. Grate colored zest from lemon and lime into a medium bowl. Add juice from lemon and lime, olive oil, garlic, salt, pepper, and cayenne. Mix well. Add chicken and turn to coat. Cover and marinate, turning occasionally, 1 to 2 hours at room temperature, or up to 12 hours refrigerated.

2. Prepare a hot fire. Remove chicken from marinade and place on an oiled grill set 4 to 6 inches from coals. Grill, turning and basting with marinade every 10 minutes, until chicken is browned outside and white throughout with no trace of pink near bone, 40 to 45 minutes.

---

45   GRILLED CHICKEN THIGHS WITH ROSEMARY-ORANGE PESTO

Prep: 30 minutes   Marinate: 2 hours   Cook: 15 to 20 minutes
Serves: 8

16 chicken thighs
2 teaspoons salt
½ teaspoon freshly ground
   pepper
1 garlic clove, minced
⅓ cup olive oil
2 tablespoons fresh lemon
   juice

1 tablespoon chopped fresh
   rosemary leaves, or 1
   teaspoon dried
   Rosemary-Orange Pesto
   (page 183)

1. Rinse chicken with cold water and pat dry. Season with salt and pepper. Place in pan with garlic, olive oil, lemon juice, and rosemary. Marinate for 2 to 3 hours at room temperature, or overnight in refrigerator.

2. Gently loosen skin from chicken meat to create a pocket. Place about 1 tablespoon Rosemary-Orange Pesto in each pocket. Press skin back down again to seal.

3. Prepare grill and wait until coals are covered with a uniform gray ash. Oil grill rack. Cook thighs, skin side down, turning carefully to keep skin intact and basting occasionally with some of the marinade, for 15 to 20 minutes, until browned outside and just cooked through with no trace of pink.

46   YAKITORI
Prep: 20 minutes   Cook: 5 to 7 minutes   Serves: 4 to 6

These light and delicate grilled Japanese chicken brochettes can be served as a main course or as an appetizer.

1 **pound skinless, boneless chicken breasts**	¼ **cup soy sauce**
2 **bunches scallions, trimmed**	1 **tablespoon sugar**
¼ **cup sake or dry white wine**	1 **teaspoon grated fresh ginger**

1. Prepare a hot fire. Rinse chicken with cold water and pat dry. Cut chicken into 1½-inch cubes. Cut scallions into 2-inch lengths, using some green tops. Thread 3 or 4 pieces of chicken onto each of 12 small metal or soaked bamboo skewers, alternating with pieces of scallion.

2. In a small bowl, mix together sake, soy sauce, sugar, and ginger. Place skewers on an oiled grill set 4 to 6 inches from coals. Grill, brushing often with soy mixture and turning occasionally, until chicken is white throughout but still moist, about 5 to 7 minutes.

47   SOUTHWESTERN CHICKEN "SUSHI"
Prep: 25 minutes   Marinate: 2 hours   Cook: 8 to 10 minutes
Serves: 8 to 12

Grilled Chili Chicken Strips (recipe follows)	1 **cup bottled salsa, mild or hot**
6 **large flour tortillas**	**Salt and freshly ground pepper**
8 **ounces cream cheese, at room temperature**	1 **large head red or green leaf lettuce, washed and well drained**
½ **teaspoon ground cumin**	
2 **15-ounce cans black beans, rinsed, drained, and coarsely mashed**	

1. Marinate and cook Chili Chicken Strips as directed in recipe that follows. Let cool, then wrap and refrigerate. Chili Chicken Strips can be prepared up to 2 days in advance.

2. Lay tortillas flat. Mix cream cheese with cumin and spread 2 generous tablespoons over each tortilla.

3. Mix together black beans and salsa. Season with salt and pepper. Spread a layer of beans over cream cheese. Top with a lettuce leaf, about 1½ tablespoons salsa, and a single long row of chicken strips down the center. Roll tortillas into a tight cylinder and use a serrated knife to cut rolls into 1-inch-thick cylinders. These can be made up to 6 hours in advance if wrapped well and refrigerated. Serve chilled or at room temperature.

48 QUICK CHICK
Prep: 5 minutes   Marinate: 5 minutes   Cook: 10 to 12 minutes
Serves: 4

If you prefer to use chicken breasts on the bone, grill them for 20 minutes.

½ cup extra-virgin olive oil
1 .06-ounce envelope Italian
   salad dressing mix

¼ cup lemon juice
4 skinless, boneless chicken
   breast halves

1. Prepare a hot fire. Combine olive oil, Italian salad dressing mix, and lemon juice. Add chicken breasts; turn to coat well. Let stand for 5 minutes.

2. Place chicken on an oiled grill 6 inches from coals. Grill, turning occasionally, for about 10 to 12 minutes, until white throughout but still moist.

49 GRILLED CURRIED CHICKEN
Prep: 10 minutes   Marinate: 1 hour   Cook: 45 minutes   Serves: 4

1 3-pound chicken, cut up
2 tablespoons minced onion
1 tablespoon curry powder
¼ cup lemon juice

¼ cup chicken broth
¼ teaspoon salt
Dash of cayenne
¼ cup vegetable oil

1. Rinse chicken with cold water and pat dry; arrange pieces in a glass or ceramic baking dish. In a small bowl, mix together onion, curry powder, lemon juice, chicken broth, salt, cayenne, and oil. Pour over chicken; turn pieces to coat. Cover with plastic wrap and marinate, turning occasionally, 1 to 3 hours at room temperature, or up to 24 hours refrigerated.

2. Prepare a hot fire. Remove chicken from marinade and place on an oiled grill set 4 to 6 inches from coals; reserve marinade. Grill, turning once, until chicken is browned on both sides, about 15 minutes per side. Brush with marinade and continue to grill, turning and basting frequently, until chicken is cooked through with no traces of pink near bone, about 15 minutes longer.

50 CHABLIS-B-Q CHICKEN
Prep: 5 minutes   Marinate: 2 hours   Cook: 35 to 45 minutes
Serves: 4

1 3-pound chicken, cut up
½ cup bottled barbecue sauce

¼ cup Chablis or other dry
   white wine

1. Rinse chicken with cold water and pat dry; arrange pieces in a glass baking dish. In a small bowl, mix together barbecue sauce and wine and pour over chicken; turn pieces to coat. Cover with plastic wrap and marinate, turning occasionally, 2 to 4 hours at room temperature, or overnight in refrigerator.

2. Prepare a hot fire. Place plain chicken pieces, skin side down, on an oiled grill set over hot coals. Grill until skin is browned, 10 to 15 minutes; turn pieces over and grill for 10 to 15 minutes, checking occasionally for flare-ups. Then begin brushing with barbecue sauce, turning chicken pieces frequently to prevent burning. Grill until chicken is cooked through with no trace of pink near bone, about 15 minutes longer.

---

51 SPICY CONFETTI CHICKEN BREASTS

Prep: 20 minutes   Marinate: 2 hours   Cook: 16 to 18 minutes
Serves: 4

4 chicken breast halves, bones
    in, skin on
    Salt and freshly ground
    pepper
¼ cup fresh orange juice
2 tablespoons chopped
    parsley

2 tablespoons olive oil
2 to 3 small fresh hot chili
    peppers, preferably a
    combination of red and
    green, seeded and minced

1. Rinse chicken with cold water and pat dry. Place in a glass baking dish and season with salt and pepper. In a small bowl, combine orange juice with parsley, olive oil, and chilies. Cover with plastic wrap and marinate 2 to 4 hours at room temperature, or overnight in refrigerator.

2. Prepare grill. Remove chicken from marinade, brushing off most of chilies and parsley clinging to meat. Reserve marinade and chilies for basting.

3. Set chicken skin side down on an oiled grill over hot coals and cook until nicely browned on bottom, about 6 to 8 minutes. Turn over and begin brushing with reserved marinade. Continue cooking and basting until chicken is just cooked through, about 10 minutes longer.

---

52 NORTH BEACH CHICKEN BREASTS

Prep: 5 minutes   Cook: 8 to 10 minutes   Serves: 6

6 skinless, boneless chicken
    breast halves
3 tablespoons olive oil
    Salt and freshly ground
    pepper

6 tablespoons Black Olive
    Pesto (page 182)
6 thin slices mozzarella
    cheese, preferably
    smoked

1. Rinse chicken with cold water and pat dry. Using a mallet or the flat side of a cleaver, pound breasts gently to flatten to an even thickness. Brush with olive oil and season with salt and pepper.

2. Place chicken skinned side down on an oiled grill over medium-hot coals. Grill until browned outside and opaque around edges, about 4 to 5 minutes. Turn chicken over and top each breast with 1 tablespoon of pesto and a slice of cheese. Continue cooking (without turning) until chicken is cooked through and cheese is melted, about 4 minutes longer.

53 CHICKEN FAJITAS
Prep: 10 minutes   Marinate: 1 hour   Cook: 10 to 15 minutes
Serves: 6

1½ pounds skinless, boneless
    chicken breasts
¼ cup bottled taco sauce
3 tablespoons lime juice
3 tablespoons tequila
2 jalapeño peppers, seeded
    and minced, or ¼
    teaspoon crushed hot red
    pepper flakes

2 garlic cloves, minced
1 teaspoon salt
½ teaspoon ground cumin
12 flour tortillas
    Salsa, guacamole, shredded
    romaine lettuce, and sour
    cream, as accompaniment

1. Rinse chicken breasts and pat dry. Trim off any fat or gristle. In a large bowl, combine taco sauce, lime juice, tequila, jalapeños, garlic, salt, and cumin. Add chicken and toss to coat. Cover and marinate, tossing occasionally, 1 to 2 hours at room temperature, or up to 12 hours refrigerated.

2. Prepare a hot fire. Set chicken on an oiled grill 4 to 6 inches from heat. Grill, turning and basting with marinade several times, until chicken is white throughout but still moist, 8 to 10 minutes. Let stand for 3 to 5 minutes before cutting or tearing into large strips.

3. While chicken is standing, heat tortillas directly on grill for 20 to 30 seconds per side, or wrap in foil in 2 packages, 6 tortillas to a package, and warm, turning several times, 3 to 5 minutes.

4. To serve, put chicken strips on tortillas. Top with salsa, guacamole, shredded lettuce, and sour cream. Roll up and eat.

54 ROSEMARY'S CHICKEN BREASTS
Prep: 10 minutes   Marinate: 30 minutes   Cook: 8 to 10 minutes
Serves: 4

4 skinless, boneless chicken
    breast halves
5 garlic cloves, minced
2 tablespoons minced fresh
    rosemary, or 1 teaspoon
    dried
1 tablespoon Dijon mustard

1 tablespoon fresh lemon
    juice
¾ teaspoon salt
¼ teaspoon freshly ground
    pepper
2 tablespoons olive oil

1. Prepare a hot fire. Rinse chicken with cold water and pat dry; place in a glass baking dish. In a small bowl, mix together garlic, rosemary, mustard, lemon juice, salt, pepper, and olive oil until well blended. Pour over chicken breasts and turn to coat well. Cover and marinate at room temperature, turning once or twice, for 30 minutes.

2. Remove chicken breasts from marinade and place on an oiled grill set 4 to 6 inches from coals. Grill chicken, turning once and basting with reserved marinade, until chicken is white throughout but still juicy, 8 to 10 minutes.

55 GRILLED CHILI CHICKEN STRIPS
Prep: 10 minutes   Marinate: 2 hours   Cook: 8 to 10 minutes
Serves: 6

6 skinless, boneless chicken
   breast halves
2 tablespoons fresh lime juice
1 garlic clove, minced
½ teaspoon salt

⅛ teaspoon freshly ground
   pepper
1 teaspoon ground chili
   powder
2 tablespoons olive oil

1. Rinse chicken with cold water and pat dry. Using a mallet or the flat side of a cleaver, gently pound breasts until they are flattened to an even thickness.

2. Combine lime juice, garlic, salt, pepper, chili powder, and olive oil in a plastic bag or nonreactive pan. Add chicken and shake or turn to coat. Seal or cover and marinate 2 hours at room temperature, or up to 24 hours refrigerated.

3. Prepare grill. Set an oiled rack over hot coals and grill chicken, turning once, until browned outside and just cooked through, about 4 to 5 minutes per side. Let cool to room temperature, then slice into long thin strips.

56 PARSLEYED CHICKEN WITH GARLIC
Prep: 25 minutes   Cook: 10 to 14 minutes   Serves: 4

For variation, substitute 8 chicken thighs or 1 whole chicken, cut up.

4 large chicken breast halves,
   boned, with skin left on
¼ cup dry white wine or
   vermouth
6 large garlic cloves, minced
⅓ cup chopped parsley,
   preferably Italian flat-leaf

¼ teaspoon salt
⅛ teaspoon freshly ground
   pepper
2 tablespoons olive oil

1. Rinse chicken with cold water and pat dry. In a small saucepan, heat wine and garlic until just simmering. Remove from heat and let cool completely.

2. Using a slotted spoon, transfer garlic to a small bowl; reserve wine. Toss garlic with parsley and season with salt and pepper. Place about 1 tablespoon of this mixture between skin and meat of each chicken breast.

3. Add olive oil and remaining parsley mixture to garlic-flavored wine and set aside. Season breasts lightly with additional salt and pepper.

4. Prepare a hot fire. Cook chicken over ash-covered coals, turning and brushing with garlic-flavored wine and oil, until browned outside and no longer pink inside, about 5 to 7 minutes per side.

57 CHICKEN LEGS TAPENADE

Prep: 15 minutes   Marinate: 2 hours   Cook: 35 minutes
Serves: 4 to 6

The marinade used in this succulent dish contains the lusty flavors so popular in southern France.

3½ pounds chicken legs	¼ cup capers, drained
1 2-ounce can flat anchovy fillets	¼ cup extra-virgin olive oil
1 6-ounce can pitted ripe olives, drained	1 teaspoon crushed hot red pepper flakes
1 tablespoon chopped fresh thyme leaves, or 1 teaspoon dried	2 large garlic cloves, minced
	½ teaspoon salt
	¼ teaspoon freshly ground pepper

1. Rinse chicken legs with cold water and pat dry. Place in a single layer in a large shallow pan.

2. Rinse and drain anchovies. In a food processor or blender, puree anchovies, olives, thyme, capers, olive oil, hot pepper, and garlic. Season tapenade with salt and pepper.

3. Brush chicken all over with half of tapenade. Reserve other half of sauce. Cover chicken and marinate 2 to 4 hours at cool room temperature, or longer refrigerated.

4. Prepare a hot fire. Place chicken legs on an oiled grill set 4 to 6 inches over coals. Grill, turning frequently and basting with reserved sauce, until chicken is cooked through, about 35 minutes total. Serve warm or at room temperature, garnished with sprigs of fresh thyme, if desired.

58 CHICKEN WINGS WAIKIKI

Prep: 15 minutes   Cook: 10 to 15 minutes   Serves: 4

12 chicken wings (2 to 3 pounds)	½ teaspoon salt
⅓ cup vegetable oil	½ cup pineapple or apricot preserves
¼ cup pineapple or lemon juice	½ cup soy sauce
	1 teaspoon Dijon mustard

1. Rinse chicken with cold water and pat dry. In a large bowl, toss chicken wings with oil, 2 tablespoons pineapple or lemon juice, and salt; set aside.

2. In a small bowl, mix together preserves, soy sauce, mustard, and remaining pineapple or lemon juice.

3. Prepare a hot fire. Remove chicken from marinade and place on an oiled grill set 4 to 6 inches over coals. Grill wings, turning frequently and basting with reserved sauce, until golden brown and cooked through, about 10 to 15 minutes.

59 GRILLED GAME HENS WITH MUSTARD BUTTER

Prep: 15 minutes   Marinate: 2 hours   Cook: 16 to 20 minutes
Serves: 4 to 6

Bits of spicy mustard butter tucked beneath the skin makes these juicy and irresistible.

4 Cornish game hens, about
    1¼ pounds each
4 garlic cloves, crushed
1 teaspoon salt
¼ teaspoon freshly ground
    pepper

1½ cups dry white wine
3 tablespoons extra-virgin
    olive oil
Mustard Butter (recipe
    follows)

1. Rinse game hens with cold water. Pat dry with paper towels. Using a cleaver or poultry shears, cut hens in half, splitting first down one side of backbone and then through breast. Place halved birds, skin side up, on a clean work surface and press down firmly with palm of your hand to flatten birds. Rub halves with crushed garlic, season with salt and pepper, and place in a nonreactive baking or roasting pan just large enough to hold hens in a single layer. Pour in wine and oil and cover with plastic wrap. Marinate 2 hours at room temperature, or as long as 48 hours refrigerated, turning hens once or twice. Let return to room temperature before grilling.

2. Prepare a hot fire. Remove birds from marinade and pat dry; reserve marinade. Using your fingers, gently loosen skin from meat to separate without tearing. Shave off slivers of cold Mustard Butter and insert about 1 tablespoon under skin of each half hen.

3. Place game hens skin side down on a well-oiled grill set about 6 inches from coals. Grill until skin is slightly browned, 8 to 10 minutes. Turn birds over and continue to cook, turning occasionally and basting with reserved marinade, until juices run clear when meat is pierced near leg joint with a fork or skewer, about 8 to 10 minutes longer. Before serving, top each cooked game hen half with an additional 1½ teaspoons Mustard Butter, if desired.

MUSTARD BUTTER

12 tablespoons (1½ sticks)
    butter, softened
2½ tablespoons Dijon mustard

1½ teaspoons mustard seeds,
    lightly crushed

1. Combine butter, Dijon mustard, and mustard seeds in a food processor or blender. Process until well blended. Chill until firm before using for grilled game hens.

2. If made in advance, butter can be wrapped tightly in plastic wrap and refrigerated up to 5 days or frozen.

60 VIETNAMESE GRILLED 5-SPICE CORNISH GAME HENS

Prep: 25 minutes   Marinate: 1 hour   Cook: 30 minutes   Serves: 4

Our friend and colleague, Joyce Jue, is a writer, teacher, lecturer, and internationally recognized authority on Asian cuisines. This recipe is her adaptation of a dish served at one of her favorite Vietnamese restaurants. It also makes a delightful appetizer over crisp shredded lettuce, in which case it will serve eight.

4 Cornish game hens	½ teaspoon 5-spice powder*
4 garlic cloves	1½ tablespoons fish sauce (nuoc
2 shallots or 3 scallions, white part only	mam)**
1½ tablespoons sugar	1½ tablespoons soy sauce
½ teaspoon salt	1½ tablespoons dry sherry
¼ teaspoon freshly ground pepper	Nuoc Cham Dipping Sauce (recipe follows)

1. Using a heavy cleaver or poultry shears, cut hens in half through breast and one side of backbone. With the palm of your hand, press down on each breast to flatten.

2. In a food processor, grind together garlic, shallots, and sugar until finely minced. Add salt, pepper, 5-spice powder, fish sauce, soy sauce, and sherry. Blend thoroughly. Rub mixture all over hens. Marinate at room temperature for 1 to 3 hours.

3. Prepare a hot fire. Cook hens on an oiled grill for 15 minutes. Turn over. Grill 15 minutes longer, or until juices run clear when pierced with tip of a knife. Serve with individual bowls of Nuoc Cham Dipping Sauce.

* *Chinese 5-spice powder is widely available in the spice section of supermarkets and in Asian markets.*
** *Fish sauce is available in Asian markets. It is called* nuoc mam *in Vietnam and* nam pla *in Thailand.*

NUOC CHAM DIPPING SAUCE

3 garlic cloves, minced	¼ cup fish sauce (nuoc mam)
2 serrano or other small hot chili peppers	⅓ cup water
3 tablespoons fresh lime juice	1 small carrot, peeled and finely shredded
1½ tablespoons sugar	

1. In a small bowl, combine garlic, chilies, lime juice, sugar, fish sauce, and water. Let stand at room temperature for 10 to 15 minutes.

2. Strain sauce through a fine sieve into a bowl; discard solids. Stir shredded carrot into sauce. Cover and refrigerate until serving time.

61   PLUM DELICIOUS GAME HENS
Prep: 15 minutes   Cook: 16 to 22 minutes   Serves: 4 to 6

4 Cornish game hens, about
   1¼ pounds each
1 teaspoon salt

½ teaspoon freshly ground
   pepper
Spicy Plum Sauce (page 185)

1. Prepare a hot fire. Rinse game hens with cold water and pat dry. Using a cleaver or poultry shears, cut hens in half, splitting first down one side of backbone and then through breast. Place halved birds, skin side up, on a clean work surface and press down firmly with palm of your hand to flatten birds. Season both sides with salt and pepper.

2. Place game hens skin side down on a well-oiled grill set 4 to 6 inches from coals. Heat Spicy Plum Sauce in a small heavy saucepan on side of grill to warm. Grill hens until skin is browned on bottom, about 6 to 8 minutes. Turn birds over and grill until second side is lightly browned, 6 to 8 minutes.

3. Brush hens with Spicy Plum Sauce. Continue to grill, turning and basting generously with sauce, until outside is nicely browned but not charred and juices run clear when meat near leg joint is pierced, about 4 to 6 minutes longer.

62   SHERRIED TURKEY QUARTERS
Prep: 15 minutes   Marinate: 2 hours   Cook: 1 hour   Serves: 6

If turkey quarters are unavailable at your supermarket, ask the butcher to quarter a whole turkey for you.

1 5- to 6-pound turkey,
   quartered
1 cup olive oil
½ cup white wine vinegar
½ cup dry sherry
2 teaspoons celery salt

2 teaspoons salt
1 tablespoon chopped fresh
   rosemary, or 1 teaspoon
   dried
4 garlic cloves, minced

1. Rinse turkey with cold water and pat dry. Place in a large nonreactive roasting pan. In a medium bowl, combine remaining ingredients. Pour over turkey, cover with plastic wrap, and marinate, turning occasionally, 2 to 3 hours at room temperature, or longer refrigerated.

2. Prepare a medium fire. Place turkey quarters on an oiled grill set 6 inches from coals; reserve marinade. Cook, turning once or twice, until browned on both sides, about 15 minutes. Reset grill to about 18 inches above coals or adjust fire to low and continue to cook, basting frequently with marinade, until turkey is cooked through and meat at thickest part of drumstick cuts easily with no trace of pink, about 45 minutes longer.

63   GRILLED TURKEY PAILLARDS
Prep: 10 minutes   Cook: 4 to 6 minutes   Serves: 4

A paillard is a large thin slice of meat ideal for quick grilling. Because the slices are so thin, we recommend cooking the meat while still chilled, so as not to overcook and dry out the turkey.

4 turkey scallopini, or 4 slices
   uncooked turkey breast
   (3/8 to 1/2 inch thick)
3 tablespoons olive oil
	1/2 teaspoon salt
	1/8 teaspoon freshly ground
	   pepper
	Lemon wedges

1. Rinse turkey under cold water and pat dry. Place each slice between 2 sheets of wax paper and pound with a mallet or flat side of a cleaver until they reach a uniform thickness of 1/8 inch. Brush both sides of each paillard with oil and season with salt and pepper. Refrigerate, covered, until ready to cook.

2. Prepare a hot fire. Place chilled turkey paillards on an oiled grill set 4 to 6 inches from coals. Cook, turning once, until lightly browned outside but still juicy inside, about 4 to 6 minutes total.

3. Serve grilled paillards with lemon wedges to squeeze over turkey.

64   GRILLED TURKEY SCALLOPINI WITH MOROCCAN SAUCE
Prep: 15 minutes   Cook: 8 to 10 minutes   Serves: 4

1/2 cup chopped cilantro
1/2 cup chopped parsley
4 large garlic cloves, crushed
1/3 cup fresh lemon juice
1 1/2 teaspoons salt
1 teaspoon paprika
1/4 teaspoon ground cumin
	1/8 teaspoon cayenne
	1/3 cup plus 2 tablespoons extra-
	   virgin olive oil
	4 turkey scallopini or thin
	   slices uncooked breast
	   meat
	Freshly ground pepper

1. Prepare a hot fire. In a medium bowl, combine cilantro, parsley, garlic, lemon juice, salt, paprika, cumin, and cayenne. Whisk in 1/3 cup olive oil. Use at once or cover sauce and let stand at room temperature for up to 2 hours.

2. If turkey slices are thicker than 1/2 inch or are uneven, pound between pieces of wax paper to thin out and even. Season lightly with additional salt and pepper. Brush with remaining 2 tablespoons olive oil. Place turkey scallopini on grill set 4 to 6 inches from coals. Grill, turning once, until lightly browned and cooked through but still moist, about 8 to 10 minutes. Top each scallopini with a generous spoonful of Moroccan sauce and pass remaining sauce on the side.

65 GRILLED TURKEY THIGHS WITH CRANBERRY CHUTNEY

Prep: 25 minutes   Cook: 40 to 55 minutes   Serves: 4

1 12-ounce package fresh or frozen cranberries	1 large garlic clove, minced
2 tart apples, skin on, cored and chopped	¼ teaspoon ground cloves
1½ cups (packed) dark brown sugar	¼ teaspoon ground allspice
½ cup raisins	Zest of 1 orange, chopped
¼ cup cider vinegar	4 boneless turkey thighs
1 teaspoon minced fresh ginger, or ¼ teaspoon dried	1 teaspoon salt
	½ teaspoon freshly ground pepper
	2 tablespoons vegetable oil

1. In a large nonreactive saucepan, combine cranberries, apples, brown sugar, raisins, vinegar, ginger, garlic, cloves, allspice, and orange zest. Boil over medium heat, stirring occasionally, until thickened, 10 to 15 minutes. Let cool, then transfer to a covered jar and refrigerate for up to 3 weeks.

2. Prepare a hot fire. Season turkey thighs with salt and pepper and brush with oil. Place skin side down on an oiled grill set 4 to 6 inches from coals. Grill, turning once or twice, until thighs are well browned outside and cooked through but still moist, about 30 to 40 minutes. Serve with cranberry chutney on the side.

---

66 YOGURT-GLAZED TURKEY BREAST

Prep: 15 minutes   Marinate: 24 hours   Cook: 40 to 50 minutes
Serves: 3 to 4

1 turkey breast half, about 2 pounds (with back and rib portions)	¼ cup plain yogurt
½ teaspoon salt	1 teaspoon Dijon mustard
⅛ teaspoon freshly ground pepper	½ cup orange juice
1 garlic clove, minced	1 tablespoon chopped fresh sage leaves, or 1 teaspoon dried
	1 teaspoon honey

1. Rinse turkey breast with cold water and pat dry. Season with salt and pepper and place in a nonreactive baking dish. In a small bowl, combine garlic, yogurt, mustard, orange juice, sage, and honey. Brush marinade over turkey, cover with plastic wrap, and refrigerate 24 to 48 hours.

2. Prepare a hot fire. Remove turkey from marinade, reserving marinade. Grill turkey over indirect heat, turning at least once, until browned outside and just cooked through inside, about 40 to 50 minutes total. Baste with reserved marinade during last 10 minutes of cooking.

67 GRILLED TURKEY HASH
Prep: 20 minutes   Cook: 13 to 15 minutes   Serves: 6

Here's a delicious way to use leftovers from a barbecued turkey dinner.

2 tablespoons vegetable oil
1 medium onion, finely
    chopped
2 garlic cloves, minced
¼ cup finely chopped green
    bell pepper
3 cups cooked turkey, diced
1 cup chopped leftover turkey
    stuffing or diced cooked
    potatoes

1 teaspoon salt
¼ teaspoon freshly ground
    pepper
½ cup toasted sliced almonds
¼ cup heavy cream

1. Heat oil in a large skillet. Add onion, garlic, and bell pepper. Cook over medium heat until onion is golden, 3 to 5 minutes. Remove from heat and let cool.

2. In a medium bowl, combine cooked onion, garlic, and green pepper with turkey, stuffing or potatoes, salt, pepper, almonds, and cream. Mix to blend well. Form into 6 patties about ¾ inch thick.

3. Prepare a hot fire. Place patties on an oiled grill 6 inches from coals and grill, turning once, until crispy brown outside, about 10 minutes.

68 GRILLED TURKEY TENDERLOINS WITH PINEAPPLE SALSA
Prep: 10 minutes   Marinate: 1 hour   Cook: 10 minutes   Serves: 6

6 turkey breast tenderloins,
    cut about 1 inch thick
1½ teaspoons salt
⅛ teaspoon freshly ground
    pepper

½ cup olive oil
¼ cup fresh lemon juice
½ cup coarsely chopped onion
Grilled Pineapple Salsa
    (recipe follows)

1. Rinse turkey with cold water and pat dry. Season with salt and pepper. Combine olive oil, lemon juice, and onion in a shallow nonreactive pan. Add turkey and turn to coat. Cover and marinate at room temperature for 1 hour.

2. Prepare a hot fire. Grill turkey over hot coals, turning once, until browned outside and just cooked through, about 5 minutes per side. Top each portion with a spoonful of Grilled Pineapple Salsa before serving. Pass remaining salsa on the side.

69 GRILLED PINEAPPLE SALSA
Prep: 15 minutes   Marinate: 2 hours   Serves: 6

1 medium pineapple, skin removed
1 medium red onion, finely chopped
2 jalapeño peppers, seeded and minced

1 garlic clove, minced
½ cup chopped fresh cilantro or mint
1 teaspoon sugar
¼ teaspoon salt

1. Prepare a hot fire. Slice pineapple into rounds ½ to ¾ inch thick. When coals are covered with gray ash, place pineapple slices on an oiled rack set 4 to 6 inches from coals. Grill, turning once or twice, until lightly browned on both sides, about 10 minutes. Let cool, then finely dice grilled pineapple, discarding tough center core.

2. Combine pineapple, red onion, jalapeño peppers, garlic, cilantro, sugar, and salt in a medium bowl. Marinate at least 2 hours at room temperature, or cover and refrigerate as long as 3 days.

70 KENTUCKY TURKEY AND BACON BROCHETTES
Prep: 10 minutes   Marinate: 2 hours   Cook: 10 minutes   Serves: 4

Economical turkey thighs get the royal treatment!

2 skinless, boneless turkey thighs
½ teaspoon salt

Kentucky Marinade (page 176)
8 strips thinly sliced bacon

1. Rinse turkey with cold water and pat dry. Cut each thigh into 8 equal pieces and season with salt. Place in a bowl with marinade and toss well. Cover and marinate 2 hours at room temperature, or as long as 48 hours refrigerated.

2. Prepare a hot fire. Cut bacon strips in half crosswise and lay flat on a clean work surface. Lift turkey from marinade and place 1 piece on each bacon slice. Wrap bacon around thigh meat and thread 4 pieces onto each of 4 oiled metal skewers, taking care that bacon is secured.

3. Place brochettes on an oiled grill set about 6 inches from coals. Grill brochettes, turning and moving occasionally and basting with reserved marinade, until bacon is well browned and turkey is cooked through, about 10 minutes.

71 TURKEY KEBABS WITH HONEY-MUSTARD SAUCE

Prep: 15 minutes   Marinate: 2 hours   Cook: 15 minutes   Serves: 4

Overcooking delicate turkey breast meat will make it dry, so be sure to remove these kebabs from the grill while the turkey is still juicy.

1½ pounds skinless, boneless turkey breast	1½ teaspoons salt
⅓ cup olive oil	½ teaspoon freshly ground pepper
½ cup dry white wine	Honey-Mustard Sauce
2 large garlic cloves, minced	(recipe follows)

1. Rinse turkey under cold running water and pat dry. Cut into 1½- to 2-inch cubes and place in a medium bowl. Add olive oil, wine, garlic, salt, and pepper; toss until well mixed. Cover with plastic wrap and marinate 2 to 4 hours at room temperature, or overnight in refrigerator.

2. Prepare a hot fire. Thread turkey pieces closely together on long metal skewers. Place on an oiled grill set 4 to 6 inches from coals and grill, turning and moving skewers occasionally, until just barely cooked, about 10 minutes. Turn again and brush with some Honey-Mustard Sauce. Grill until kebabs are browned outside and just cooked through, about 5 minutes longer. Transfer kebabs to a platter and pour on remaining sauce before serving.

HONEY-MUSTARD SAUCE

1 cup heavy cream	1 tablespoon coarse-grained
3 tablespoons dry white wine	mustard
1 tablespoon honey	

1. In a medium saucepan, boil cream over medium-high heat on stove until it is reduced by half, about 6 to 8 minutes.

2. Stir in wine, honey, and mustard. Cook just until heated through, about 1 minute. Remove from heat. (This sauce can be prepared up to 2 days ahead and refrigerated, covered. Reheat on stove or side of grill before using.)

72 TURKEY AND PARMESAN BURGERS WITH GRILLED CALIFORNIA SALSA
Prep: 10 minutes   Cook: 16 to 20 minutes   Serves: 6

2 pounds ground turkey
¼ cup heavy cream
½ cup grated Parmesan cheese
1 tablespoon chopped fresh
    basil, or 1 teaspoon dried

1½ teaspoons salt
½ teaspoon freshly ground
    pepper
    Grilled California Salsa
    (recipe follows)

1. Prepare a hot fire. Place turkey in a large bowl and as quickly and lightly as possible, mix in cream, cheese, basil, salt, and pepper. Lightly form meat mixture into 6 patties about 1 inch thick.

2. Place patties on an oiled grill set 4 to 6 inches from coals. Grill, turning once or twice, until patties are well browned on both sides and no longer pink in the center, about 16 to 20 minutes. Top each burger with a spoonful of Grilled California Salsa.

73 GRILLED CALIFORNIA SALSA
Prep: 5 minutes   Cook: 20 minutes   Makes: 1½ cups

Grilling vegetables gives a delightful smoky flavor to familiar salsa. Although it is best served the day it is made, leftover sauce can be stored in a covered jar in the refrigerator for up to 2 days.

5 large tomatoes
1 large onion
1 tablespoon olive oil
3 Anaheim or other mild
    chilies

1 small fresh hot chili pepper,
    such as jalapeño or
    serrano

1. Prepare a hot fire. Core tomatoes and slice in half. Cut onion into 1-inch-thick slices. Lightly brush cut sides of tomato and both sides of onion slices with oil.

2. Place tomato halves, onion slices, whole Anaheim chilies, and hot pepper on an oiled grill set 4 to 6 inches from coals. Grill tomatoes until soft, 3 to 5 minutes. Grill onion, turning once, until browned outside and just tender, about 15 to 20 minutes.

3. Grill Anaheim chilies and hot pepper, turning frequently, until skin is charred all over, about 12 to 15 minutes for Anaheim, 5 minutes for small hot pepper. As soon as chilies are cooked, enclose in a plastic bag for 10 minutes. (If you have a small grill, cook vegetables in batches.)

4. Peel tomatoes. Chop tomatoes and onion and place in a medium bowl. Peel charred skin off chilies and remove stems and seeds. Chop chilies and add to bowl. Toss to mix. Serve at room temperature.

74 GRILLED TURKEY SAUSAGE WITH CILANTRO PESTO

Prep: 10 minutes   Cook: 12 to 15 minutes   Serves: 4 to 6

2 cups cilantro leaves (about ½ pound), well washed and dried
½ cup flat-leaf Italian parsley leaves
1 large garlic clove, peeled
½ cup grated Parmesan cheese
⅓ cup hulled pumpkin seeds (pepitas) or pine nuts

1 tablespoon fresh lime or lemon juice
¼ cup extra-virgin olive oil
½ teaspoon salt
¼ teaspoon freshly ground pepper
2 pounds turkey sausage

1. Prepare a hot fire. In a food processor or blender, combine cilantro, parsley, garlic, Parmesan cheese, pumpkin seeds, lime juice, olive oil, salt, and pepper. Purée to a coarse paste. Set cilantro pesto aside.

2. Prick each sausage several times with tines of a fork to allow fat to escape while cooking. Place sausages on an oiled grill set 6 inches from coals. Cook, turning occasionally, until outside is browned and no pink remains in center, about 12 to 15 minutes. Serve with a spoonful of cilantro pesto on the side. (Any leftover pesto can be stored in a tightly covered jar in refrigerator for 5 days, or frozen.)

---

75 SCOTCH-SOAKED BUTTERFLIED QUAIL

Prep: 20 minutes   Marinate: 2 hours   Cook: 8 to 10 minutes
Serves: 4 to 6

These dark-meat birds make a spectacular entrée. Quail cooks very quickly and tastes best when the breast meat is still slightly pink.

12 quail, 3 to 4 ounces each, thawed if frozen
1 medium onion
½ cup Scotch whiskey
2 tablespoons extra-virgin olive oil

1 tablespoon chopped fresh rosemary, or 1 teaspoon dried
1 teaspoon salt
¼ teaspoon freshly ground pepper

1. Rinse quail with cold water and pat dry. Using a cleaver or poultry shears, cut through backbone of each bird. Place quail, skin side up, on a flat surface and press down firmly to flatten birds. Place in a nonreactive baking or roasting pan just large enough to hold quail in a single layer.

2. In a food processor or blender, purée onion, Scotch, olive oil, rosemary, salt, and pepper until smooth. Pour over quail, cover with plastic wrap, and marinate, turning occasionally, 2 hours at room temperature, or up to 48 hours refrigerated. Let return to room temperature before grilling.

3. Prepare a hot fire. Remove birds from marinade; reserve marinade. Place quail skin side up on a well-oiled grill set 6 inches over coals. Cook, turning

occasionally and basting with reserved marinade, until skin is browned and breast meat is just pink in center, about 8 to 10 minutes.

76 GRILLED BREAST OF DUCK A L'ORANGE
Prep: 5 minutes   Marinate: 30 minutes   Cook: 14 to 18 minutes
Serves: 2

1 whole duck breast, bone in and skin on	½ cup dry white wine
1 cup orange juice	4 sprigs fresh thyme, or ½ teaspoon dried

1. Rinse duck breast with cold water and pat dry. Use a sharp knife to score several diagonal slash marks in the skin. Place in a shallow glass baking dish or pie pan.

2. Combine orange juice, wine, and thyme. Pour over duck breast and cover with plastic wrap. Marinate at least 30 minutes at room temperature, or overnight in refrigerator.

3. Prepare a hot fire. Remove duck from marinade and pat dry with a paper towel; reserve marinade. Grill duck breast 8 to 10 minutes on each side, brushing occasionally with marinade, until skin is slightly charred and meat is just cooked through but still juicy.

77 LORETTA'S BARBECUED DUCK
Prep: 15 minutes   Cook: 1¼ hours   Serves: 2 to 4

¾ cup ketchup	1½ teaspoons chili powder
¾ cup water	¼ teaspoon cayenne
¼ cup red wine vinegar	1 4½- to 5-pound duck, quartered
1 medium onion, chopped	½ teaspoon salt
2 tablespoons brown sugar	
1 tablespoon chopped fresh thyme, or ¾ teaspoon dried	

1. In a small nonreactive saucepan, combine ketchup, water, vinegar, onion, brown sugar, thyme, chili powder, and cayenne. Bring to a boil over medium-high heat. Reduce heat to medium-low and simmer uncovered, stirring occasionally, until barbecue sauce is slightly thickened, about 30 minutes.

2. Remove all excess fat from duck. Rinse with cold water and pat dry. Season with salt.

3. Prepare a medium-hot fire. Place duck, skin side up, on an oiled grill set 6 inches from coals. Grill, turning and moving pieces frequently to avoid flare-ups, until duck is lightly browned on both sides, about 15 minutes. Continue to cook, basting with barbecue sauce and turning, until skin is well browned and meat is cooked through, about 30 minutes longer. Serve with remaining barbecue sauce on the side.

78 GRILLED DUCK BREASTS WITH QUICK APPLE AND APRICOT CHUTNEY
Prep: 30 minutes   Cook: 28 to 40 minutes   Serves: 6

This unusual condiment is great with grilled pork chops, too.

- 1 **pound unpeeled tart apples, diced**
- ½ **cup coarsely chopped dried apricots**
- ¾ **cup cider vinegar**
- ½ **lemon, seeded and chopped (skin and all)**
- ¾ **cup (packed) light brown sugar**
- ¼ **cup minced fresh ginger**
- 2 **garlic cloves, minced**
- 2 **shallots, chopped**
- ½ **cup golden raisins**
- 2½ **teaspoons salt**
  Pinch of cayenne
- ½ **cup chopped walnuts or pecans**
- 3 **whole duck breasts, boned, skinned, and split in half (about 1½ pounds total)**
- 2 **tablespoons olive oil**
- ½ **teaspoon freshly ground pepper**

1. In a medium nonreactive saucepan, combine apples, apricots, vinegar, lemon, brown sugar, ginger, garlic, shallots, raisins, ½ teaspoon salt, and cayenne. Boil gently, uncovered, until thickened, 20 to 30 minutes. Let cool to room temperature, then stir in nuts. Store chutney tightly covered in refrigerator for up to 2 weeks before serving.

2. Prepare a hot fire. Rinse duck breasts under cold water and pat dry. Brush both sides with olive oil. Season with 2 teaspoons salt and pepper. Place on an oiled grill set 6 inches from coals. Grill, turning once, until browned outside and just cooked through but still moist, about 8 to 10 minutes. Serve with apple and apricot chutney.

79 GINGERED DUCK BREASTS WITH NECTARINES
Prep: 15 minutes   Marinate: 2 hours   Cook: 12 to 14 minutes Serves: 4

Duck breasts, which can be found in butcher shops and are becoming increasingly available in supermarkets, make an excellent choice for entertaining.

- 2 **whole duck breasts, boned, skinned, and split (about 1 pound total)**
- 2 **tablespoons dry sherry**
- 2 **tablespoons soy sauce**
- 2 **tablespoons peanut oil**
- 1 **tablespoon minced fresh ginger**
- ½ **teaspoon Asian sesame oil**
- 1 **teaspoon salt**
- ¼ **teaspoon freshly ground pepper**
- 2 **firm ripe nectarines**

1. Rinse duck breasts with cold water and pat dry. In a glass baking dish, combine sherry, soy sauce, peanut oil, ginger, and sesame oil. Season duck breasts with salt and pepper and add to soy mixture. Turn to coat. Marinate duck in soy mixture, turning once or twice, for 2 hours at room temperature, or longer in refrigerator.

2. Prepare a hot fire. Halve and pit nectarines and brush with some of marinade. Place on an oiled grill set 6 inches from coals and cook, turning once, until nectarines just begin to soften, about 4 minutes. Remove and set aside.

3. Lift duck from marinade and pat dry. Place on an oiled grill and cook, turning once and brushing with marinade, until browned outside and just cooked through but still moist, about 8 to 10 minutes. Serve duck with grilled nectarine halves.

Chapter 3

Wholly Hamburgers and Hot Dogs

For many Americans, especially kids, the preferred meal in a bun has to be the hamburger, seconded only by the hot dog. And if you're under five, the hot dog might well win out. What's a barbecue without a burger and a frank, anyway?

For hamburgers, we prefer to use freshly ground chuck, because its natural fat content makes for a juicier burger. If you use a leaner meat, simply add 2 tablespoons ice water to add moisture. (Also use this trick with ground turkey, lamb, or veal.) When you're forming the burgers, remember that over-handling any ground meat will toughen the texture of the finished burger—so easy does it!

Burgers sometimes puff up during grilling. If they look too thick to bite into, flatten slightly once with a wide metal spatula right after turning them over. Resist the temptation to keep pressing down on them as you stand over the grill, because you'll lose tasty juices.

Whether you call them hot dogs, frankfurters, or weiners, remember to prick them with the tines of a fork or the tip of a knife before grilling to prevent them from bursting. Almost all franks are precooked, so they need only to be heated through and browned to your taste.

Hamburgers and hot dogs are fast food, even if you prepare them at home. And nothing is easier if you're grilling for a crowd. Here are more than two dozen ways to serve them to kids of all ages. We guarantee you'll never be bored with the same old hot dog or hamburger anymore.

80   THE BASIC BURGER
Prep: 10 minutes   Cook: 8 to 12 minutes   Serves: 4

1⅓ pounds ground chuck
1½ teaspoons salt
½ teaspoon freshly ground
   pepper
4 hamburger buns, onion
   rolls, or other bread

Optional: Mustard,
ketchup, mayonnaise,
sliced sweet onion or
grilled onion slices,
pickles or pickle relish,
sliced tomatoes, lettuce
leaves

1. Prepare a hot fire. In a medium bowl, working as quickly and gently as possible, mix ground beef with salt and pepper. Divide mixture into quarters and lightly form into 4 patties ¾ to 1 inch thick.

2. Place patties on an oiled grill set 4 to 6 inches from coals. Grill, turning once, until outside is well browned but inside is still pink and juicy, about 8 to 12 minutes for rare to medium rare, or longer if desired.

3. Meanwhile, open buns and rolls. Toast on sides of grill until warm and lightly browned. Place cooked burgers in buns and let everyone choose their own fixings.

> **NOTE:** *If cooking for a crowd, you may want to wrap buns together in aluminum foil and warm the package on the side of the grill, rather than toasting them individually.*

81   CHEESEBURGERS
Prep: 10 minutes   Cook: 8 to 12 minutes   Serves: 4

1⅓ pounds ground chuck
1½ teaspoons salt
½ teaspoon freshly ground
   pepper
4 slices cheese, such as
   American, Swiss, or
   Cheddar
4 hamburger buns, onion
   rolls, or other bread

Optional: Mustard,
ketchup, mayonnaise,
sliced sweet onion or
grilled onion slices,
pickles or pickle relish,
sliced tomatoes, lettuce
leaves

1. Prepare a hot fire. In a medium bowl, working as quickly and gently as possible, mix ground beef with salt and pepper. Divide mixture into quarters and lightly form into 4 patties ¾ to 1 inch thick.

2. Place patties on an oiled grill set 4 to 6 inches from coals. Grill, turning once, until outside is well browned but inside is still pink and juicy, about 8 to 12 minutes for rare to medium rare, or longer if desired. About 30 seconds before moving burgers from grill, top each with a slice of cheese.

3. Meanwhile, open buns or rolls and toast on sides of grill until warm and lightly browned. Place cooked cheeseburgers in buns and let everyone choose their own fixings.

82 CHILI BURGERS
Prep: 10 minutes   Cook: 8 to 12 minutes   Serves: 4

1⅓ pounds ground chuck
1½ teaspoons salt
½ teaspoon freshly ground
    pepper
1 garlic clove, crushed
2 teaspoons chili powder
½ teaspoon ground cumin
2 cups chili con carne, canned
    or homemade

4 hamburger buns, onion
    rolls, or other bread
Optional: Chopped raw
    onion, grated Cheddar
    cheese, sour cream, sliced
    black olives, sliced
    tomatoes, lettuce

1. Prepare a hot fire. In a medium bowl, working as quickly and gently as possible, mix ground beef with salt, pepper, garlic, chili powder, and cumin. Divide mixture into quarters and lightly form into 4 patties ¾ to 1 inch thick. Warm chili con carne in a small heavy saucepan on side of grill.

2. Place patties on an oiled grill set 4 to 6 inches from coals. Grill, turning once, until outside is well browned but inside is still pink and juicy, about 8 to 12 minutes for rare to medium rare, or longer if desired.

3. Meanwhile, open buns or rolls and toast on sides of grill until warm and lightly browned. Place cooked burgers in buns, top with a big spoonful of chili, and let everyone choose their own fixings. Pass any remaining chili on the side.

83 PIZZA BURGERS
Prep: 10 minutes   Cook: 8 to 12 minutes   Serves: 4

1⅓ pounds ground chuck
1 teaspoon oregano
1½ teaspoons salt
½ teaspoon freshly ground
    pepper
4 hamburger buns, hard rolls,
    or Italian bread

¼ cup sliced black olives or
    sautéed mushroom and/
    or green bell pepper slices
½ cup bottled pizza or
    marinara sauce
4 slices mozzarella

1. Prepare a hot fire. In a medium bowl, working as quickly and gently as possible, mix ground beef with oregano, salt, and pepper. Divide mixture into quarters and lightly form into 4 patties ¾ to 1 inch thick. Warm pizza sauce in a butter warmer or very small saucepan on edge of grill.

2. Place patties on an oiled grill set 4 to 6 inches from coals. Grill, turning once, until outside is lightly charred but inside is still pink and juicy, about 8 to 12 minutes for rare to medium rare, or longer if desired. About 30 seconds before removing burgers from grill, top each with a slice of mozzarella.

3. Meanwhile, open buns and toast on sides of grill until warm and lightly browned. Place cooked burgers in buns. Top each burger with 1 tablespoon sliced olives and about 1½ tablespoons pizza sauce. Serve at once.

84   SAN FRANCISCO BURGERS
Prep: 15 minutes   Cook: 13 to 19 minutes   Serves: 4

1⅓ pounds ground chuck
1 garlic clove, crushed
1½ tablespoons minced fresh
    basil, or ½ teaspoon dried
1½ teaspoons salt
½ teaspoon freshly ground
    pepper
2 tablespoons extra-virgin
    olive oil
1 large onion, thickly sliced

4 slices Monterey Jack cheese
4 crusty French or Italian rolls,
    preferably sourdough
Optional: Pesto (page 182; or
    your favorite brand),
    Dijon mustard, ketchup,
    mayonnaise, sliced
    tomatoes, shredded
    romaine lettuce

1. Prepare a hot fire. In a medium bowl, working as quickly and gently as possible, mix ground beef with garlic, basil, salt, pepper, and 1 tablespoon olive oil. Divide into quarters and lightly form into 4 rectangular patties, ¾ to 1 inch thick, shaped to fit into French rolls.

2. Brush onion slices with remaining olive oil and place on an oiled grill set 4 to 6 inches from coals. Grill, turning once, until lightly browned and tender, 5 to 7 minutes. As onions cook, move them to sides of grill.

3. Place burgers on grill and cook, turning once, until outside is well browned but inside is still pink and juicy, about 8 to 12 minutes for rare to medium rare, or longer if desired. About 30 seconds before removing burgers from grill, top each with a slice of Jack cheese.

4. Meanwhile, split open rolls and toast on sides of grill until warm and lightly browned. Place cooked burgers in rolls and top with grilled onions. Let everyone choose their own fixings.

85   TACO BURGERS
Prep: 10 minutes   Cook: 8 to 12 minutes   Serves: 4

1⅓ pounds ground chuck
¼ cup crushed tortilla chips
2 tablespoons bottled taco
    sauce
1 teaspoon salt
½ teaspoon freshly ground
    pepper
4 cornmeal or other
    hamburger buns

Optional: Sliced pickled
    jalapeño peppers,
    shredded Cheddar
    cheese, chopped
    scallions, sliced tomatoes,
    shredded iceberg lettuce,
    additional taco sauce

1. Prepare a hot fire. In a medium bowl, working as quickly and gently as possible, mix ground beef with crushed tortilla chips, taco sauce, salt, and pepper. Divide mixture into quarters and lightly form into 4 patties ¾ to 1 inch thick.

2. Place patties on an oiled grill set 4 to 6 inches from coals. Grill, turning once, until outside is well browned and inside is slightly charred but still pink and juicy, about 8 to 12 minutes for rare to medium rare, or longer if desired.

3. Meanwhile, open buns and toast on sides of grill until warm and lightly browned. Place cooked burgers in buns and let everyone choose their own fixings.

---

86 HERBED BURGUNDY BURGERS
Prep: 10 minutes   Cook: 8 to 12 minutes   Serves: 4

1⅓ pounds ground chuck
2 tablespoons dry red wine
1 tablespoon chopped fresh herbs (such as thyme, chives, sage, and/or parsley), or 1 teaspoon dried
1½ teaspoons Dijon mustard
1½ teaspoons salt
½ teaspoon freshly ground pepper

4 hamburger buns, onion rolls, or other bread
Optional: Mustard, ketchup, mayonnaise, sliced sweet onion or grilled onion slices, pickles or pickle relish, sliced tomatoes, lettuce leaves

1. Prepare a hot fire. In a medium bowl, working as quickly and gently as possible, mix ground beef with wine, herbs, mustard, salt, and pepper. Divide mixture into quarters and lightly form into 4 patties ¾ to 1 inch thick.

2. Place patties on an oiled grill set 4 to 6 inches from coals. Grill, turning once, until outside is slightly charred but inside is still pink and juicy, about 8 to 12 minutes for rare to medium rare, or longer if desired.

3. Meanwhile, open buns and toast on sides of grill until warm and lightly browned. Place cooked burgers in buns and let everyone choose their own fixings.

87 BURIED BRIE BURGERS
Prep: 10 minutes   Cook: 8 to 12 minutes   Serves: 4

1⅓ pounds ground chuck
1½ teaspoons salt
½ teaspoon freshly ground
   pepper
3 tablespoons Brie cheese
4 hamburger buns, onion
   rolls, or French bread

Optional: Dijon mustard,
   ketchup, mayonnaise,
   sliced sweet onion or
   grilled onion slices,
   pickles or pickle relish,
   sliced tomatoes, lettuce

1. Prepare a hot fire. In a medium bowl, working as quickly and gently as possible, mix ground beef with salt and pepper. Divide mixture into quarters and lightly form into 4 patties ¾ to 1 inch thick. Press your thumb into patties to make a large indentation. Fill each with ¾ tablespoon Brie. Pinch meat to seal cheese inside.

2. Place patties on an oiled grill set 4 to 6 inches from coals. Grill, turning once, until well browned outside but still pink and juicy inside, about 8 to 12 minutes, or longer if desired.

3. Meanwhile, open buns and toast on sides of grill until warm and lightly browned. Place cooked burgers in buns and let everyone choose their own fixings.

88 BARBECUED BURGERS
Prep: 10 minutes   Cook: 8 to 12 minutes   Serves: 4

1⅓ pounds ground chuck
1½ teaspoons salt
½ teaspoon freshly ground
   pepper
1 cup barbecue sauce, bottled
   or homemade
4 hamburger buns, onion
   rolls, or other bread

Optional: Mustard, sliced
   sweet onion or grilled
   onion slices, pickles or
   pickle relish,
   mayonnaise, sliced
   tomatoes, lettuce

1. Prepare a hot fire. In a medium bowl, working as quickly and gently as possible, mix ground beef with salt and pepper. Divide mixture into quarters and lightly form into 4 patties ¾ to 1 inch thick. Warm barbecue sauce in a small heavy saucepan on edge of grill.

2. Place patties on an oiled grill set 4 to 6 inches from coals. Grill, turning once, until outside is well browned but inside is still pink and juicy, about 8 to 12 minutes for rare to medium rare, or longer if desired. Just before removing burgers from grill, baste generously with warm barbecue sauce. Turn over and baste again to coat both sides.

3. Meanwhile, open buns and toast on sides of grill until warm and lightly browned. Place cooked burgers in buns and let everyone choose their own fixings. Pass remaining barbecue sauce on the side.

89 BURGERS CHINOISE
Prep: 10 minutes   Cook: 8 to 12 minutes   Serves: 4

1⅓ pounds ground chuck
1 teaspoon minced fresh
  ginger
1 garlic clove, crushed
1½ teaspoons salt
½ teaspoon freshly ground
  pepper

⅓ cup hoisin sauce
4 sesame seed buns
  Optional: Shredded Napa
  cabbage or iceberg
  lettuce, mayonnaise,
  sliced sweet onion

1. Prepare a hot fire. In a medium bowl, working as quickly and gently as possible, mix ground beef with ginger, garlic, salt, and pepper. Divide mixture into quarters and lightly form into 4 patties ¾ to ½ inch thick.

2. Place patties on an oiled grill set 4 to 6 inches from coals. Grill, turning once, until well browned outside but still pink and juicy inside, about 8 to 12 minutes, or longer if desired. Just before removing burgers from grill, baste generously with hoisin sauce, turn over, and baste again to coat both sides.

3. Meanwhile, open buns and toast on sides of grill until warm and lightly browned. Place cooked burgers in buns and let everyone choose their own fixings.

90 CALIFORNIA BURGERS
Prep: 10 minutes   Cook: 8 to 12 minutes   Serves: 4

1⅓ pounds ground chuck
1½ teaspoons salt
½ teaspoon freshly ground
  pepper
4 slices Pepper Jack, Chili
  Jack, or Monterey Jack
  cheese
4 hamburger buns, pita
  pockets, or onion rolls

1 large avocado, sliced
½ cup alfalfa sprouts
  Optional: Honey mustard,
  Russian dressing,
  ketchup, mayonnaise,
  sliced sweet onion or
  grilled onion slices,
  pickle relish or dill pickle
  slices, sliced tomatoes

1. Prepare a hot fire. In a medium bowl, working as quickly and gently as possible, mix ground beef with salt and pepper. Divide mixture into quarters and lightly form into 4 patties ¾ to 1 inch thick.

2. Place patties on an oiled grill set 4 to 6 inches from hot coals. Grill, turning once, until outside is well browned but inside is still pink and juicy, about 8 to 12 minutes for rare to medium rare, or longer if desired. About 30 seconds before removing burgers from grill, top each with a slice of Jack cheese.

3. Meanwhile, open buns and toast on sides of grill until warm and lightly browned. Place cooked burgers in buns, top each with 2 or 3 slices avocado and 2 tablespoons sprouts, and serve at once. Let everyone choose their own additional fixings.

91 BACON AND CHEESE BURGERS
Prep: 10 minutes   Cook: 8 to 12 minutes   Serves: 4

1⅓ pounds ground chuck
1½ teaspoons salt
½ teaspoon freshly ground
    pepper
  4 to 8 slices cooked bacon
  4 slices cheese, such as Swiss,
    Cheddar, or American
  4 hamburger buns, onion
    rolls, or other bread

Optional: Mustard,
    ketchup, mayonnaise,
    sliced sweet onion or
    grilled onion slices,
    pickles or pickle relish,
    sliced tomatoes, lettuce
    leaves

1. Prepare a hot fire. In a medium bowl, working as quickly and gently as possible, mix ground beef with salt and pepper. Divide mixture into quarters and lightly form into 4 patties ¾ to 1 inch thick.

2. Place patties on an oiled grill over hot coals. Grill, turning once, until outside is well browned but inside is still pink and juicy, about 8 to 12 minutes for rare to medium rare, or longer if desired. Just before removing burgers from grill, top each with 1 or 2 slices of bacon and a slice of cheese.

3. Meanwhile, open buns and toast on sides of grill until warm and lightly browned. Place cooked burgers in buns and let everyone choose their own fixings.

---

92 BURGER-BABS
Prep: 20 minutes   Cook: 10 to 15 minutes   Serves: 4

1½ pounds ground chuck
  1 egg, lightly beaten
  1 teaspoon salt
¼ teaspoon freshly ground
    pepper
  8 large pimiento-stuffed
    olives
  8 cherry tomatoes

  8 small white boiling onions,
    peeled
  1 cup ketchup
  1 tablespoon prepared white
    horseradish
½ teaspoon Worcestershire
    sauce
  1 teaspoon prepared mustard

1. Prepare a hot fire. In a medium bowl, mix ground beef with egg and season with salt and pepper. Shape mixture into 24 small meatballs about 1½ inches in diameter.

2. Thread meatballs, olives, tomatoes, and onions onto 4 oiled, long metal skewers, alternating ingredients and dividing them equally among skewers. In a small bowl, mix together ketchup, horseradish, Worcestershire, and mustard. Brush over meatballs and vegetables.

3. Place kebabs on an oiled grill set 4 to 6 inches from coals. Grill, turning skewers and basting with sauce several times, until meat is well browned and onions are crisp-tender, about 10 to 15 minutes.

93 HAMBURGER AU POIVRE
Prep: 10 minutes   Cook: 8 to 12 minutes   Serves: 4

1⅓ pounds ground chuck
1 tablespoon Dijon mustard
1½ teaspoons salt
¾ teaspoon freshly ground
   pepper
2½ tablespoons coarsely
   cracked black
   peppercorns

4 hamburger buns, French
   rolls, or other bread
Optional: Dijon mustard,
   ketchup, mayonnaise,
   sliced sweet onion or
   grilled onion slices,
   pickles or pickle relish,
   sliced tomatoes, lettuce

1. Prepare a hot fire. In a medium bowl, working as quickly and gently as possible, mix ground beef with mustard, salt, ground pepper, and 1½ teaspoons coarsely cracked peppercorns. Divide mixture into quarters and lightly form into 4 patties, ¾ to 1 inch thick. Sprinkle remaining cracked pepper over both sides of patties. Press gently to help pepper adhere.

2. Place patties on an oiled grill set 4 to 6 inches from coals. Grill, turning once, until outside is well browned but inside is still pink and juicy, about 8 to 12 minutes for rare to medium rare, or longer if desired.

3. Meanwhile, open buns and toast on sides of grill until warm and lightly browned. Place cooked burgers in buns and let everyone choose their own fixings.

94 MONSTER BURGER
Prep: 10 minutes   Cook: 20 to 25 minutes   Serves: 4 to 6

If you don't have a grill basket to make a monster burger, form the mixture into individual stuffed burgers.

1½ pounds ground beef
¼ cup quick-cooking rolled
   oats
1 egg, beaten
2 tablespoons ketchup
½ teaspoon salt

⅛ teaspoon freshly ground
   pepper
½ cup grated sharp Cheddar
   cheese
¼ cup minced onion

1. Prepare a hot fire. In a medium bowl, as quickly and lightly as possible, mix together beef, oats, egg, ketchup, salt, and pepper. Divide mixture in half and pat into 2 7-inch circles on individual sheets of wax paper. Scatter cheese and onions over 1 meat circle to within 1 inch of edge. Lift second sheet of wax paper and invert other meat circle onto cheese and onion mixture; peel off wax paper. Press and pinch to seal edges of burger.

2. Lift wax paper holding burger and invert onto a well-oiled grill basket; peel off wax paper and close basket. Place grill basket on a rack set 6 inches from coals. Grill, turning once or twice until burger is nicely browned outside and cheese inside has melted, about 20 to 25 minutes. Remove burger from basket and cut into wedges to serve.

95 OLYMPIC BURGERS
Prep: 10 minutes   Cook: 8 to 12 minutes   Serves: 4

1⅓ pounds ground chuck
1 garlic clove, crushed
1 teaspoon oregano
¾ teaspoon salt
½ teaspoon coarsely ground pepper
6 tablespoons crumbled feta cheese (about 1½ ounces)

4 hamburger buns or pita breads
Optional: Ketchup, mustard, Greek olives, sliced red onions, sliced tomatoes, lettuce

1. Prepare a hot fire. In a medium bowl, working as quickly and gently as possible, mix ground beef with garlic, oregano, salt and pepper. Divide mixture into quarters and then halve again; lightly form into 8 patties about ½ inch thick.

2. Sprinkle 1½ tablespoons crumbled feta over 4 patties. Top them with remaining meat and pinch edges to seal cheese inside.

3. Place patties on an oiled grill set 4 to 6 inches from coals. Grill, turning once, until outside is well browned but inside of meat is still pink and juicy, about 8 to 10 minutes for rare to medium rare, or longer if desired.

4. Meanwhile, open buns and toast on sides of grill until warm and lightly browned. Placed cooked burgers in buns and let everyone choose their own fixings.

---

96 ROQUEFORT BURGERS
Prep: 10 minutes   Cook: 8 to 12 minutes   Serves: 4

1 ounce Roquefort cheese (about 2 tablespoons)
1½ tablespoons butter, softened
1½ teaspoons Cognac or brandy Dash cayenne
1⅓ pounds ground chuck
1½ teaspoons salt
½ teaspoon freshly ground pepper

4 hamburger buns, onion rolls, or other bread
Optional: Mustard, ketchup, mayonnaise, sliced sweet onion or grilled onion slices, pickles or pickle relish, sliced tomatoes, lettuce

1. Prepare a hot fire. In a small bowl, combine Roquefort, butter, Cognac, and cayenne. Blend until smooth. Set Roquefort butter aside.

2. In a medium bowl, working as quickly and gently as possible, mix ground beef with salt and pepper. Divide mixture into quarters and lightly form into 4 patties ¾ to 1 inch thick. Press your thumb into patties to make large indentation. Fill each with about 2 teaspoons Roquefort butter. Pinch meat to seal filling inside.

3. Place patties on an oiled grill set 4 to 6 inches from coals. Grill, turning once, until outside is well browned but inside is still pink and juicy, about 8 to 12 minutes for rare to medium rare, or longer if desired.

4. Meanwhile, open buns or rolls and toast on sides of grill until warm and lightly browned. Place cooked burgers in buns and let everyone choose their own fixings.

---

97   MEATLOAF BURGERS
Prep: 15 minutes   Cook: 8 to 12 minutes   Serves: 4

1⅓ pounds ground chuck or a
    combination of beef,
    veal, and pork
  1 egg, lightly beaten
  ¼ cup minced onion
  ¼ cup chopped green bell
    pepper
  ¼ cup fresh bread crumbs
  ¼ cup ketchup or chili sauce
  1 teaspoon salt

  ½ teaspoon freshly ground
    pepper
  4 hamburger buns, onion
    rolls, or other bread
Optional: Mustard,
    ketchup, mayonnaise,
    sliced sweet onion or
    grilled onion slices,
    pickles or pickle relish,
    sliced tomatoes, lettuce

1. Prepare a hot fire. In a medium bowl, working as quickly and gently as possible, mix ground meat with egg, onion, green pepper, bread crumbs, ketchup, salt, and pepper. Divide mixture into quarters and lightly form into 4 patties ¾ to 1 inch thick.

2. Place patties on an oiled grill set 4 to 6 inches from coals. Grill, turning and gently flattening once with a wide spatula, until well browned outside but still pink and juicy inside, about 8 to 12 minutes for rare to medium rare, or longer if desired. If using ground pork, be sure to cook meat until well done.

3. Meanwhile, open buns and toast on sides of grill until warm and lightly browned. Place cooked burgers in buns and let everyone choose their own fixings.

98   THE CLASSIC FRANKFURTER
Prep: 5 minutes   Cook: 8 to 10 minutes   Serves: 4

1 pound frankfurters
8 hot dog buns or other bread
   or rolls

Optional: Mustard,
   ketchup, pickle relish,
   chopped onion

1. Prepare a hot fire. Using a knife or the tines of a fork, prick franks several times to prevent bursting. Grill hot dogs, turning occasionally, until exterior is browned and bubbly, about 8 to 10 minutes.

2. Meanwhile, open buns and toast on sides of grill until warm and lightly browned. Place cooked frankfurters in buns and let everyone choose their own fixings.

   NOTE: *If cooking for a crowd, you may want to wrap rolls in foil and warm package on grill for convenience.*

99   CHEESY-DOES-IT DOGS
Prep: 5 minutes   Cook: 8 to 10 minutes   Serves: 4

1 pound frankfurters
8 strips American, sharp
   Cheddar, or Swiss
   cheese, about 4 inches
   long and ½ inch wide
8 strips thinly sliced bacon

8 hot dog buns or other bread
   or rolls
Optional: Mustard,
   ketchup, pickle relish,
   chopped onion

1. Prepare a hot fire. Cut a lengthwise slice ⅜ inch to ½ inch deep in each hot dog and fill with a strip of your favorite cheese. Wrap a strip of bacon around each dog. Grill hot dogs, turning occasionally, until exterior is browned and bubbly, about 8 to 10 minutes.

2. Meanwhile, open buns and toast on sides of grill until warm and lightly browned. Place cooked frankfurters in buns and let guests choose their own fixings.

100   BBQ'D DOGS
Prep: 5 minutes   Cook: 8 to 10 minutes   Serves: 4

1 pound frankfurters
½ cup barbecue sauce, bottled
   or homemade
8 hot dog buns

Optional: Mustard,
   ketchup, pickle relish,
   chopped onion

1. Prepare a hot fire. Butterfly hot dogs or make several shallow slashes on opposite sides. Grill for 2 minutes, turning frequently. Continue to grill, brushing repeatedly with barbecue sauce, until hot dogs are heated through and nicely browned and glazed, about 6 to 8 minutes longer.

2. Meanwhile, open buns and toast on sides of grill until warm and lightly browned. Place cooked hot dogs in buns and let everyone choose their own fixings.

---

101   BACON 'N' CHEDDAR DOGS
Prep: 5 minutes   Cook: 10 minutes   Serves: 4

1 pound frankfurters
8 strips sharp Cheddar cheese,
   about 4 inches long and
   ½-inch wide
8 strips thinly sliced bacon

8 hot dog buns or other bread
   or rolls
Optional: Mustard,
   ketchup, pickle relish,
   chopped onion

1. Prepare a hot fire. Cut a lengthwise slice ⅜ inch to ½ inch deep in each hot dog and fill with a strip of sharp Cheddar cheese. Wrap each stuffed frankfurter spirally with a strip of bacon, securing each end with a toothpick. Grill hot dogs, turning occasionally, until bacon is browned and cheese is melted, about 10 minutes.

2. Meanwhile, open buns or rolls and toast on sides of grill until warm and lightly browned. Remove toothpicks and place cooked frankfurters in buns. Let everyone choose their own fixings.

---

102   FRANKFURTERS FRANÇAISE
Prep: 5 minutes   Cook: 8 to 10 minutes   Serves: 4

1 pound frankfurters
2 long narrow French breads
   (baguettes), cut into 4 4-
   inch pieces each, or 8 4-
   inch French rolls

Optional: Dijon mustard;
   Brie, Camembert, or
   Roquefort cheese;
   cornichons

1. Prepare a hot fire. If using French bread, prick franks several times with tines of a fork to prevent bursting. If using rolls, butterfly franks. Grill hot dogs, turning occasionally, until browned and bubbly outside, about 8 to 10 minutes.

2. Meanwhile, split open bread or rolls and toast on sides of grill until warm and lightly browned. Place cooked frankfurters in bread and let everyone choose their own fixings.

103   GERMAN-STYLE FRANKS
Prep: 5 minutes   Cook: 8 to 10 minutes   Serves: 4

1 **pound frankfurters**
8 **hot dog buns, Kaiser rolls,
   or rye bread**
	**Optional: Dusseldorf
	   mustard, chopped onion,
	   sauerkraut, shredded
	   Muenster cheese**

1. Prepare a hot fire. Using a knife or tines of a fork, prick franks several times to prevent bursting. Grill franks, turning occasionally, until browned and bubbly outside, about 8 to 10 minutes.

2. Meanwhile, open buns and toast on sides of grill until warm and lightly browned. Place cooked franks in buns and let everyone choose their own fixings.

104   FRANKFURTERS OLÉ
Prep: 5 minutes   Cook: 8 to 10 minutes   Serves: 4

1 **pound frankfurters**
8 **corn or flour tortillas**
   **Optional: Shredded
      Cheddar or Monterey
      Jack cheese, Salsa Fresca
      (page 161) or bottled salsa,**
	**guacamole or avocado slices,
	   sour cream, sliced pickled
	   jalapeño peppers, sliced
	   black olives, shredded
	   iceberg lettuce**

1. Prepare a hot fire. Using a knife or tines of a fork, prick each frank several times. Grill, turning occasionally, until browned and bubbly outside, about 8 to 10 minutes.

2. Meanwhile, quickly warm tortillas on edge of grill, turning once, until softened, about 2 minutes. Place cooked frankfurters on warm tortillas and let everyone choose their own fixings. Fold or roll up to eat.

105   MIDDLE EASTERN-STYLE FRANKFURTERS
Prep: 5 minutes   Cook: 8 to 10 minutes   Serves: 4

1 **pound frankfurters**
8 **pita breads**
   **Optional: Crumbled feta
      cheese, cucumber slices,**
	**yogurt with chopped mint,
	   Tabbouleh (page 163),
	   Hummus (page 155)**

1. Prepare a hot fire. Butterfly franks. Grill, turning occasionally, until browned and bubbly outside, about 8 to 10 minutes.

2. Meanwhile, open pita breads and quickly toast on sides of grill, turning once, until warmed through, 2 to 3 minutes. Place cooked frankfurters in pita breads and let everyone choose their own fixings.

106 HOT DOGS ITALIANO
Prep: 5 minutes   Cook: 8 to 10 minutes   Serves: 4

1 cup tomato sauce,
    homemade or canned
1 pound frankfurters
4 Italian hero rolls, or 8 hot
    dog buns

Optional: Grilled onion
    slices, shredded
    Mozzarella cheese, strips
    of green bell pepper, or
    Roasted Red and Yellow
    Peppers (page 117)

1. Prepare a hot fire. Place tomato sauce in small saucepan on edge of grill to warm. With tip of a knife or tines of a fork, prick each frankfurter several times. Grill, turning occasionally, until browned and bubbly outside, about 8 to 10 minutes.

2. Meanwhile, open rolls or buns and toast on edge of grill until warm and lightly browned. Place 2 cooked franks in each roll or 1 in each bun and top with a spoonful of tomato sauce. Let everyone choose their own fixings. Pass any remaining tomato sauce on the side.

107 SHISH-KE-DOGS
Prep: 5 minutes   Cook: 8 to 10 minutes   Serves: 4

1 pound frankfurters
1 medium onion, cut into
    1-inch pieces
1 green bell pepper, cut into
    1-inch squares
1 medium zucchini, cut into
    1-inch pieces

2 tablespoons olive oil
Optional: Mustard,
    ketchup, pickle relish,
    steak sauce, hot pepper
    sauce

1. Prepare a hot fire. Cut hot dogs into 1-inch pieces. Thread pieces onto long metal skewers, alternating pieces of meat with onion, green pepper, and zucchini.

2. Brush vegetables with olive oil. Place hot dog kebabs on an oiled grill set 4 to 6 inches from heat. Grill, turning and brushing vegetables with oil several times, until hot dogs are browned and bubbly outside and vegetables are crisp-tender, about 8 to 10 minutes. Serve on plates with a knife and fork and let everyone choose their own fixings.

Chapter 4

Grilling Magic with Meats

Nothing can rival the aroma of a sizzling slab of meat hot off the grill. This chapter will give you lots of ideas for barbecuing beef, pork, sausages, ham, lamb, veal, and venison.

Most meats are cooked quickly over a hot fire. Since they grill for such a short time, it's a good idea to marinate them beforehand for extra flavor. For tougher cuts, long marinating will tenderize as well. And don't forget to trim off all excess fat before cooking. Besides reducing calories, it will prevent flare-ups that can char the meat.

Whole roasts and ribs require longer, slower cooking. If you have time, let bulkier cuts come to room temperature before grilling. It will reduce the cooking time and yield more even results. Butterflying a larger piece of meat—leg of lamb, for example—allows it to cook quicker and more evenly.

If you have an instant-reading thermometer, here is a handy guideline for doneness.

Rare	*120 to 125*
Medium Rare	*130 to 135*
Medium	*140 to 145*
Medium Well	*150 to 155*
Well Done	*160 to 170*

If you don't have a thermometer, touch the meat. If it feels very soft and doesn't spring back, it's still raw. If it springs back but still feels somewhat soft in the center, it's rare. If it's firm, it's well done.

You can always cut into the meat, but you'll lose juices. Also, most meats continue to cook for several minutes after they're removed from the heat, so it's a good idea to let large steaks and roasts stand for about 5 to 10 minutes to finish cooking and allow the juices to return to the center of the meat before carving.

108   BEEF FAJITAS

Prep: 10 minutes   Marinate: 1 hour   Cook: 10 to 15 minutes
Serves: 6

1½ pounds beef skirt or flank
    steak
¼ cup fresh lime juice
¼ cup tequila
2 tablespoons olive oil
2 jalapeño peppers, thinly
    sliced, or ¼ to ½ teaspoon
    crushed hot red pepper
    flakes

3 garlic cloves, minced
1 teaspoon salt
½ teaspoon ground cumin
12 flour tortillas
    Salsa, guacamole, and sour
        cream, as accompaniment

1. Trim all fat and loose membrane from meat. In a nonreactive pan, combine lime juice, tequila, olive oil, jalapeños, garlic, salt, and cumin. Add steak and turn to coat. Cover and marinate, turning occasionally, 1 to 2 hours at room temperature, or up to 24 hours refrigerated.

2. Prepare a hot fire. Set steak on an oiled grill 4 to 6 inches from heat. Grill, turning once, until browned outside but still pink and juicy inside, 10 to 15 minutes for rare to medium rare. Let stand 5 minutes before carving crosswise, against the grain, on the diagonal into thin slices.

3. While meat is standing, heat tortillas by setting them directly on grill for about 30 seconds per side, or by wrapping them in foil in 2 packages of 6 each and warming, turning several times, for about 5 minutes. Place steak slices on tortillas, top with salsa, guacamole, and sour cream, and roll up.

---

109   HERBED FLANK STEAK WITH DIJON MUSTARD

Prep: 20 minutes   Marinate: 1 hour   Cook: 10 to 15 minutes
Serves: 6

2½ pounds flank steak
¼ cup Dijon mustard
¼ cup dry red wine
2 tablespoons olive oil
1 garlic clove, minced
1 large shallot or small onion,
    minced
1 tablespoon chopped fresh
    basil, or 1 teaspoon dried

1 tablespoon chopped fresh
    oregano, or 1 teaspoon
    dried
1 tablespoon chopped fresh
    thyme, or 1 teaspoon
    dried
1½ teaspoons salt
¼ teaspoon freshly ground
    pepper

1. Trim any excess fat from flank steak and place in a large nonreactive pan. In a small bowl, mix together mustard, wine, olive oil, garlic, shallot, basil, oregano, thyme, salt, and pepper. Rub mustard mixture all over flank steak. Cover with plastic wrap and marinate 1 to 3 hours at room temperature, or up to 24 hours refrigerated.

2. Prepare a hot fire. Remove steak from marinade, scraping as much marinade as possible back into pan. Place steak on an oiled grill set 4 to 6 inches from coals. Grill, brushing once or twice with reserved marinade, until steak is browned on bottom, about 5 to 7 minutes. Turn and grill until second side is well browned and inside is still pink and juicy, about 5 to 7 minutes longer for rare, 7 to 8 minutes for medium rare.

3. Transfer steak to a carving board and let stand for about 5 minutes before cutting thin slices on a diagonal against the grain.

---

110 GRILLED STEAK AU POIVRE

Prep: 10 minutes   Cook: 6 to 10 minutes   Serves: 4

4 shell or rib-eye steaks, cut ¾ inch thick, boned and trimmed
1½ teaspoons olive oil
1 teaspoon salt

3 to 4 tablespoons coarsely cracked peppercorns
Creamy Cognac Sauce (recipe follows)

1. Prepare a hot fire. Rub steaks lightly with oil and season with salt. Spread crushed pepper on wax paper and press both sides of each steak into peppercorns to coat.

2. Cook steaks on an oiled grill set 4 to 6 inches from coals, turning once or twice, until nicely browned outside yet still pink and juicy inside, about 6 to 8 minutes for rare, 8 to 10 for medium rare. Serve with Creamy Cognac Sauce, if desired.

CREAMY COGNAC SAUCE

2 tablespoons butter
4 shallots, minced
2 tablespoons Cognac or brandy
⅓ cup dry red wine
3 tablespoons heavy cream

1½ cups brown beef gravy, homemade or store-bought
Salt and freshly ground pepper

1. In a large skillet, melt butter over medium heat. Add shallots and cook just until softened but not browned, 1 to 2 minutes. Add Cognac and, standing back, ignite with a long-handled match. When flames subside, add wine and bring to a boil. Continue cooking until liquid reduces by half, about 3 to 5 minutes.

2. Whisk in cream and gravy and bring to a boil. Cook until sauce is just thick enough to coat back of a spoon, about 5 minutes. Season with salt and pepper. Serve with Grilled Steak au Poivre.

111 SOY-GLAZED FLANK STEAK

Prep: 10 minutes   Marinate: 1 hour   Cook: 10 to 12 minutes
Serves: 4 to 6

¼ cup soy sauce
3 tablespoons honey
2 tablespoons red wine
   vinegar
2 scallions, minced
2 large garlic cloves, minced

2 teaspoons minced fresh
   ginger
½ cup olive oil
1 flank steak, about 1½
   pounds

1. In a small bowl, mix together soy sauce, honey, vinegar, scallions, garlic, and ginger. Whisk in olive oil. Place steak in a glass or ceramic baking dish and pour in marinade; turn to coat both sides of meat. Cover with plastic wrap and marinate, turning occasionally, 1 to 2 hours at room temperature, or up to 24 hours refrigerated.

2. Prepare a hot fire. Remove steak from marinade, scraping off and reserving as much marinade as possible. Place steak on an oiled grill set 4 to 6 inches from coals. Grill, turning and brushing with marinade several times, until outside is well browned and inside is still pink and juicy, about 10 to 12 minutes. Transfer to a cutting board or platter and let rest about 5 minutes before carving on the diagonal into thin slices.

112 GRILLED TENDERLOIN OF BEEF WITH HORSERADISH SAUCE

Prep: 15 minutes   Marinate: 2 hours   Cook: 40 minutes   Serves: 12

Here's a perfect recipe for easy entertaining.

2 cups sour cream
⅔ cup prepared white
   horseradish
2 tablespoons fresh lemon
   juice
   Freshly ground white
   pepper
1 whole beef tenderloin,
   trimmed of excess fat and
   tied (about 5 pounds)

1½ cups dry red wine
3 garlic cloves, minced
2 teaspoons salt
1 teaspoon freshly ground
   black pepper
½ cup olive oil

1. In a medium bowl, combine sour cream, horseradish, lemon juice, and white pepper. Mix to blend well. Cover and refrigerate horseradish sauce until ready to use.

2. Place beef in a nonreactive dish. In a medium bowl, mix together wine, garlic, salt, black pepper, and olive oil. Pour over meat. Cover with plastic wrap and marinate, turning once or twice, 2 to 4 hours at room temperature, or overnight in refrigerator.

3. Prepare a hot fire. When coals are covered with gray ash, lift meat from marinade and place on an oiled grill set 4 to 6 inches from coals. Grill, turning and moving frequently, until well browned outside and rare to medium rare inside, about 40 minutes. An instant-reading thermometer inserted in thickest part of meat should read 130 to 135 degrees. Let meat rest 5 to 10 minutes before carving. Serve with horseradish sauce on the side.

---

113 CHARCOAL-BROILED STEAK WITH CHEDDAR-SCALLION BUTTER

Prep: 5 minutes   Cook: 8 to 12 minutes   Serves: 6

Serve this with baked or grilled potatoes, as the Cheddar-Scallion Butter is perfect on both.

6 steaks, such as filet mignon or top sirloin, about 1 inch thick Olive oil	Salt and freshly ground pepper Cheddar-Scallion butter (recipe follows)

1. Prepare a hot fire. If steaks contain an outer edge of fat, slash fat diagonally (avoiding the meat) at 1-inch intervals to prevent meat from curling as it cooks, or trim off fat entirely. Brush both sides of steaks lightly with oil and season well with salt and pepper.

2. Cook steaks on an oiled grill set 4 to 6 inches over charcoal, turning once or twice, until well browned outside but still pink and juicy inside, about 8 to 12 minutes for medium rare. Serve each steak with a dollop of Cheddar-Scallion Butter.

CHEDDAR-SCALLION BUTTER

8 tablespoons (1 stick) butter, softened ½ cup sliced scallions ½ teaspoon dry mustard	2 cups finely shredded Cheddar cheese (about ½ pound)

Combine all ingredients and mix by hand or in a food processor until well blended. Serve on warm steaks and potatoes.

114 EAST-WEST CHUCK ROAST

Prep: 5 minutes   Marinate: 8 hours   Cook: 40 to 45 minutes
Serves: 6 to 8

This untraditional pot roast cooked on the grill is low in cost and high in flavor. Marinating the meat overnight ensures both tenderness and tastiness.

1 4- to 5-pound beef chuck roast, bone in, about 2 inches thick	1 medium onion, coarsely chopped
1 cup dry red wine	2 large garlic cloves, minced
⅓ cup soy sauce	¼ teaspoon freshly ground pepper
3 tablespoons olive oil	

1. Remove excess fat from roast and place meat in a nonreactive roasting pan or baking dish. Add wine, soy sauce, olive oil, onion, garlic, and pepper; turn meat once or twice to coat well. Cover with plastic wrap and marinate in refrigerator at least 8 and up to 48 hours, turning occasionally. Let meat return to room temperature before grilling.

2. Prepare a medium-hot fire. Remove meat from marinade and pat dry with paper towels; reserve marinade. Place roast on an oiled grill set 4 to 6 inches above off-set coals. Grill indirectly, turning and moving meat once or twice and basting occasionally with reserved marinade, until meat is well browned outside and tender, pink, and juicy inside, about 40 to 45 minutes. Center of roast should register about 140° on an instant-reading thermometer for medium. Let stand for 5 to 10 minutes before carving on the diagonal against the grain into thin slices.

115 GRILLED RIB STEAKS WITH ROQUEFORT BUTTER

Prep: 5 minutes   Cook: 8 to 12 minutes   Serves: 8

8 beef rib steaks, cut 1 inch thick	8 tablespoons (1 stick) unsalted butter, softened
3 tablespoons olive oil	½ cup crumbled Roquefort cheese
1 teaspoon salt	Dash of cayenne
¼ teaspoon freshly ground pepper	1½ teaspoons minced parsley

1. Prepare a hot fire. Rub steaks with oil and season with salt and pepper.

2. In a food processor or blender, combine butter, cheese, cayenne, and parsley. Process until well blended. (Roquefort butter can be refrigerated up to 3 days.)

3. When coals are hot, place steaks on an oiled grill and cook, turning occasionally, until well browned outside and still pink and juicy inside, about 8 to 12 minutes. Top each steak with a dollop of Roquefort butter.

116 CHARRED STEAK-ON-THE-ROCKS
Prep: 5 minutes   Cook: 20 minutes   Serves: 4 to 6

Sometimes it's fun to break the rules a bit, as in this case where meat is coated with a salt crust and buried right in the coals to cook. This method is convenient for picnics at the beach or camping.

1 2-pound boneless steak, such as London broil, cut 2 inches thick	¾ cup Dijon mustard
	2½ cups rock salt

1. Prepare a hot fire with a bed of coals about 3 inches thick and twice as long as the steak. Allow at least 30 minutes for the coals to turn ash white.

2. Remove all visible fat from steak. Spread half the mustard over top and sides of meat and press half of salt into mustard as thick as it will stick. Place meat salt side down directly onto coals and cook until salt crust is charred, about 10 minutes. Brush remaining mustard over exposed raw meat and press remaining salt into it. Using 1 or 2 large spatulas, turn steak over onto another section of hot coals to cook until charred, about 10 minutes longer.

3. Remove meat from coals; knock off any of the charred crust that did not fall off during turning. Let meat rest about 5 minutes before slicing on the diagonal against grain to serve.

---

117 MIDDLE EASTERN BEEF KEBABS
Prep: 15 minutes   Marinate: 1 hour   Cook: 12 to 15 minutes
Serves: 6 to 8

Serve these savory beef kebabs with a knife and fork, or slip them into pita breads that you've warmed on the grill and top with Hummus (page 155)

3 pounds boneless beef, such as top sirloin, cut into 1½-inch cubes	3 tablespoons olive oil
	1½ teaspoons ground cumin
3 garlic cloves, minced	1 teaspoon salt
3 tablespoons fresh lemon juice	½ teaspoon freshly ground pepper

1. In a large bowl, toss beef with garlic, lemon juice, olive oil, cumin, salt, and pepper. Cover and marinate, tossing occasionally, 1 to 2 hours at room temperature, or up to 24 hours refrigerated. If chilled, let meat return to room temperature before grilling.

2. Prepare a hot fire. Thread beef onto skewers, reserving marinade. Place kebabs on an oiled grill set 4 to 6 inches from coals. Grill, turning frequently and basting with marinade, until browned outside but still pink and juicy inside, about 12 to 15 minutes.

118   BARCELONA BEEF KEBABS

Prep: 15 minutes   Marinate: 2 hours   Cook: 10 to 15 minutes
Serves: 6 to 8

3 pounds boneless beef, such as top round, cut into 2-inch cubes
¼ cup orange juice
¼ cup tomato juice
2 tablespoons fresh lime or lemon juice
3 tablespoons extra-virgin olive oil
2 garlic cloves, minced

1 tablespoon chopped fresh oregano, or 1 teaspoon dried
1 teaspoon paprika
1 teaspoon ground cumin
1 teaspoon salt
½ teaspoon crushed hot red pepper flakes
3 medium onions, cut into 8 wedges each

1. Place beef cubes in a large bowl. Add orange juice, tomato juice, lime juice, olive oil, garlic, oregano, paprika, cumin, salt, and hot pepper flakes. Toss to coat meat. Cover with plastic wrap and marinate, tossing occasionally, 2 to 4 hours at room temperature, or up to 48 hours refrigerated.

2. Prepare a hot fire. Remove meat from marinade; reserve marinade. Thread beef cubes and onion wedges alternately onto 6 to 8 long metal skewers.

3. Place kebabs on an oiled grill set 4 to 6 inches over coals. Grill, turning and moving skewers and brushing with reserved marinade, until beef is well browned outside and tender, pink, and juicy inside, about 10 to 15 minutes.

119   BACON-WRAPPED MEAT LOAF

Prep: 20 minutes   Cook: 30 minutes   Serves: 8 to 10

4 pounds ground chuck or sirloin
¼ cup ketchup
3 tablespoons Worcestershire sauce
2 tablespoons hot pepper sauce
1 tablespoon cayenne
1 tablespoon salt

1 teaspoon garlic salt
¼ teaspoon freshly ground pepper
2 pounds sliced bacon
4 large tomatoes, sliced ½ inch thick
2 large onions, sliced ⅜ inch thick

1. As quickly and lightly as possible, mix ground meat with ketchup, Worcestershire sauce, hot sauce, cayenne, 2 teaspoons salt, garlic salt, and pepper. Shape mixture into a rectangular loaf about 9½ × 11 inches and 1½ inches thick. Prepare a medium-hot fire.

2. Use a grill basket about 10 inches wide, 12 inches long, and 2½ inches deep. Line bottom of basket with half the bacon. Place meat mixture on top. Place sliced tomatoes on top of meat and season with ½ teaspoon salt. Place sliced onions on top of tomatoes and season with remaining ½ teaspoon salt. Cover onions with remaining sliced bacon. Close top of grill basket to hold contents securely.

3. Place basket on an oiled grill set 4 to 6 inches from coals. Cook, turning and moving grill basket frequently to avoid flare-ups, until bacon is cooked through, meat loaf is set, and beef is cooked through but still slightly pink in center, about 30 minutes.

---

120 PORK BROCHETTES WITH CARIBBEAN DIPPING SAUCE

Prep: 35 minutes   Marinate: 1 hour   Cook: 15 minutes   Serves: 6

3 pounds boneless pork
    shoulder, trimmed of
    excess fat and cut into
    ¾-inch cubes
⅓ cup dry white wine
3 garlic cloves, minced

⅔ cup olive oil
1 teaspoon salt
¼ teaspoon freshly ground
    pepper
Caribbean Dipping Sauce
    (recipe follows)

1. In a medium bowl, combine pork with wine, garlic, olive oil, salt, and pepper. Cover and marinate 1 to 2 hours at room temperature, tossing occasionally, or overnight in refrigerator. Meanwhile, make Caribbean Dipping Sauce.

2. Prepare a hot fire. Thread meat onto oiled metal skewers and grill, turning and basting occasionally, until pork is well browned and cooked through, with no trace of pink in center, about 15 minutes. Serve with sauce for dipping.

CARIBBEAN DIPPING SAUCE

¼ pound salt pork, finely
    diced
1 medium onion, chopped
1 jalapeño or other chili
    pepper, seeded and
    minced
2 garlic cloves, minced
½ pound ripe tomatoes,
    peeled, seeded, and
    chopped (1¼ cups)

Pinch of freshly grated
    nutmeg
Pinch of ground cinnamon
Pinch of ground ginger
Pinch of ground cloves
Pinch of salt
¼ cup chopped cilantro or
    parsley

1. In a large skillet, cook salt pork over medium-high heat, stirring occasionally, until lightly browned, about 5 minutes. Add onion, jalapeño pepper, and garlic. Cook until onion is softened but not browned, 3 to 5 minutes. Stir in tomatoes, nutmeg, cinnamon, ginger, cloves, salt, and cilantro.

2. Continue cooking, stirring, until sauce has thickened enough to coat back of a spoon, about 10 to 15 minutes longer. Let cool, then cover and refrigerate. Serve at room temperature or slightly chilled.

121 FRUITED PORK KEBABS

Prep: 20 minutes   Marinate: 30 minutes   Cook: 10 to 15 minutes
Serves: 2

This was inspired by Madeleine Kamman's recipe for Pork and Prune Skewers.

¾ pound boneless pork shoulder, cut into 12 1½-inch cubes
½ teaspoon salt
⅛ teaspoon freshly ground pepper
10 moist pitted prunes
2 tablespoons olive oil

Juice of 1 medium orange (about ⅓ cup)
Grated zest of 1 medium orange (about 1 tablespoon)
1 medium onion, peeled, quartered, and separated into thin wedges

1. Combine pork with salt, pepper, prunes, olive oil, orange juice, and orange zest. Cover and set aside to marinate 30 minutes at room temperature, or overnight in refrigerator.

2. Thread onion wedges, pork, and prunes onto 2 oiled long metal skewers, alternating in that order. Reserve any extra marinade for basting.

3. Prepare grill. Cook pork on an oiled rack set 4 to 6 inches over hot coals. Turn and baste occasionally until pork is nicely browned and just cooked through, about 10 to 15 minutes.

---

122 TOM'S MONGOLIAN PORK CHOPS

Prep: 20 minutes   Marinate: 1 hour   Cook: 10 to 15 minutes
Serves: 6

This recipe is from Tom Roach, a highly respected baker and confectioner from California's Napa Valley. Serve these chops plain or with Tom's Tomato Chutney (page 162).

1 cup rice wine vinegar*
½ cup soy sauce
2 tablespoons brown bean sauce*
1 cup chopped scallions
½ cup chopped cilantro

2 teaspoons chopped fresh or freeze-dried chives
5 garlic cloves, minced
1 teaspoon ground coriander
6 boneless pork loin chops, cut ½ to ¾ inch thick

1. In a large shallow baking dish, combine rice wine vinegar, soy sauce, brown bean sauce, scallions, cilantro, chives, garlic, and ground coriander. Add pork chops and turn to coat. Cover and marinate, turning occasionally, 1 to 2 hours at room temperature, or up to 24 hours refrigerated.

2. Prepare a hot fire. Grill pork chops, turning once, until cooked through and white in center but still moist, 10 to 15 minutes.

* *Available in Asian markets and in the international foods section of many supermarkets.*

123 CURRIED PORK CHOPS WITH NECTARINE CHUTNEY

Prep: 20 minutes   Marinate: 1 hour   Cook: 16 to 20 minutes
Serves: 6

This spicy and sweet combination of flavors makes a wonderful warm-weather dinner.

4 large garlic cloves	½ teaspoon salt
1 2-inch piece of fresh ginger, peeled and coarsely chopped	3 tablespoons fresh lemon juice
	½ cup olive oil
6 whole cloves	6 pork loin chops, cut 1 inch thick
2 tablespoons curry powder	
1 teaspoon ground cumin	Nectarine Chutney (recipe follows)
1 teaspoon paprika	

1. In a food processor or blender, purée garlic with ginger and cloves. Add curry, cumin, paprika, and salt; mix, then blend in lemon juice and olive oil.

2. Lay pork chops in a single layer in a glass or ceramic baking dish. Add curry mixture and turn to coat both sides of chops with marinade. Cover and marinate 1 to 2 hours at room temperature, or overnight in refrigerator. Let meat return to room temperature before grilling.

3. Prepare a hot fire. When coals are covered with gray ash, scrape away excess marinade from chops and place on grill 4 to 6 inches from coals. Grill, turning and basting occasionally with marinade, until just cooked through with no trace of pink in center, about 16 to 20 minutes.

NECTARINE CHUTNEY

1 cup (packed) light brown sugar	2 tablespoons minced fresh ginger
½ cup apple cider vinegar	1 large garlic clove, minced
4 or 5 nectarines (about 1½ pounds), skins on, pitted and diced	½ teaspoon curry powder
	⅛ teaspoon cayenne
1 cup raisins	Dash of salt
1 whole lemon, seeded and chopped (skin and all)	

1. In a medium nonreactive saucepan, cook brown sugar in vinegar over medium heat, stirring to dissolve sugar. Bring to a boil. Add nectarines, raisins, lemon, ginger, garlic, curry, cayenne, and salt. Return to a boil and cook for 2 minutes.

2. Remove from heat and let cool. Store chutney, covered, in refrigerator for up to 2 weeks, or freeze. Serve at room temperature or slightly chilled.

124 HERB-STUFFED LOIN OF PORK
Prep: 30 minutes   Cook: 45 minutes   Serves: 6

1½ pounds boneless pork loin
2 tablespoons Dijon mustard
2 garlic cloves, crushed
3 tablespoons chopped fresh or freeze-dried chives
2 tablespoons chopped fresh sage, or 1½ teaspoons dried
1 tablespoon chopped fresh thyme, or 1 teaspoon dried

2 teaspoons chopped fresh rosemary, or ½ teaspoon dried
1 teaspoon salt
1 tablespoon coarsely cracked black pepper
2 tablespoons olive oil

1. Trim all excess fat from meat. Cut down length of loin halfway through and open up like a book to butterfly roast, or ask your butcher to do it for you.

2. Combine mustard and garlic; rub all over meat. Combine chives, sage, thyme, and rosemary. Sprinkle herbs evenly over opened side of pork. Season with ½ teaspoon salt and 1 teaspoon pepper. Fold roast back together and tie with butcher's twine or kitchen string that has been moistened with water to prevent burning. Season outside of pork loin with remaining salt and pepper; rub with olive oil.

3. Prepare a medium fire. Place pork on an oiled grill set 4 to 6 inches from coals. Grill pork loin, turning and changing position occasionally, until golden brown and crisp outside and white throughout but still moist, about 45 minutes. (Fire will probably be low by the time meat is done.) Let roast stand 5 to 10 minutes before carving.

125 PORKBURGERS WITH ONION SAUCE
Prep: 20 minutes   Cook: 10 minutes   Serves: 8

2 pounds ground pork
¼ cup dry bread crumbs
1 egg, beaten
2 tablespoons water
2 tablespoons ketchup

2 teaspoons salt
½ teaspoon onion powder
¼ teaspoon freshly ground pepper
Onion Sauce (page 186)

1. Prepare a hot fire. In a large bowl, as lightly and quickly as possible combine pork with bread crumbs, egg, water, ketchup, salt, onion powder, and pepper. Shape into 8 patties about ¾ inch thick.

2. Place burgers on an oiled grill set 4 to 6 inches from coals. Grill burgers, turning once or twice, until well browned and just cooked through, about 10 minutes. Serve with Onion Sauce on hamburger buns.

126 PORK TENDERLOIN WITH RED ONION CONFIT

Prep: 40 minutes   Marinate: 30 minutes   Cook: 15 to 20 minutes   Serves: 4

This dish is suitable for even the most elegant dinner party.

2 **pounds boneless pork tenderloin (either 1 large or 2 smaller tenderloins)**
2 **teaspoons salt**
½ **teaspoon freshly ground pepper**

1 **tablespoon chopped fresh thyme, or 1 teaspoon dried**
2 **tablespoons olive oil Red Onion Confit (recipe follows)**

1. Trim fat and silver membrane off pork. Place meat in a baking dish and rub with salt, pepper, thyme, and olive oil. Cover with plastic wrap and marinate at room temperature for 30 minutes. Meanwhile, make Red Onion Confit and prepare a hot fire.

2. Grill pork tenderloins on an oiled grill set 4 to 6 inches from coals, turning, until just cooked through with no trace of pink in center, about 15 to 20 minutes. Meat should register 160° to 165° on an instant-reading thermometer. Allow meat to rest 5 to 10 minutes before slicing thin. Serve on a bed of Red Onion Confit.

RED ONION CONFIT

2 **tablespoons olive oil**
4 **large red onions, thinly sliced**
2 **tablespoons sugar**
¼ **teaspoon salt**
¼ **cup currants or raisins**
¾ **cup dry red wine**

¼ **cup balsamic vinegar**
2 **tablespoons crème de cassis (black currant liqueur)**
1½ **teaspoons chopped fresh thyme, or ½ teaspoon dried**

1. Heat oil in a large nonreactive skillet over medium-low heat. Add red onions and cook until softened but not browned, 5 to 7 minutes. Add sugar, salt, currants, and wine. Bring to a boil, reduce heat, and simmer until nearly all liquid is gone, about 20 minutes.

2. Stir in vinegar, cassis, and thyme and cook, stirring frequently, until onions have turned a deep golden brown, about 10 minutes. Serve warm or at room temperature. This keeps well in the refrigerator for several days.

127   PORK KEBABS WITH SPICED PLUM SAUCE
Prep: 10 minutes   Marinate: 30 minutes   Cook: 12 to 14 minutes
Serves: 4 to 6

2 pounds boneless pork loin,
    trimmed and cut into
    1-inch cubes
¾ teaspoon salt
¼ teaspoon freshly ground
    pepper
1 tablespoon olive oil
1 tablespoon lemon juice

1 garlic clove, crushed
1 10-ounce jar plum jam or
    preserves
1 tablespoon dry white wine
    or fresh lemon juice
¼ teaspoon ground ginger
¼ teaspoon ground cardamom
⅛ teaspoon ground cloves

1. In a medium bowl, toss pork with salt, pepper, olive oil, lemon juice, and garlic. Marinate at room temperature 30 to 60 minutes, tossing once or twice. If using bamboo skewers, soak in water at least 30 minutes to prevent burning.

2. Meanwhile, in a small saucepan, warm jam over medium heat, stirring until melted, about 2 minutes. Stir in remaining ingredients. Simmer 2 minutes. Let cool slightly before serving, or serve cold. This sauce will keep almost indefinitely in refrigerator.

3. Prepare a hot fire. Thread pork onto skewers and place on an oiled grill 4 to 6 inches from coals. Grill, turning frequently, until meat is browned outside and no longer pink inside, about 8 to 10 minutes. Serve pork kebabs with spiced plum sauce on the side.

128   MISSISSIPPI SPARERIBS
Prep: 10 minutes   Cook: 1¾ hours   Serves: 6

The long simmering time in water removes a great deal of fat from spareribs prior to grilling, which prevents flare-ups on the grill.

3 pounds pork spareribs
½ cup chili sauce or ketchup
½ cup (packed) brown sugar
1 tablespoon cider vinegar

2 tablespoons Worcestershire
    sauce
⅛ teaspoon cayenne

1. Simmer spareribs in a large pot of salted water until just tender, about 1½ hours. Drain and place ribs in a shallow baking dish; let cool.

2. In a small bowl, mix together chili sauce, brown sugar, vinegar, Worcestershire sauce, and cayenne. Spread over meaty side of spareribs, reserving extra for basting.

3. Prepare a medium-hot fire. Place meat on an oiled grill set 4 to 6 inches from coals. Grill, turning frequently and basting with reserved sauce, until ribs are brown and crusty, about 15 minutes.

129 CANTON-STYLE SPARERIBS
Prep: 10 minutes   Marinate: 1 hour   Cook: 1 hour   Serves: 4

4 pounds pork spareribs
½ cup soy sauce
2 tablespoons dry sherry
3 tablespoons crushed
   pineapple

2 tablespoons sugar
2 tablespoons honey
2 garlic cloves, crushed
1 teaspoon salt

1. Trim excess fat from ribs and place them in a large shallow pan. Mix together all remaining ingredients and pour over ribs. Cover with plastic wrap and marinate, turning occasionally, 1 to 2 hours at room temperature, or up to 24 hours refrigerated.

2. Prepare a medium-hot fire. Remove ribs from marinade; reserve marinade. Place ribs on an oiled grill set 4 to 6 inches from off-set coals. Grill ribs indirectly, turning occasionally and brushing with marinade, until crusty outside and tender and juicy inside, about 1 hour.

130 KANSAS CITY–STYLE SPARERIBS
Prep: 10 minutes   Cook: 1¼ hours   Serves: 6

This spicy mustard glaze is a nice change from the tomato-based sauces so often used on ribs. Baking these in advance makes the grilling a snap.

6 garlic cloves, crushed
8 to 9 pounds pork spareribs
   (about 3 racks)
2 teaspoons salt
½ teaspoon freshly ground
   pepper

1 cup (packed) dark brown
   sugar
¾ cup coarse grainy mustard
⅓ cup cider vinegar
¼ cup molasses
1½ tablespoons dry mustard

1. Preheat oven to 350°. Rub garlic into both sides of ribs and season with salt and pepper. Arrange ribs meaty side down on a large baking sheet. Bake 1 hour, turning ribs after 20 minutes. (Ribs can be baked a day ahead. Remove to a rack and let drain and cool. Then wrap in plastic wrap and refrigerate.)

2. In a medium nonreactive saucepan, combine brown sugar, grainy mustard, vinegar, molasses, and dry mustard. Bring to a boil, reduce heat, and simmer, stirring to dissolve sugar, 5 minutes. Remove glaze from heat and let cool slightly.

3. Prepare a hot fire. Place prebaked ribs meaty side up on an oiled grill set 4 to 6 inches from coals. Spread one third of glaze over ribs and cook until bottom is browned, about 5 minutes. Turn, spread half of remaining glaze over ribs, and cook until meaty side is browned and crisp, about 5 minutes. Turn again and spread remaining glaze on top. Grill until bottom side is well browned and crisp, about 5 minutes longer. Cut into individual ribs or portions for serving.

131 ST. JOE RIBS
Prep: 15 minutes   Cook: 2¼ hours   Serves: 6 to 8

Prebaking ribs with a coating of flour makes them extra crispy.

7 to 8 pounds country pork ribs, or 3 or 4 racks of beef back ribs	2 cups chili sauce
1 cup flour	½ cup minced onion
1 tablespoon paprika	2 tablespoons brown sugar
2 teaspoons minced garlic	2 tablespoons cider vinegar
¼ teaspoon freshly ground pepper	2 teaspoons dry mustard
	6 dashes of hot pepper sauce
	4 dashes of Worcestershire sauce

1. Preheat oven to 325°. Trim any excess fat from ribs. Mix together flour, paprika, garlic, and pepper. In a sturdy plastic bag, combine ribs and seasoned flour in batches and shake to coat well. Set ribs on a rack in a large roasting pan and bake until ribs are browned and tender and an instant-reading thermometer inserted in thickest part of meat registers 150°, about 1½ hours for country pork ribs, 45 minutes for beef back ribs. Remove from oven and let cool. (Ribs can be baked up to 2 hours ahead. Set aside, uncovered, at room temperature.)

2. Meanwhile, in a medium nonreactive saucepan, combine chili sauce, onion, brown sugar, vinegar, mustard, hot sauce, and Worcestershire sauce. Bring to a boil over medium-high heat. Reduce heat to low and simmer until barbecue sauce is slightly thickened, about 15 minutes. Remove from heat and let cool to room temperature.

3. Prepare a medium-hot fire. Pour sauce over ribs; turn to coat thoroughly. Grill ribs 4 to 6 inches from coals, turning and basting frequently with sauce, until ribs are crisp, about 30 minutes.

---

132 SPARERIBS IN THE NUDE
Prep: 2 minutes   Cook: 1 hour   Serves: 4 to 6

These are so tasty, no one will miss the traditional barbecue sauce.

6 pounds pork spareribs	1 tablespoon freshly ground pepper
2 tablespoons salt	

1. Prepare a medium-hot fire. Season ribs liberally with salt and pepper and place on an oiled grill set 4 to 6 inches from coals.

2. Grill, turning once or twice, until ribs are well browned outside and meat is tender and cooked through, with no trace of pink near bone, about 1 hour. Cut into portions to serve.

133 HELEN'S BARBECUED SPARERIBS

Prep: 20 minutes   Cook: 1 to 1¼ hours   Serves: 4 to 6

These ribs are completely cooked on the grill. The spicy sauce is added only during the final half hour.

2 garlic cloves, minced	2 tablespoons Worcestershire
2 tablespoons butter, melted	sauce
2 tablespoons prepared	2 dashes of hot pepper sauce
mustard	1 teaspoon salt
¼ cup (packed) brown sugar	1½ cups water
1 cup ketchup	4 pounds spareribs or loin
¾ cup chili sauce	back ribs
1 tablespoon celery seeds	

1. In a medium nonreactive saucepan, sauté garlic in butter over medium heat until softened but not browned, 2 to 3 minutes. Add mustard, brown sugar, ketchup, chili sauce, celery seeds, Worcestershire, hot sauce, salt, and water and bring to a boil. If made in advance, let cool, cover, and refrigerate until ready to baste ribs.

2. Prepare a medium fire. Place ribs, bone side down, on an oiled grill set 6 inches from coals. Grill until brown, about 20 minutes; turn meaty side down and cook until browned, about 15 minutes longer. Turn meaty side up again and continue to grill without turning 20 to 30 minutes, basting with sauce every 5 to 10 minutes. Brush sauce on both sides of ribs and let cook 2 to 3 minutes on each side to glaze well.

---

134 GRILLED SAUSAGES WITH PEGGY'S PEAR-MUSTARD SAUCE

Prep: 10 minutes   Cook: 8 to 10 minutes   Serves: 6 to 8

Try this delicious sauce with ham or other pork.

2 16-ounce cans pears in heavy	⅛ teaspoon salt
syrup, drained	½ teaspoon freshly ground
2 tablespoons hot-sweet or	pepper
Dijon mustard	2 pounds sweet or hot Italian
1 tablespoon cider vinegar	sausages
1 tablespoon honey	

1. Purée pears in a food processor or blender. Add mustard, vinegar, honey, salt, and pepper. Blend well. (This sauce can be made several days in advance and stored in the refrigerator.)

2. Prepare a hot fire. Pour sauce into a heavy medium saucepan and set on side of grill to warm. Prick each sausage in several places with tines of a fork. Grill, turning, until lightly browned and cooked through, 8 to 10 minutes. Serve sausages hot with pear-mustard sauce on the side.

135   SAUSAGES AND SPUDS
Prep: 10 minutes   Cook: 17 to 22 minutes   Serves: 6

1 pound small red potatoes, cut into 1-inch wedges
1½ pounds spicy sausage, such as linguica, Louisiana hots, or hot Italian sausage, cut into 1-inch pieces
2 green bell peppers, cut into 1-inch squares
3 tablespoons olive oil

1. In a large saucepan of boiling salted water, cook potatoes until just barely softened, about 7 minutes. Drain, rinse under cold running water, and drain well.

2. Prepare a hot fire. Thread sausages, potatoes, and green peppers onto 6 long metal skewers, alternating ingredients.

3. Place skewers on an oiled grill set 4 to 6 inches from coals. Grill, brushing potatoes and peppers with oil and turning skewers frequently, until sausages are browned outside and cooked through and potatoes are tender when pierced with a knife, about 10 to 15 minutes.

136   GRILLED SAUSAGE AND PEPPER HEROES
Prep: 10 minutes   Cook: 10 to 15 minutes   Serves: 6

2 cups pizza sauce, bottled or homemade
3 green bell peppers
6 Italian sausages, hot or sweet
6 Italian or French rolls, split

1. Prepare a hot fire. Set pizza sauce in a small saucepan on side of grill and let warm. Grill whole bell peppers, turning frequently, until skin is charred, 10 to 15 minutes. Remove from grill and enclose in a plastic bag until cool enough to handle, 5 to 10 minutes. Remove peppers from bag and peel away charred skin under cold running water. Remove stems and seeds, pat peppers dry, and cut into 1-inch strips.

2. Meanwhile, slice down length of sausages without cutting all the way through to split them open. Prick casings several times with tines of a fork and place on an oiled grill set 4 to 6 inches from coals. Grill sausages, turning once or twice and basting often with some of pizza sauce, until crusty brown outside with no trace of pink inside, 8 to 10 minutes.

3. If space permits, while sausages are cooking, open rolls and toast cut side down on grill, 1 to 2 minutes. Otherwise, wrap in aluminum foil and set on grill, turning once or twice, until heated through, 2 to 3 minutes.

4. To serve, place a grilled sausage in a heated roll, heap on some pepper strips, and top with pizza sauce.

137 KIELBASA KEBABS

Prep: 20 minutes   Marinate: 1 hour   Cook: 10 to 15 minutes
Serves: 4

These also make excellent appetizers if threaded in small amounts onto little bamboo skewers.

½ cup dry white wine
½ cup water
2 cups tomato sauce
1 tablespoon chili powder
1½ pounds fully cooked
    Kielbasa sausage, cut into
    1-inch pieces

1 small green or red bell
    pepper, cut into 1-inch
    pieces
1 small onion, cut into 1-inch
    pieces
¼ pound medium mushrooms

1. If using wooden skewers, soak in water at least 30 minutes to avoid burning. In a medium saucepan, combine wine, water, tomato sauce, and chili powder. Bring to a boil over medium heat. Reduce heat and simmer until marinade is slightly thickened, about 5 minutes. Remove from heat and let cool to room temperature.

2. Meanwhile, thread sausage, bell pepper, onion, and mushrooms onto skewers. Place in a glass or ceramic baking dish. Pour cooled marinade over kebabs. Cover with plastic wrap and marinate, turning several times, 1 to 2 hours at room temperature, or longer in refrigerator.

3. Prepare a hot fire. Remove kebabs from marinade; reserve marinade. Place kebabs on an oiled grill set 4 to 6 inches from coals. Grill, turning skewers and basting kebabs with reserved marinade, until sausage is browned and vegetables are crisp-tender, about 10 to 15 minutes.

---

138 GRILLED BRATWURST

Prep: 5 minutes   Cook: 10 to 12 minutes   Serves: 6

1½ pounds bratwurst (about 6
    sausages)

Optional: Orange Maple
    Glaze (page 185)

1. Prepare a hot fire. Prick each sausage several times with tines of a fork. Place on an oiled rack set 4 to 6 inches from coals and grill, turning frequently, until cooked through, 10 to 12 minutes.

2. If desired, after grilling for only 5 minutes, brush bratwurst with Orange Maple Glaze. Continue to grill, turning and basting frequently, until cooked through and nicely glazed, about 5 to 7 minutes.

139 AUNT VIRGINIA'S GRILLED HAM

Prep: 10 minutes   Marinate: 1 hour   Cook: 10 to 15 minutes
Serves: 4

Sweet and spicy, a lot like Aunt Virginia!

1 1½-pound slice cooked ham,
   cut 1 inch thick
1 cup ginger ale
1 cup orange juice
½ cup (packed) brown sugar

3 tablespoons vegetable oil
1 tablespoon cider vinegar
2 teaspoons dry mustard
¾ teaspoon ground ginger
¼ teaspoon ground cloves

1. Remove any visible fat from ham and place in a shallow dish. Combine all remaining ingredients and pour over ham. Let marinate at room temperature 1 hour, or refrigerate overnight, spooning marinade over ham several times.

2. Prepare a medium fire. Place ham on an oiled grill set 4 to 6 inches from coals. Cook 10 to 15 minutes, turning once or twice and brushing with reserved marinade, until ham is lightly browned. Heat any remaining marinade and serve as a sauce on the side.

140 GRILLED HAM SLICES

Prep: 5 minutes   Marinate: 1 hour   Cook: 10 to 15 minutes
Serves: 6

½ cup orange marmalade
¾ cup Dijon mustard
1 teaspoon Worcestershire
   sauce

¾ cup water
6 6- to 8-ounce slices fully
   cooked ham, cut about 1
   inch thick

1. In a small bowl, combine marmalade, mustard, Worcestershire sauce, and water; pour into a large baking dish. Add ham slices and turn to coat. Marinate at room temperature 1 hour, or longer in refrigerator.

2. Prepare a medium fire. Remove ham from marinade, reserving marinade for basting.

3. Place ham on an oiled grill set 4 to 6 inches from coals. Grill 10 to 15 minutes, turning frequently and basting with marinade during the last 5 minutes of cooking, until well browned outside and heated through.

141   HAM AND PINEAPPLE KEBABS
Prep: 10 minutes   Cook: 4 to 5 minutes   Serves: 4

1 8-ounce can unsweetened
   pineapple chunks,
   drained
1½ pounds lean cooked ham in
   1 piece, cut into 1½-inch
   cubes

8 maraschino cherries,
   stemmed
½ cup soy sauce
2 tablespoons dry sherry
1 tablespoon brown sugar
½ teaspoon ground ginger

1. If using bamboo skewers, soak in water for at least 30 minutes to prevent burning. Prepare a medium-hot fire.

2. Thread pineapple, ham, and cherries onto 4 6- to 8-inch skewers, dividing ingredients equally among skewers. In a small bowl, mix together soy sauce, sherry, brown sugar, and ginger. Liberally brush soy sauce mixture over skewered ingredients.

3. Place kebabs on an oiled grill set 4 to 6 inches from coals. Cook, turning once or twice and brushing with soy sauce mixture each time, until lightly browned, about 5 minutes.

142   GRILLED GEORGIA PEACHES AND HAM
Prep: 10 minutes   Cook: 4 to 5 minutes   Serves: 4

1 cup water
1 tablespoon lemon juice
4 fresh peaches
½ cup peach jam

¼ cup orange juice or canned
   peach nectar
2 1-pound fully cooked, bone-
   in ham steaks

1. In a large bowl, combine water and 2 teaspoons lemon juice. Fill a large saucepan with water and bring to a boil. Drop in peaches and boil 1 to 2 minutes, just until skins loosen. Gently drain and rinse under cold running water. Peel off skins, halve peaches, and drop into lemon water.

2. In a small bowl, combine peach jam, orange juice, and remaining 1 teaspoon lemon juice. Set glaze aside.

3. Prepare a hot fire. Place ham steaks on an oiled grill set 4 to 6 inches from coals. Drain peach halves well and place on sides of grill. Brush ham steaks and peach halves with glaze and grill, turning once or twice and brushing with glaze, until ham is well browned and ham and peaches are heated through, about 4 to 5 minutes.

143   VINTNER'S LAMB

Prep: 15 minutes   Marinate: 24 hours   Cook: 30 to 40 minutes
Serves: 6

A butterflied leg of lamb is ideal for company. Start this a day ahead. It is delicious and easy to carve, and the uneven thickness ensures both rare and well-done meat.

1 5- to 6-pound leg of lamb, boned, butterflied, and trimmed of fat (about 3 pounds after boning)	3 tablespoons Tarragon Mustard (page 13) or Dijon mustard
Salt and freshly ground pepper	3 large garlic cloves, minced
⅓ cup mixed chopped fresh herbs, such as tarragon, thyme, rosemary, and parsley, or 2 tablespoons dried	¼ cup olive oil
	1 cup dry red wine

1. Lay meat flat in a large nonreactive pan and season well with salt and pepper, rubbing into all sides of meat.

2. Mix herbs with mustard, garlic, and oil and rub over meat to coat. Drizzle wine over lamb, cover with plastic wrap, and refrigerate 24 hours, turning meat occasionally. Let meat return to room temperature before grilling.

3. Prepare a hot fire. Lift meat from marinade, reserving liquid, and place on an oiled grill set about 6 inches from heat. Grill, brushing several times with reserved marinade, 15 to 20 minutes per side, or until an instant-reading thermometer inserted in the thickest part registers 135° for medium rare.

4. Transfer cooked meat to a cutting board and allow to rest 5 to 10 minutes before carving.

144   MINTED BUTTERFLIED LEG OF LAMB

Prep: 10 minutes   Marinate: 2 hours   Cook: 30 to 40 minutes
Serves: 6

1 5- to 6-pound leg of lamb, boned, butterflied, and trimmed of fat (about 3 pounds after boning)	½ cup chopped fresh mint
	½ teaspoon ground cumin
1 cup plain yogurt	1½ teaspoons salt
4 large garlic cloves, minced	½ teaspoon freshly ground pepper

1. Lay meat flat in a large nonreactive pan. In a small bowl, combine yogurt, garlic, mint, cumin, salt, and pepper. Rub seasoned yogurt all over lamb. Cover and marinate 2 to 3 hours at room temperature, or up to 24 hours refrigerated. Let meat return to room temperature before grilling.

2. Prepare a hot fire. Remove meat from marinade, scraping off marinade into pan. Pat lamb dry with paper towels. Place on an oiled grill set 4 to 6 inches from coals. Grill, turning once and brushing with marinade several times, until lamb is browned outside and tender, pink, and juicy inside, about 30 to 40 minutes. An instant-reading thermometer inserted in thickest part of meat will register 130° to 135° for medium rare.

3. Transfer meat to a carving board and let rest for 5 to 10 minutes before slicing.

---

145 GRILLED LAMB PATTIES WITH MINT SALSA

Prep: 5 minutes   Cook: 10 to 15 minutes   Serves: 4

1⅓ pounds lean ground lamb	2 garlic cloves, minced
¼ cup chopped parsley	1 teaspoon salt
2 tablespoons chopped fresh mint, or 1½ teaspoons dried	½ teaspoon freshly ground pepper
2 tablespoons fresh lemon juice	Mint Salsa (recipe follows)

1. Prepare hot fire. In a large bowl, as quickly and lightly as possible, mix together lamb, parsley, mint, lemon juice, garlic, salt, and pepper until well blended. Form into 4 patties about 1 inch thick.

2. Place patties on an oiled grill rack set 4 to 6 inches from coals and cook, turning once or twice, until well browned outside and just slightly pink in center, about 10 to 15 minutes.

MINT SALSA

4 large ripe tomatoes (about 2 pounds), seeded and diced *	2 fresh jalapeño peppers, seeded and minced
1 cup chopped onion	2 tablespoons fresh lime juice
½ cup finely chopped fresh mint leaves	½ teaspoon salt
	⅛ teaspoon freshly ground pepper

In a medium bowl, combine tomatoes, onion, mint, jalapeños, lime juice, salt, and pepper. Stir gently to mix. Set aside at room temperature for up to 2 hours before serving.

* If ripe summer tomatoes are unavailable, substitute 2 28-ounce cans peeled whole tomatoes, coarsely chopped and well drained.

146 GRILLED LAMB CHOPS WITH MINTED CUCUMBER SAUCE

Prep: 30 minutes   Cook: 6 to 9 minutes   Serves: 6

¾ cup peeled, seeded, minced cucumber
½ teaspoon salt
1 cup plain yogurt or sour cream
1 tablespoon chopped fresh mint,* or 1 teaspoon dried

2 small garlic cloves—1 minced, 1 cut in half
Freshly ground pepper
6 round-bone shoulder lamb chops, cut ¾ inch thick
1 tablespoon olive oil

1. Place cucumber in a sieve, sprinkle with salt, and set aside to drain for 30 minutes.

2. Meanwhile, in a small bowl, combine yogurt, mint, and minced garlic. Add well-drained cucumber and season with additional salt and pepper. Cover and refrigerate minted cucumber sauce until ready to serve.

3. Prepare a hot fire. Rub lamb chops with cut garlic. Brush with olive oil and season with additional salt and pepper. Grill over hot coals, turning once, until medium rare, about 6 to 9 minutes. Serve with a dollop of minted cucumber sauce on top. Pass remaining sauce on the side.

* *In the absence of fresh mint, cilantro, dill, rosemary, or chives are other good choices.*

147 LAMB-IN-A-POCKET

Prep: 15 minutes   Cook: 30 seconds   Serves: 6

A delicious sandwich for casual get-togethers. Have plenty of napkins on hand!

1 cup plain yogurt
1 cup sour cream
1 small garlic clove, crushed
Dash of salt
6 pita breads, cut in half to make 12 pockets

Minted Butterflied Leg of Lamb (page 86), thinly sliced
Mint Salsa (page 87)
12 green leaf lettuce leaves

1. In a small bowl, combine yogurt, sour cream, garlic, and salt. (This can be done in advance, covered, and refrigerated.)

2. Quickly grill pita bread over a low fire, turning once, about 30 seconds, just until heated through. (Or warm in oven.)

3. Have each guest create his or her own sandwich by filling the pocket with a combination of Minted Butterflied Leg of Lamb, Mint Salsa, lettuce, and yogurt sauce.

148 GOOD THYME LAMB CHOPS
Prep: 10 minutes   Marinate: 1 hour   Cook: 15 minutes   Serves: 4

8 lamb loin chops, cut about 1 inch thick
3 tablespoons chopped fresh thyme leaves, or 2 teaspoons dried
1 tablespoon fresh lemon juice

3 garlic cloves, minced
3 tablespoons extra-virgin olive oil
2 teaspoons salt
½ teaspoon freshly ground pepper

1. Place lamb chops in a glass or ceramic dish. In a small bowl, mix together thyme, lemon juice, garlic, olive oil, salt, and pepper. Rub seasonings into both sides of meat. Cover with plastic wrap and marinate at room temperature 1 to 2 hours or up to 24 hours in refrigerator.

2. Prepare a hot fire. When coals are ready, place chops on a well oiled grill. Cook, turning once or twice, until browned outside and still pink inside, about 15 minutes.

---

149 GRILLED RACK OF LAMB
Prep: 15 minutes   Marinate: 2 hours   Cook: 15 to 20 minutes   Serves: 4

2 racks of lamb, trimmed of excess fat (2½ to 3 pounds each)
¾ cup honey
¼ cup Dijon mustard
2 tablespoons beef broth

2 tablespoons Worcestershire sauce
1½ teaspoons chopped fresh marjoram, or ½ teaspoon dried

1. Place lamb in a pan just large enough to hold racks. In a medium bowl, combine honey, mustard, broth, Worcestershire sauce, and marjoram. Whisk to blend well. Spread mustard mixture all over meat. Cover with plastic wrap and marinate 2 hours at room temperature, or longer in refrigerator. Let meat return to room temperature before grilling, if necessary.

2. Prepare a hot fire. Remove lamb from marinade, scraping off and reserving as much as possible. Place racks of lamb meaty side down on an oiled grill set 4 to 6 inches from coals. Grill, turning once or twice, until lightly browned outside, about 8 minutes.

3. Continue to grill, turning and basting with reserved marinade, until lamb is well browned outside but still pink and juicy inside, about 7 to 12 minutes longer. Let stand for about 5 minutes before dividing into chops and serving.

150 LAMB CHOPS WITH LEMON AND BASIL
Prep: 10 minutes   Marinate: 2 hours   Cook: 10 to 12 minutes
Serves: 4

4 lamb shoulder chops, cut
 ½ to ¾ inch thick
1 garlic clove, minced
2 tablespoons chopped fresh
 basil, or 1 teaspoon dried

Juice of 1 lemon
Grated zest of 1 lemon
1 teaspoon salt
¼ teaspoon lemon pepper
¼ cup olive oil

1. Place lamb chops in a glass or ceramic dish. In a small bowl, mix together garlic, basil, lemon juice, lemon zest, salt, lemon pepper, and olive oil. Pour over lamp chops, cover with plastic wrap, and marinate, turning once or twice, 2 to 3 hours at room temperature or up to 24 hours in refrigerator.

2. Prepare a hot fire. Place chops on an oiled grill set 4 to 6 inches from coals. Grill, turning once and brushing with any reserved marinade, until well browned outside and still pink inside, about 10 to 12 minutes.

151 LAMB BROCHETTES
Prep: 30 minutes   Marinate: 2 hours   Cook: 10 to 15 minutes
Serves: 4 to 6

2½ pounds boneless leg of
 lamb, trimmed of all fat
 and cut into 1½-inch
 cubes
½ teaspoon salt
¼ teaspoon freshly ground
 pepper
3 large garlic cloves, minced
2 tablespoons fresh lemon
 juice

Grated zest of 1 lemon
⅓ cup olive oil
1 tablespoon chopped fresh
 thyme, or 1 teaspoon
 dried
2 medium onions
½ pound thinly sliced center-
 cut bacon

1. In a large bowl, combine lamb cubes, salt, pepper, garlic, lemon juice, lemon zest, olive oil, and thyme. Toss until meat is well coated. Cover with plastic wrap and marinate, tossing occasionally, 2 to 4 hours at room temperature, or as long as 3 days in refrigerator.

2. Prepare a hot fire. Peel onions and quarter lengthwise. Separate layers into individual crescents.

3. Cut bacon slices in half horizontally and lay flat on a clean work surface. Place a piece of lamb on each slice and wrap with bacon.

4. Oil metal skewers and begin threading a piece of onion, concave side up, then a piece of bacon-wrapped lamb and another slice of onion, concave side down, to encase the lamb. Continue with another piece of onion, more lamb, and more onion until all the lamb has been threaded. Do not crowd these too much; allow space for bacon to cook.

5. Grill brochettes over hot coals, turning occasionally, until cooked through, about 10 to 15 minutes for medium rare.

---

152 BAA-BAA KEBABS
Prep: 15 minutes   Marinate: 1 hour   Cook: 10 to 15 minutes
Serves: 4

1½ pounds lean boneless lamb,
    cut into 1½-inch cubes
¾ cup red wine vinegar
½ cup olive oil
¼ cup dry red wine
4 medium onions—
    1 chopped, 3 quartered
1 teaspoon salt
½ teaspoon freshly ground
    pepper

2 garlic cloves, crushed
1 bay leaf
¼ teaspoon cinnamon
⅛ teaspoon ground cloves
1 small eggplant (about
    ¾ pound), skin on, cut
    into 1-inch cubes

1. Place lamb in a medium bowl and toss with vinegar, ¼ cup olive oil, wine, chopped onion, salt, pepper, garlic, bay leaf, cinnamon, and cloves. Cover with plastic wrap and marinate, tossing occasionally, 1 to 2 hours at room temperature, or up to 24 hours refrigerated.

2. Prepare a hot fire. Remove lamb from marinade and pat dry on paper towels. Thread lamb, onion quarters, and eggplant cubes onto 4 long metal skewers. Brush liberally with some of remaining olive oil.

3. Place skewers on an oiled grill set 4 to 6 inches from coals. Grill, turning skewers and brushing frequently with olive oil, until eggplant is tender and lamb is browned outside but still pink and juicy inside, 10 to 15 minutes.

---

153 LAMB CHOPS WITH MINT PESTO
Prep: 10 minutes   Marinate: 2 hours   Cook: 6 to 8 minutes
Serves: 2 to 3

6 rib lamb chops (about
    1¼ pounds total)
2 garlic cloves, minced
½ teaspoon salt
½ teaspoon freshly ground
    pepper

2 tablespoons chopped fresh
    mint leaves, or
    2 teaspoons dried
2 tablespoons olive oil
    Mint Pesto (page 181)

1. Place lamb chops in a baking dish and season with garlic, salt, pepper, mint, and olive oil. Cover with plastic wrap and marinate for 2 to 4 hours at room temperature, turning once or twice, or overnight in refrigerator.

2. Prepare a hot fire. Grill chops 4 to 6 inches from coals, turning occasionally, until outside is well browned and inside is still pink, about 6 to 8 minutes total for medium rare. Serve with Mint Pesto.

154 VEAL CHOPS WITH SAGE

Prep: 10 minutes   Marinate: 1 hour   Cook: 10 to 12 minutes
Serves: 6

6 veal loin chops, cut ¾ inch
   thick
2 tablespoons chopped fresh
   sage, or 1½ teaspoons
   ground dried
3 garlic cloves, crushed

1½ teaspoons salt
¼ teaspoon freshly ground
   pepper
3 tablespoons dry white wine
   or fresh lemon juice
3 tablespoons olive oil

1. Rub veal chops with sage, garlic, salt, and pepper. Drizzle wine and olive oil over meat. Cover with plastic wrap and marinate, turning occasionally, 1 to 2 hours at room temperature, or overnight in refrigerator.

2. Prepare a hot fire. Grill veal chops, turning once or twice, until browned outside and just barely pink at center, about 10 to 12 minutes total.

155 GRILLED VEAL RIB CHOPS WITH CRANBERRIES IN CABERNET

Prep: 20 minutes   Cook: 20 to 25 minutes   Serves: 6

This spirited cranberry sauce is also wonderful with grilled pork, chicken, and duck.

1½ cups sugar
1 cup Cabernet Sauvignon or
   other dry red wine
1 12-ounce package fresh or
   frozen cranberries,
   picked over for stems
1 cinnamon stick
1 orange, halved and studded
   with 2 cloves

6 veal rib chops, about 10
   ounces each
¼ cup olive oil
1½ teaspoon salt
¾ teaspoon freshly ground
   pepper

1. Combine sugar and wine in a medium nonreactive saucepan and bring to a boil over medium heat, stirring to dissolve sugar. Add cranberries, cinnamon stick, and orange with cloves. Boil gently until berries just begin to burst, 5 to 10 minutes.

2. Remove from heat and discard cinnamon, orange, and cloves. Let cool to room temperature. (Cranberries in Cabernet can be stored in a tightly covered jar in the refrigerator for up to 2 months.)

3. Prepare a medium-hot fire. Rub veal chops with olive oil and season with salt and pepper. When coals are hot, place chops on an oiled grill and cook, turning once, until browned outside and still pink inside, about 9 minutes. Serve grilled chops and pass cranberries in Cabernet on the side.

156 KASS'S VEAL KEBABS

Prep: 15 minutes   Marinate: 2 hours   Cook: 8 to 12 minutes
Serves: 8

2 pounds boneless veal
shoulder, cut into 1-inch
cubes
½ cup olive oil
2 tablespoons dry white wine
or lemon juice
2 tablespoons chopped
parsley
2 teaspoons salt

1 teaspoon grated fresh lemon
zest
1 teaspoon grated fresh
orange zest
2 garlic cloves, minced
½ teaspoon freshly ground
pepper
2 medium zucchini, cut into
1-inch pieces

1. In a medium bowl, combine veal cubes, olive oil, wine, parsley, salt,
lemon zest, orange zest, garlic, and pepper. Toss to blend well and coat
meat. Cover with plastic wrap and marinate, stirring once or twice, 2 to 3
hours at room temperature, or up to 24 hours refrigerated. If using bamboo
skewers, soak in water at least 30 minutes to prevent scorching.

2. Prepare a hot fire. Alternately thread veal and zucchini onto skewers and
place on an oiled grill 4 to 6 inches from coals. Grill, turning occasionally and
basting with any remaining marinade, until meat is browned outside and
barely pink in center and zucchini is crisp-tender, about 8 to 12 minutes.

157 GRILLED VEAL BURGERS WITH SWEDISH SAUCE

Prep: 15 minutes   Cook: 10 to 15 minutes   Serves: 6

½ cup applesauce
½ cup prepared white
horseradish
½ cup sour cream
1 teaspoon lemon juice
½ teaspoon sugar

2¼ teaspoons salt
2 pounds ground veal
½ teaspoon freshly ground
pepper
2 garlic cloves, minced

1. In a small bowl, combine applesauce, horseradish, sour cream, lemon
juice, sugar, and ¼ teaspoon salt. Cover and refrigerate until ready to serve.

2. Prepare a hot fire. In a large bowl, mix together veal, 2 teaspoons salt,
pepper, and garlic as quickly and as lightly as possible. Gently form into 6
patties about 1 inch thick. Place on an oiled grill 4 to 6 inches from coals
and cook, turning once or twice, until meat is well browned outside and still
slightly pink in center, about 10 to 15 minutes. Serve with Swedish sauce.

158   GRILLED VENISON STEAKS WITH CUMBERLAND SAUCE

Prep: 10 minutes   Marinate: overnight   Cook: 5 to 30 minutes
Serves: 6

This sauce also goes well with grilled pork or poultry.

6 4-ounce venison steaks, about ¾ inch thick	½ cup olive oil
1 teaspoon salt	2 large shallots, minced
¼ teaspoon freshly ground pepper	⅓ cup red currant jelly
	⅓ cup tawny port wine
¼ cup plus ⅓ cup orange juice	2 teaspoons cornstarch
5 tablespoons fresh lemon juice	1 tablespoon cold water

1. Place steaks in a large glass or ceramic dish and season with salt and pepper. In a small bowl, mix together ¼ cup orange juice, 2 tablespoons lemon juice, and the olive oil and pour over meat. Cover and marinate, turning once or twice, overnight in refrigerator.

2. In a small nonreactive saucepan, combine shallots, jelly, ⅓ cup orange juice, and port. Simmer 10 minutes. Stir in 3 tablespoons lemon juice.

3. In a small bowl, dissolve cornstarch in water and whisk into warm sauce. Cook over medium heat, stirring frequently, until sauce boils and thickens, 3 to 5 minutes. Let Cumberland sauce cool, then refrigerate until serving time.

4. Return steaks to room temperature while you prepare a hot fire. Lift meat from marinade and grill, turning occasionally and basting with reserved marinade, until meat is well browned outside and still slightly pink inside, about 10 to 15 minutes. Serve with Cumberland sauce chilled or at room temperature.

Chapter 5

Fish on the Fire

Whether your fish comes out of the ocean, a freshwater stream, or the local market, these recipes will show it off to its very best advantage.

When choosing fish, keep in mind that fillets with the skin on are much easier to cook on the grill than skinless fillets. Set them skin side down first, then turn carefully with a wide metal spatula. Because of its delicacy and tendency to break apart, fish should be turned only once.

Here, too, are recipes for all those great shellfish we enjoy so much—shrimp, scallops, lobster, clams, oysters, and mussels, grilled most easily speared, skewered, or cooked in the shell.

Remember the easy test for doneness for all fish, shrimp, and scallops: they should be opaque through to the center, but still moist and tender. As with meat, fish will continue cooking for a minute or two after it is removed from the fire, so be sure to take it off the grill as soon as it is just done. You can always put it back on for a little longer, but once it's overcooked, there's no repair.

---

159 GRILLED WHOLE FISH
Prep: 10 minutes   Cook: 25 to 35 minutes   Serves: 12 to 15

1 8- to 10-pound fish, such as salmon or cod, cleaned, head and tail left intact	¼ teaspoon freshly ground pepper
⅓ cup olive oil	2 lemons, sliced
1½ teaspoons salt	1 large onion, thinly sliced
	2 fresh parsley sprigs

1. Prepare a medium-hot fire. Rinse fish with cold water and pat dry. Brush fish, including cavity, with 2 tablespoons oil and season with salt and pepper. Place lemon slices, onion, and parsley in center cavity; skewer or sew shut with kitchen twine.

2. Transfer fish directly to a well-oiled grill or fish grill basket. Grill until bottom skin turns golden, about 10 minutes. Brush with remaining oil and carefully turn fish over using 1 or 2 large spatulas, or turn basket. Continue cooking and brushing with oil until fish is opaque in center, about 25 to 35 minutes.

160 ALI'S GRILLED SALMON SANDWICH
Prep: 5 minutes   Cook: 8 minutes   Serves: 4

4 4- to 6-ounce salmon fillets,
   skinned
⅓ cup extra-virgin olive oil
   Salt and freshly ground
   pepper
8 slices French or Italian bread

About ½ cup Rémoulade
   Sauce (recipe follows)
1 bunch watercress, or lettuce
   leaves
   Lemon wedges

1. Prepare a medium-hot fire. Brush both sides of fish with olive oil and season with salt and pepper. Place fish on an oiled grill set 4 to 6 inches from coals. Grill, turning once, until fish is just barely opaque in center, about 3 minutes per side.

2. Brush both sides of bread with olive oil and grill, turning once, until golden brown on both sides, about 1½ to 2 minutes total.

3. Spread Rémoulade Sauce on one side of each bread slice. Place a slice of bread, sauced side up, on each of 4 plates. Cover with watercress or lettuce and then a salmon fillet. Top with remaining slice of bread. Serve additional sauce and lemon wedges on the side.

RÉMOULADE SAUCE

1 cup mayonnaise
1 tablespoon drained capers,
   coarsely chopped
1 scallion, minced

1 teaspoon Dijon mustard
1 teaspoon chopped dill
   pickles

Combine all ingredients in a small bowl. Stir to blend well. Cover and refrigerate until ready to use. Sauce may be kept in a tightly covered jar in refrigerator for up to 7 days.

161 TERIYAKI SALMON STEAKS
Prep: 10 minutes   Cook: 10 to 12 minutes   Serves: 4

3 tablespoons soy sauce
3 tablespoons dry vermouth
   or sherry
1½ tablespoons sugar
1 teaspoon finely chopped
   fresh ginger

1 garlic clove, minced
4 salmon steaks, cut 1 inch
   thick (about 5 to 6 ounces
   each)
1 tablespoon vegetable oil

1. Prepare a hot fire. In a small bowl, combine soy sauce, vermouth, sugar, ginger, and garlic. Set teriyaki sauce aside.

2. Brush salmon with oil and place on an oiled grill set 4 to 6 inches from coals. Grill, brushing fish several times with teriyaki sauce, until lightly browned on bottom, about 5 to 6 minutes.

3. Using a wide spatula, carefully turn salmon steaks over and brush cooked side with teriyaki sauce. Continue to grill, basting frequently, until second side is browned and salmon is just opaque in center, about 5 to 6 minutes longer.

---

162 GRILLED SALMON FILLETS WITH DILL SAUCE
Prep: 10 minutes   Cook: 8 to 10 minutes   Serves: 4

½ cup mayonnaise	1½ teaspoons fresh lemon juice
½ cup sour cream	¼ teaspoon freshly ground
2 tablespoons minced fresh dill, or 2 teaspoons dried	pepper
2 tablespoons minced parsley	4 7-ounce salmon fillets
1 scallion, minced	2 tablespoons olive oil
	½ teaspoon salt

1. In a small bowl, combine mayonnaise, sour cream, dill, parsley, scallion, lemon juice, and ⅛ teaspoon pepper. Cover dill sauce and refrigerate until serving time.

2. Prepare a hot fire. Brush both sides of salmon with oil and season with salt and remaining ⅛ teaspoon pepper. Place fish on an oiled grill set 4 to 6 inches from coals. Grill, turning once, until salmon is lightly browned outside and just opaque in center, about 8 to 10 minutes. Serve with dill sauce on the side.

---

163 GRILLED SALMON WITH GUACAMOLE
Prep: 15 minutes   Cook: 10 to 12 minutes   Serves: 4

4 salmon steaks, cut 1 inch thick (about 6 ounces each)	2 ripe avocados
	2 tablespoons fresh lime juice
¾ teaspoon salt	1 jalapeño pepper, minced, or
¼ teaspoon freshly ground pepper	¼ teaspoon hot pepper sauce
2 tablespoons olive oil	1 tablespoon minced scallion

1. Prepare a hot fire. Rinse salmon steaks and pat dry. Season with ½ teaspoon salt and ⅛ teaspoon pepper and rub olive oil over both sides.

2. In a medium bowl, mash avocados with a fork to make a coarse purée. Add lime juice, minced jalapeño, scallion, and remaining ¼ teaspoon salt and ⅛ teaspoon pepper. Blend well.

3. Set fish steaks on an oiled grill 4 to 6 inches from heat. Grill, turning once, until fish is just opaque at center, 10 to 12 minutes. Top each salmon steak with a dollop of guacamole. Pass remaining guacamole on the side.

164   FRESH TROUT DILLED AND GRILLED
Prep: 5 minutes   Cook: 10 to 12 minutes   Serves: 4

Substitute frozen trout, thawed, when necessary.

4 whole fresh trout, cleaned	2 large garlic cloves, minced
⅓ cup olive oil	¼ cup chopped fresh dill, or 1
Salt and freshly ground	tablespoon dried
pepper	

1. Prepare a hot fire. Brush insides of trout with some of the oil and season cavities with salt and pepper.

2. Combine garlic with dill. Stuff each trout with one quarter of the mixture.

3. Brush outside of fish with oil and place on an oiled grill set 6 inches from coals. Cook for 10 to 12 minutes, turning once, until browned outside and just opaque near bone.

165   GRILLED SWORDFISH WITH MELON SALSA
Prep: 5 minutes   Marinate: 1 hour   Cook: 10 to 12 minutes
Serves: 8

8 swordfish steaks, cut about	¼ cup fresh lime or lemon
1 inch thick (about	juice
½ pound each)	1 garlic clove, minced
⅓ cup vegetable oil	Melon Salsa (recipe follows)
⅓ cup soy sauce	

1. Arrange swordfish steaks in a single layer in a large shallow baking dish. Combine oil, soy sauce, lime juice, and garlic and pour over fish. Cover and marinate in refrigerator for 1 to 2 hours, turning occasionally.

2. Prepare a hot fire. Oil grill rack. When coals are covered with gray ash, grill swordfish, turning once and moving as necessary to ensure even cooking, until just opaque at center, 10 to 12 minutes total. Serve with Melon Salsa.

MELON SALSA

1½ cups finely diced cantaloupe	3 tablespoons fresh lime juice
or casaba melon	2 tablespoons chopped fresh
1½ cups finely diced honeydew	cilantro or mint
melon	1 jalapeño pepper, seeded and
1½ cups finely diced Crenshaw	minced, or ¼ teaspoon
melon	cayenne

Combine all ingredients in a medium bowl. Cover and refrigerate for up to 2 days.

166   STUFFED SWORDFISH
Prep: 20 minutes   Cook: 8 to 12 minutes   Serves: 4

2   tablespoons butter
3   tablespoons olive oil
1   tablespoon plus 1 teaspoon
    chopped fresh tarragon,
    or 1½ teaspoons dried
4   6- to 8-ounce swordfish
    steaks, about 1 inch thick

1   teaspoon salt
¼   teaspoon freshly ground
    pepper
2   ounces Jarlsberg cheese, cut
    into thin strips (about ½
    cup)

1. Prepare a medium-hot fire. In a small saucepan, heat butter, olive oil, and 1 tablespoon fresh tarragon or 1 teaspoon dried over low heat just until butter has melted.

2. With the point of a sharp knife, cut a small deep incision in the side of each fish steak and carefully swivel knife blade back and forth to form a pocket. Season outside of fish with salt and pepper. Mix remaining tarragon with cheese and stuff into each pocket, spreading as evenly as possible. Brush each side of fish with some tarragon butter.

3. Place swordfish on an oiled grill set 6 inches from coals. Grill, turning once and brushing with tarragon butter, until fish is just cooked through and cheese is melted, about 8 to 12 minutes. Serve immediately, with any remaining tarragon butter drizzled over fish.

167   CRISPY GRILLED CATFISH FILLETS WITH TARTAR SAUCE
Prep: 10 minutes   Cook: 8 to 10 minutes   Serves: 4

Don't forget to make some of Sarah's Hush Puppy Muffins (page 168) to go with your catfish.

1   cup mayonnaise
1   tablespoon chopped parsley
1   tablespoon sweet pickle
    relish
1   tablespoon drained capers
1   tablespoon chopped green
    olives

4   7-ounce catfish fillets
¼   cup buttermilk
3   drops hot pepper sauce
½   cup yellow cornmeal

1. In a small bowl, combine mayonnaise, parsley, pickle relish, capers, and olives. Cover and refrigerate tartar sauce until serving time.

2. Prepare a hot fire. Pat fillets dry with paper towels. In a shallow dish, mix buttermilk with hot sauce. Dip catfish in milk, then dredge lightly in cornmeal to coat.

3. Place fish on a well-oiled grill set 4 to 6 inches from coals. Grill, turning once, until fish is browned and crisp outside and just opaque throughout, about 8 to 10 minutes. Serve with tartar sauce.

168 GRILLED HALIBUT WITH MARTINI BUTTER

Prep: 10 minutes   Marinate: 30 minutes   Cook: 10 to 12 minutes
Serves: 6

For those who yearn for a good steak and a martini!

6 7-ounce halibut steaks, cut about 1 inch thick	½ teaspoon freshly ground pepper
⅓ cup olive oil	Martini Butter (recipe follows)
3 tablespoons dry vermouth	
1½ teaspoons salt	

1. Brush fish on both sides with olive oil and vermouth. Season with salt and pepper. Cover with plastic wrap and marinate 30 minutes at room temperature.

2. Prepare a hot fire. Oil grill and set 4 to 6 inches from coals. Grill halibut, turning once and moving as necessary to prevent scorching, until fish is just opaque in center, about 10 to 12 minutes total. Serve with a dollop of Martini Butter on top of each steak.

MARTINI BUTTER

2 tablespoons gin	8 tablespoons (1 stick) unsalted butter, at room temperature
1 tablespoon dry vermouth	
⅓ cup pimiento-stuffed green olives (about 12 medium olives)	½ teaspoon grated lemon zest
	Dash of cayenne

1. In a small nonreactive saucepan, boil gin and vermouth over high heat until liquid is reduced to 1 tablespoon, 2 to 4 minutes. Remove from heat and let cool.

2. In a food processor or blender, combine reduced gin mixture, olives, butter, lemon zest, and cayenne. Process until olives are minced and mixture is well blended. Martini butter can be stored several days in refrigerator or weeks in freezer.

169 GRILLED CAJUN SNAPPER

Prep: 10 minutes   Cook: 8 to 10 minutes   Serves: 4

4 red snapper fillets, about 8 ounces each	1 tablespoon plus 1 teaspoon Cajun Spice Blend (page 185)
1 tablespoon olive oil	

1. Prepare a hot grill. Rub snapper fillets with olive oil. Season each fillet with 1 teaspoon Cajun Spice Blend, sprinkling it over both sides of fish.

2. Set fish fillets skin side up on an oiled grill 4 to 6 inches from heat. Grill 4 to 5 minutes, until bottom is browned. Carefully turn fish over with a wide metal spatula. Grill 4 to 5 minutes longer, until skin is browned and fish is opaque throughout.

---

170 GRILLED SNAPPER FILLETS WITH ANCHOVY SAUCE

Prep: 10 minutes   Cook: 8 to 12 minutes   Serves: 4

1 cup mayonnaise
2 tablespoons chopped
    parsley
1 tablespoon minced
    anchovies, or 1 teaspoon
    anchovy paste
2 tablespoons capers, drained
1 teaspoon Dijon mustard

2 pounds red snapper fillets,
    cut into 4 serving pieces
2 tablespoons olive oil
½ teaspoon salt
⅛ teaspoon freshly ground
    pepper
1 lemon, quartered

1. In a small bowl, mix together mayonnaise, parsley, anchovies, capers, and mustard. Cover and refrigerate anchovy sauce until serving time.

2. Prepare a hot fire. Brush both sides of snapper with olive oil and season with salt and pepper. Place fish fillets on an oiled grill set 4 to 6 inches from coals. Grill, turning once, until fish is lightly browned outside and just opaque throughout, about 8 to 12 minutes. Serve each fillet with a dab of anchovy sauce and a lemon wedge. Pass the remaining sauce on the side.

---

171 SHARK!!!!

*Prep: 10 minutes   Marinate: 30 minutes   Cook: 10 to 12 minutes
Serves: 8*

Tuna or swordfish can be successfully prepared in the same manner.

½ cup fresh orange or lemon
    juice
1 tablespoon minced fresh
    oregano, or 2 teaspoons
    dried
1½ teaspoons minced parsley

2 teaspoons salt
½ teaspoon freshly ground
    pepper
1 cup olive oil
6 to 8 8-ounce shark steaks,
    cut 1 inch thick

1. In a bowl, combine orange juice, oregano, parsley, salt, and pepper. Whisk in oil. Arrange shark steaks in a single layer in a large glass baking dish and pour marinade over them. Cover and marinate at room temperature, turning once, for 30 minutes.

2. Prepare a hot fire. Remove shark steaks from marinade; reserve marinade. Place fish on an oiled grill set 4 to 6 inches from coals. Grill, turning once and basting with reserved marinade, until just opaque throughout, about 10 to 12 minutes.

172   ITALIAN GRILLED TUNA
Prep: 10 minutes   Marinate: 30 minutes   Cook: 13 to 15 minutes
Serves: 6

¾ cup extra-virgin olive oil
½ cup minced parsley
½ cup jarred marinated roasted
    red peppers, drained and
    diced
½ cup thinly sliced scallions
¼ cup fresh lemon juice
2 tablespoons capers, drained

2 tablespoons minced fresh
    oregano, or 2 teaspoons
    dried
¼ teaspoon salt
6 8-ounce tuna steaks, about
    ¾ inch thick
⅛ teaspoon freshly ground
    pepper

1. In a medium saucepan, combine ½ cup olive oil with parsley, red peppers, scallions, 2 tablespoons lemon juice, capers, oregano, and salt. Simmer over low heat 5 minutes, stirring occasionally, to blend flavors. Remove from heat and set aside.

2. Place tuna in a single layer in a glass baking dish. Drizzle remaining ¼ cup olive oil and 2 tablespoons lemon juice over fish. Season with pepper. Turn to coat both sides. Cover with plastic wrap and marinate at room temperature 30 minutes.

3. Prepare a hot fire. Place fish on an oiled grill set 4 to 6 inches from coals. Reheat sauce by placing saucepan on side of grill. Grill tuna, turning once, until opaque throughout but still moist, about 8 to 10 minutes. Transfer to a serving plate and spoon sauce over each steak.

173   GRILLED TUNA STEAKS WITH DILL PESTO
Prep: 10 minutes   Cook: 6 to 10 minutes   Serves: 4

2½ cups loosely packed
    chopped fresh dill
¼ cup lightly toasted walnuts
    or pine nuts
2 to 3 garlic cloves, peeled
¾ cup plus 1 tablespoon extra-
    virgin olive oil

½ teaspoon salt
½ teaspoon freshly ground
    pepper
4 tuna steaks, cut ½ inch thick
    (1½ to 2 pounds total)

1. Combine dill, nuts, garlic, ¾ cup olive oil, salt, and pepper in a food processor or blender. Purée to a coarse paste. Set dill pesto aside at room temperature.

2. Prepare a hot fire; lightly oil grill rack. Brush tuna on both sides with remaining 1 tablespoon olive oil and season with additional salt and pepper. Grill over hot coals, turning once, until browned outside and just opaque throughout, 3 to 5 minutes per side. Serve fish warm or at room temperature, with a spoonful of dill pesto on top of each steak. Pass remaining pesto on the side.

174   GRILLED TUNA STEAK WITH LEMON-CAPER BUTTER

Prep: 10 minutes   Cook: 10 to 12 minutes   Serves: 6

8 tablespoons (1 stick)
    unsalted butter, softened
3 tablespoons fresh lemon
    juice
½ teaspoon grated lemon zest

2 teaspoons Dijon mustard
2 teaspoons capers, drained
6 8-ounce tuna steaks, cut
    ¾ inch thick
¼ cup vegetable oil

1. Mix together butter, 2 tablespoons lemon juice, lemon zest, mustard, and capers. Set lemon-caper butter aside.

2. Prepare a hot fire. Brush tuna steaks with oil. Drizzle remaining 1 tablespoon lemon juice over fish. Place steaks on an oiled grill set 4 to 6 inches from coals. Grill, turning once, until firm and opaque at center, about 10 to 12 minutes.

3. Remove from heat and top each steak with 1 tablespoon lemon-caper butter.

175   COCONUT MACADAMIA MONKFISH KEBABS

Prep: 30 minutes   Cook: 6 minutes   Serves: 4

1 cup unsweetened pineapple
    chunks, fresh or canned
½ cup macadamia nuts
¼ cup canned cream of coconut
1 pound monkfish
    (membrane removed), cut
    into ¾-inch cubes
¼ cup olive oil

¼ tablespoon lemon or
    pineapple juice
2 garlic cloves, minced
½ teaspoon salt
¼ teaspoon freshly ground
    pepper
1 small red bell pepper, cut
    into 1-inch squares
1 small yellow bell pepper,
    cut into 1-inch squares

1. In a food processor or blender, purée pineapple, macadamia nuts, and coconut cream. Transfer to a small nonreactive saucepan, bring to a boil, reduce heat, and simmer for 1 minute.

2. In a large bowl, combine monkfish cubes, olive oil, lemon juice, garlic, salt, and pepper. Marinate at room temperature, tossing occasionally, for 30 minutes. If using bamboo skewers, soak in water for at least 30 minutes to prevent burning.

3. Prepare a hot fire. Lift fish cubes from marinade and thread onto skewers, alternating red and yellow pepper squares between each piece of fish. Reserve marinade.

4. Place kebabs on an oiled grill set 4 to 6 inches from coals. Cook, turning occasionally and brushing with reserved marinade, until fish is firm, lightly browned, and opaque throughout, 6 to 8 minutes.

176 GRILLED SZECHWAN SARDINES
Prep: 5 minutes   Cook: 6 to 8 minutes   Serves: 6

¼ teaspoon Chinese hot chili
   oil
½ cup peanut or other mild
   vegetable oil
   Szechwan Seasoned Salt
   (recipe follows)

3 pounds fresh or frozen
   sardines, cleaned and
   gutted
   Lemon wedges

1. Prepare a hot fire. Place a screen or sheet of heavy-duty aluminum foil on grill set about 6 inches from coals. Using a skewer or 2-tined fork, poke about a dozen holes in foil.

2. Combine chili oil with peanut oil. Brush foil lavishly with oil mixture and sprinkle with a generous amount of Szechwan Seasoned Salt. Lay sardines on foil, brush with oil, and sprinkle with more seasoned salt. Grill, carefully turning once, until golden, about 3 to 4 minutes per side. Serve warm, with lemon wedges.

SZECHWAN SEASONED SALT

⅓ cup Szechwan peppercorns
   (available at Asian
   markets)

3 tablespoons coarse (kosher)
   salt

1. Preheat a wok or large heavy skillet over high heat. Add peppercorns and salt. Reduce heat to medium and stir until peppercorns are fragrant and lightly browned, about 2 minutes. Pour into a bowl and let cool.

2. Coarsely grind salt and pepper mixture in a blender or food processor. Store in an airtight jar.

177 MACKEREL FILLETS WITH GRILLED RED PEPPER SALSA
Prep: 15 minutes   Cook: 8 to 10 minutes   Serves: 4

1½ pounds mackerel fillets
 1 tablespoon lemon juice
 2 tablespoons olive oil
½ teaspoon salt

¼ teaspoon freshly ground
   pepper
   Grilled Red Pepper Salsa
   (recipe follows)

1. Prepare a hot fire. Arrange mackerel fillets in a single layer in a glass or ceramic dish. Brush with lemon juice and olive oil. Season with salt and pepper.

2. Set fish skin side up on an oiled grill set 4 to 6 inches from coals. Grill, carefully turning once with a wide metal spatula, until fish is just opaque throughout but still moist, 8 to 10 minutes. Top each fillet with a spoonful of Grilled Red Pepper Salsa and pass the remainder on the side.

178 GRILLED RED PEPPER SALSA
Prep: 5 minutes   Cook: 10 to 15 minutes   Makes: about 1 cup

This savory sauce is a wonderful accompaniment to grilled fish. It also makes a terrific appetizer spread, served with Italian Garlic Toasts (page 17) or croutons of crusty French bread.

2 large or 3 medium red bell peppers
¼ cup chopped oil-cured black olives
2 tablespoons drained capers
2 tablespoons extra-virgin olive oil

1 garlic clove, crushed
2 tablespoons chopped Italian flat-leaf parsley
1½ teaspoons fresh lemon juice
¼ to ½ teaspoon crushed hot red pepper flakes
⅛ teaspoon salt

1. Prepare a hot fire. Set peppers on grill and cook, turning frequently, until skin is charred and blackened all over, 10 to 15 minutes. Immediately seal peppers in a plastic or brown paper bag and let stand for 10 minutes.

2. Rub peppers under cold running water to remove charred skin. Remove and discard stems and seeds. Finely chop peppers and place in a small bowl.

3. Add all remaining ingredients to roasted peppers and stir to blend well. Let stand at room temperature for up to 3 hours, or cover and refrigerate for up to 3 days.

179 GRILLED LOBSTER
Prep: 10 minutes   Cook: 10 to 12 minutes   Serves: 4

Lobster from the grill is succulent, with a hint of smoke. Serve simply with lemon wedges and melted butter.

4 live lobsters, 1¼ pounds each
2 teaspoons olive oil
1½ teaspoons minced fresh thyme, or ½ teaspoon dried

Salt and freshly ground pepper
8 tablespoons (1 stick) unsalted butter
Lemon wedges

1. Prepare a hot fire. Bring a stockpot of water to a boil. Plunge lobsters into pot head first, cover immediately, and boil 1 to 2 minutes, until lobsters have begun to turn red. Remove and let stand just until cool enough to handle; then split lobsters down back. Bend shell back to expose tail meat.

2. Brush lobster with olive oil and season lightly with thyme, salt, and pepper. Place back side down on an oiled grill set 4 to 6 inches from coals. Grill, covered, 3 minutes. Turn lobsters over and grill, covered, until lobster meat is translucent throughout but still juicy, 7 to 9 minutes longer.

3. While lobster is grilling, melt butter in a small pot on side of grill. Serve lobster with melted butter and lemon wedges.

180 GRILLED CLAM FONDUE
Prep: 15 minutes   Cook: 3 to 5 minutes   Serves: 4 to 6

8 tablespoons (1 stick)
unsalted butter
36 hard-shelled clams, such as
littlenecks, well scrubbed

1 loaf crusty French or Italian
bread, cut into 1-inch
cubes

1. Prepare a hot fire. Place butter in a heavy 1½- to 2-quart saucepan on side of grill, preferably not directly over coals. Let melt while clams cook.

2. Place clams directly on grill and cook, turning once, until shells pop open, about 3 to 5 minutes. Use tongs to lift opened clams from grill and drain clam juices into pot of butter. (Discard any clams that do not open.)

3. Place open clams in a serving dish alongside a basket of bread cubes. To eat, alternately spear clams and chunks of bread with a fork and dunk them in warm butter mixture.

181 GRILLED OYSTERS AND MUSSELS ON THE HALF SHELL WITH CHIVE BUTTER
Prep: 10 minutes   Cook: 1½ to 4 minutes   Serves: 4

2 dozen fresh oysters in the
shell
2 dozen mussels, preferably
cultivated, in the shell
3 tablespoons minced chives

8 tablespoons (1 stick) butter,
softened
1 teaspoon fresh lemon juice
Salt and freshly ground
pepper

1. Wash oyster shells to remove any sand. Scrub mussels thoroughly; discard any with open shells that do not close. With a small sharp knife, cut off hairy brown "beards."

2. Prepare a hot fire. In a small bowl, blend chives, butter, and lemon juice. Season with salt and pepper. Place chive butter in a small heavy saucepan at edge of grill to melt.

3. Place shellfish directly on grill (deep side of oysters down) and cook until shells open, about 2 to 3 minutes for mussels, 3 to 4 minutes for oysters. As soon as shellfish open, transfer with tongs to a serving platter. Do not overcook and try not to lose flavorful juices in shells. (Discard any oysters or mussels that do not open.)

4. As soon as oysters and mussels are taken from grill, encourage guests to remove top shells, spoon about ½ teaspoon chive butter over each oyster and mussel, and eat directly from shells.

182 GALVESTON-STYLE SHRIMP
Prep: 30 minutes   Cook: 4 to 6 minutes   Serves: 8

1 onion, quartered	1½ tablespoons Worcestershire
1½ cups white wine vinegar	sauce
1 cup ketchup	2 teaspoons hot pepper sauce
¼ cup apple juice	2 garlic cloves, chopped
¼ cup (packed) brown sugar	½ teaspoon cayenne, or to taste
¼ cup vegetable oil	½ teaspoon turmeric
2 tablespoons Dijon mustard	3 pounds large shrimp
1½ tablespoons celery seed	

1. In a blender or food processor, purée onion with vinegar until smooth. Add ketchup, apple juice, brown sugar, oil, mustard, celery seed, Worcestershire, hot sauce, garlic, cayenne, and turmeric and blend well.

2. Transfer mixture to a medium nonreactive saucepan and bring to a boil. Reduce heat to medium and simmer, stirring frequently, until sauce is slightly thickened, about 20 minutes. Let cool. (The sauce can be prepared up to 1 week ahead and kept in a covered jar in the refrigerator.)

3. Soak bamboo skewers in water for at least 30 minutes to prevent burning. Prepare hot fire. Shell shrimp, leaving tails on. Split each shrimp lengthwise, down back, cutting only about halfway through, and remove vein. Flatten to butterfly. Thread 2 shrimp lengthwise onto each bamboo skewer. Brush shrimp with sauce.

4. Cook shrimp on an oiled grill set 4 to 6 inches from coals, brushing often with sauce and turning once, until shrimp are firm to the touch and opaque throughout, about 4 to 6 minutes. Serve warm or at room temperature, using reserved sauce as a dip.

183 MEXICALI SHRIMP KEBABS
Prep: 25 minutes   Marinate: 1 hour   Cook: 4 to 6 minutes
Serves: 6 to 8

2 pounds large shrimp,	¼ cup tequila
shelled and deveined	¼ teaspoon cayenne
½ cup Garlic Oil (page 180) or	2 garlic cloves, minced
olive oil	½ cup chili sauce
1 teaspoon salt	

1. Place shrimp in a medium bowl. Add oil, salt, tequila, cayenne, garlic, and chili sauce. Cover and refrigerate 1 to 2 hours.

2. Prepare a hot fire. Remove shrimp from marinade and thread onto long metal skewers. Place on an oiled rack above ashen coals and grill, basting frequently with marinade and turning once, until shrimp are pink and loosely curled, about 2 to 3 minutes per side.

184 SPEARED SCALLOPS AND SHRIMP
Prep: 20 minutes   Cook: 10 to 15 minutes   Serves: 4 to 6

This rich and flavorful kebab makes an excellent dinner for special friends.

6 slices lean bacon	1 teaspoon salt
1 pound sea scallops	¼ teaspoon freshly ground
8 tablespoons (1 stick) butter,	pepper
cut into tablespoons	1 pound large shrimp, shelled
2 tablespoons fresh lemon	and deveined
juice	6 large mushrooms, halved
1 garlic clove, minced	

1. Prepare a hot fire. If using bamboo skewers, soak in water for at least 30 minutes to prevent burning.

2. Cut bacon slices in half. Wrap a half strip of bacon around each scallop.

3. In a small saucepan, melt butter with lemon juice and garlic. Warm over low heat until butter melts, about 2 minutes. Season with salt and pepper.

4. On each of 4 long metal skewers, thread a shrimp, a mushroom half, and a bacon-wrapped scallop. Repeat, ending with a shrimp. Brush each skewer with melted butter mixture.

5. Place skewers on an oiled grill set 6 inches from coals. Grill, turning once or twice and basting frequently with butter mixture, until shrimp are pink and scallops are opaque throughout, about 8 to 13 minutes.

---

185 GRILLED SHRIMP KEBABS WITH QUICK COCKTAIL SAUCE
Prep: 10 minutes   Cook: 4 to 6 minutes   Serves: 4 to 6

1 cup ketchup	¼ cup chopped parsley
1 tablespoon prepared white	2 scallions, minced
horseradish	1½ pounds large shrimp,
1 tablespoon fresh lemon	shelled and deveined
juice	2 tablespoons olive oil

1. In a small bowl, combine ketchup, horseradish, lemon juice, parsley, and scallions. Cover and refrigerate cocktail sauce until serving time. If using bamboo skewers, soak in water at least 30 minutes to prevent burning.

2. Prepare a hot fire. Thread shrimp on skewers and brush with olive oil. Place on an oiled grill set 4 to 6 inches from coals. Grill, turning once, until shrimp turn pink and begin to curl, about 4 to 6 minutes. Serve with cocktail sauce for dipping.

186   SHELLFISH BROCHETTES HAWAIIAN
Prep: 25 minutes   Marinate: 30 minutes   Cook: 5 minutes
Serves: 6

½ cup dry sherry
2 tablespoons Asian sesame oil
2 tablespoons grated fresh ginger
1 large garlic clove, minced
1 teaspoon soy sauce
¾ pound sea scallops
12 large shrimp, shelled and deveined

½ pound fresh ripe pineapple, cut into 6 wedges, or 1 8-ounce can unsweetened pineapple rings, cut into wedges
1 medium onion, cut lengthwise into 6 wedges
1 large green pepper, seeded and cut into 1-inch squares

1. Combine sherry, sesame oil, ginger, garlic, and soy sauce in a medium bowl. Add scallops and shrimp; toss to coat. Cover with plastic wrap and marinate at room temperature 30 minutes.

2. Prepare a hot fire. Remove shellfish from marinade and pat dry. Reserve marinade. Thread shrimp and scallops onto 6 long metal skewers, alternating shellfish with pineapple, onion, and green pepper. Grill over hot coals, turning several times and basting with reserved marinade, until shrimp turn pink and scallops are just opaque throughout, about 5 minutes.

187   CURRIED SCALLOP KEBABS WITH SAFFRON MAYONNAISE
Prep: 15 minutes   Cook: 5 to 7 minutes   Serves: 6

¼ teaspoon saffron threads
2 teaspoons plus 3 tablespoons fresh lemon juice
1 cup mayonnaise
1½ pounds sea scallops

3 cups cherry tomatoes
1½ teaspoons curry powder
1 teaspoon salt
Dash of cayenne
2 tablespoons olive oil

1. If using bamboo skewers, soak in water at least 30 minutes to prevent burning. Place saffron in a small bowl and crush with a spoon. Stir in 2 teaspoons lemon juice to soften saffron. Stir saffron-lemon juice into mayonnaise until color is uniformly yellow. Cover and refrigerate until serving time. (Saffron mayonnaise will keep at least 7 days in refrigerator.)

2. Thread scallops and cherry tomatoes onto skewers. In a small bowl, combine remaining 3 tablespoons lemon juice, curry powder, salt, and cayenne. Gradually whisk in olive oil. Brush mixture over kebabs.

3. Prepare a hot fire. When coals are ashen, place kebabs on an oiled rack and grill, turning frequently and basting with marinade, until scallops are lightly browned outside and just opaque inside, about 5 to 7 minutes. Serve kebabs with a dollop of saffron mayonnaise.

Chapter 6

Grilling Vegetables and Grains

Isn't it time you got those vegetables out of the frying pan and into the fire? Grilling is often associated with burgers and ribs, but nearly all vegetables can be grilled successfully. The smoky fragrance and crusty exterior imparted by the coals accentuate the natural goodness of everything from artichokes to zucchini.

Kids who eat nothing but hot dogs and hamburgers will reach out their hands for grilled vegetables, especially if they are served to them on a stick. Small vegetables, such as tiny new potatoes, benefit from the convenience of grilling on thin bamboo skewers.

A light coating of oil prevents vegetables from drying out and sticking to the grill rack, and additional flavors, such as herbs and spices, can be added for variety.

Because many vegetable recipes take up so little room on the grill, use an existing fire whenever possible. Cook them before the main course or at the same time on the side of the grill.

When space on the grill is limited, cook the vegetables first. They can be held at the sides of the grill while the rest of the meal is prepared, or they can be served at room temperature. Corn for a crowd can be boiled briefly in advance to soften and then quickly browned on the grill at the last minute.

---

188 GRILLED CARROTS
Prep: 5 minutes   Cook: 20 minutes   Serves: 6

Grilling carrots accentuates their natural sweetness. Serve with just a splash of balsamic vinegar or top with a dab of butter. Or why not baste them during the last 5 minutes of cooking with your favorite glaze or barbecue sauce?

1½ pounds medium carrots,   1 to 2 tablespoons olive oil
       trimmed and scrubbed

Prepare a hot fire. Rub carrots with oil and place on an oiled grill set 4 to 6 inches from coals. Grill, turning occasionally, until outside is browned and inside is tender when pierced with a fork, about 20 minutes.

189   CORN ON THE COB WITH CHILI BUTTER

Prep: 10 minutes   Marinate: 10 minutes   Cook: 10 to 15 minutes
Serves: 4 or 8

Corn grilled in its own husk is one of summer's great pleasures. We like to serve this as a first course so it receives all the attention it deserves.

8 ears fresh corn	1½ tablespoons chili powder
8 tablespoons (1 stick) butter, cut into bits	1 teaspoon fresh lime or lemon juice
2 scallions, chopped	Salt
1 garlic clove, crushed	

1. Prepare a medium fire. Gently peel back corn husks, leaving them attached at base. Remove and discard as much corn silk as possible.

2. In a food processor or blender, combine butter, scallions, garlic, chili powder, and lime juice. Process until chili butter is well blended.

3. Rub about 2 teaspoons chili butter over kernels in each ear. Fold husks back over corn and tie securely in place with kitchen string or a strip of corn husk. Soak corn in a large bowl of cold water 10 minutes to prevent burning. Squeeze out excess water.

4. Place damp corn on an oiled grill set 4 to 6 inches from coals. Grill, turning and moving ears frequently, until outside leaves are lightly charred. Peel off husks and eat with additional chili butter and salt.

190   CORN HUSKERS' CORN

Prep: 5 minutes   Cook: 15 to 20 minutes   Serves: 4 or 8

Here's an authentic Nebraskan recipe from the heart of the Midwestern corn belt. This preparation is easy on the cook, since guests can husk their own corn.

8 ears unhusked corn, freshly picked	Butter
1 gallon ice water	Salt and freshly ground pepper

1. Prepare a hot fire. As soon as possible after corn is picked, drop ears into pot of ice water and soak at least 10 minutes. Drain before grilling.

2. Place unhusked ears of corn on an oiled grill set 4 to 6 inches from coals. Grill, turning frequently, until husks blacken, 15 to 20 minutes. Remove from grill and use gloves, if necessary, to remove husks, or wait until corn cools slightly. Serve with butter and salt and pepper.

191   GRILLED CORN SALSA

Prep: 10 minutes   Cook: 10 to 15 minutes   Makes: about 1½ cups
Serves 6 to 8

This tangy relish makes a great accompaniment to grilled fish or beef.

3 ears corn, husked	1½ tablespoons lime juice
1 tablespoon olive oil	½ teaspoon ground cumin
1 large tomato	¼ teaspoon salt
1 to 2 jalapeño peppers	⅛ teaspoon freshly ground
1 garlic clove, minced	pepper

1. Prepare a hot fire. In a large saucepan of boiling water, cook corn 2 minutes; drain. (Corn can be precooked up to a day in advance.)

2. Brush corn with oil and set on grill 4 to 6 inches from heat. Grill, turning, until lightly browned all over, 5 to 7 minutes. Remove and set aside.

3. Place tomato and jalapeños on grill. Grill tomato, turning, until skin is slightly charred and tomato is softened, 3 to 5 minutes. Grill jalapeños, turning, until skin is charred, about 5 minutes.

4. Cut corn kernels off cob and place in a medium bowl. Peel tomatoes and jalapeños. Remove seeds. Chop tomatoes and mince jalapeños. Add to corn. Add garlic, lime juice, cumin, salt, and pepper. Toss to mix well. Serve at room temperature.

---

192   BREADED TOMATOES TERRIFIC

Prep: 15 minutes   Cook: 8 to 10 minutes   Serves: 6

This preparation works equally well with green tomatoes from your garden.

½ cup flour	1 teaspoon salt
2 eggs	¼ teaspoon freshly ground
⅓ cup yellow cornmeal	pepper
⅓ cup grated Parmesan cheese	4 medium tomatoes, sliced ¼
2 tablespoons chopped fresh	inch thick
oregano, or 1 teaspoon	
dried	

1. Place flour in a small bowl or on a sheet of wax paper. In a small shallow bowl, lightly beat eggs. In another bowl or on a sheet of wax paper, combine cornmeal, cheese, oregano, salt, and pepper. Mix until blended.

2. Working with 1 tomato slice at a time, dip first in flour, then in egg, and finally in seasoned cornmeal, coating both sides completely. As they are coated, place tomato slices on a rack or baking sheet in a single layer.

3. Prepare a hot fire. Place tomato slices on an oiled grill set 4 to 6 inches from coals. Grill, turning once, until tomato slices are golden and crisp outside and heated through, about 8 to 10 minutes.

193   GRILLED LEEKS WITH CREAM VINAIGRETTE

Prep: 15 minutes   Cook: 20 to 25 minutes   Marinate: 15 minutes
Serves: 4

12 small to medium leeks	½ teaspoon salt
¼ cup extra-virgin olive oil	¼ teaspoon freshly ground
¾ cup heavy cream	pepper
2 tablespoons white wine	2 tablespoons minced chives
vinegar	or parsley

1. Trim roots and dark green tops from leeks, leaving 2 to 3 inches of light green. Slit leeks lengthwise and rinse very well under cold running water. Let soak in a bowl of cold water for 10 minutes, then rinse thoroughly again. Drain well and pat dry.

2. Prepare a medium fire or use an existing fire. Brush olive oil all over leeks. Place on an oiled grill set 4 to 6 inches from coals. Grill, turning frequently and basting with olive oil occasionally, until leeks are browned and tender, 20 to 25 minutes.

3. In a wide bowl, blend cream, vinegar, salt, and pepper. Add grilled leeks and toss to coat. Let stand at room temperature at least 15 minutes or up to 3 hours before serving. Transfer leeks to individual plates. Drizzle a little cream vinaigrette over each serving. Garnish with chives.

194   SKEWERED MARINATED VEGETABLES ITALIANO

Prep: 10 minutes   Marinate: 1 hour   Cook: 10 minutes   Serves: 4

1 medium yellow summer	8 cherry tomatoes
squash, cut into ¾-inch	8 medium mushrooms
pieces	¾ cup bottled Italian salad
1 medium zucchini, cut into	dressing
¾-inch pieces	

1. In a large bowl, combine squash, zucchini, tomatoes, and mushrooms with salad dressing. Toss to coat well. Cover with plastic wrap and marinate 1 to 4 hours at room temperature, or overnight in refrigerator.

2. Prepare a hot fire. Thread vegetables separately onto 4 long metal skewers, so that each skewer is filled with the same vegetable. Place on an oiled grill set 4 to 6 inches from coals. Grill, turning frequently and brushing with reserved marinade, until each vegetable is cooked, 2 to 3 minutes for the tomatoes, 8 to 10 minutes for the squash and zucchini, and 10 minutes for the mushrooms.

3. To serve, slide vegetables off skewers and toss in a serving bowl, or arrange decoratively on a platter.

195 GRILLED ARTICHOKES WITH ROASTED GARLIC MAYONNAISE

Prep: 10 minutes   Cook: 18 to 20 minutes   Serves: 4 to 6

These beautiful vegetables can easily be prepared a day in advance. Serve with fresh lemon wedges and a dollop of Roasted Garlic Mayonnaise.

2 tablespoons lemon juice
1 pound medium or large artichokes
Olive oil

Lemon wedges
Roasted Garlic Mayonnaise (recipe follows)

1. Prepare a hot fire. Add lemon juice to a large bowl filled with 1½ quarts cold water. Trim each artichoke; cut off stems and top third. Bend back and snap off outer leaves around bottom. Cut medium artichokes in half lengthwise or large artichokes into quarters. Remove fuzzy "choke" inside with a melon baller or spoon. As soon as each artichoke is cut, immediately drop into lemon water to prevent discoloration.

2. Bring a large pot of salted water to a boil. Boil artichokes until tender, 8 to 10 minutes. Drain and rinse under cold running water; drain well. Brush artichokes with olive oil.

3. Place artichokes on an oiled grill set 4 to 6 inches from coals. Grill, turning, moving occasionally, and basting with olive oil if they seem dry, until lightly browned, about 10 minutes. Serve warm or at room temperature, with lemon wedges and Roasted Garlic Mayonnaise.

196 ROASTED GARLIC MAYONNAISE

Prep: 2 minutes   Cook: 30 to 40 minutes   Makes: 1 cup

This mayonnaise can be made up to a week in advance, and roasting the garlic takes up very little space on the grill, so try to use an existing fire.

6 to 8 garlic cloves
1 cup mayonnaise

2 teaspoons fresh lemon juice
Dash of cayenne

1. Use an existing medium fire or the very edge of the grill if your fire is hot. Wrap unpeeled garlic cloves in a single layer in a double thickness of aluminum foil. Set on grill about 6 inches from heat and roast, turning occasionally, until garlic is soft, 30 to 40 minutes.

2. Squeeze roasted garlic into a food processor or blender, discarding skins. Add mayonnaise, lemon juice, and cayenne and purée until smooth. Cover and refrigerate for up to 7 days before using.

197   GRILLED SCALLIONS
Prep: 10 minutes   Cook: 3 to 5 minutes   Serves: 8

32 scallions	1 teaspoon salt
⅓ cup olive oil	⅛ teaspoon freshly ground
1 large garlic clove, minced	pepper

1. Prepare a medium-hot fire. Trim off roots from scallions. Trim tops to leave 2 inches of green. In a shallow baking dish, combine olive oil, garlic, salt, and pepper. Add scallions and toss to coat.

2. Remove scallions from oil and place diagonally on an oiled grill set 4 to 6 inches from coals. Grill, turning frequently and basting with oil, until lightly browned and tender, about 3 to 5 minutes.

198   POTATOES ON A POLE
Prep: 5 minutes   Cook: 17 to 20 minutes   Serves: 4 to 6

These practical potatoes can be prepared a day in advance and warmed on the grill just before serving.

2 pounds tiny new potatoes or small red potatoes, cut in half	¼ cup olive oil Coarse (kosher) salt

1. If using bamboo skewers, soak in water at least 30 minutes to prevent burning. Scrub potatoes and boil or steam until almost tender, 7 to 10 minutes. Drain potatoes. When cool enough to handle, thread potatoes on skewers and brush with some of olive oil. (If made in advance, these can sit at room temperature for several hours, or be refrigerated overnight. Let return to room temperature before grilling.)

2. Prepare a hot fire. Place skewers on an oiled grill and cook, turning frequently and brushing with remaining olive oil, until browned outside and fork-tender inside, about 10 minutes. Sprinkle with salt.

199   GRILLED POTATO SLICES
Prep: 10 minutes   Cook: 20 minutes   Serves: 4 to 6

¼ cup olive oil	4 baking potatoes
¼ cup bottled Italian dressing	

1. Prepare a hot fire. In a small bowl, combine olive oil and salad dressing. Whisk to blend well.

2. Scrub potatoes. Without peeling, cut each potato lengthwise into ⅛- to ¼-inch-thick slices. Brush with oil and salad dressing mixture.

3. Place potato slices on an oiled grill set 4 to 6 inches from coals. Cook, turning and basting with oil mixture every 5 minutes, until potatoes are crisp outside and tender inside, about 15 to 20 minutes. Serve warm.

200 SOY-GRILLED SWEET POTATO SLICES

Prep: 5 minutes   Marinate: 30 minutes   Cook: 34 minutes
Serves: 6

2 pounds sweet potatoes
¼ cup soy sauce
1 tablespoon rice wine
    vinegar or white wine
    vinegar

1 tablespoon minced fresh
    ginger
1 large garlic clove, minced
¼ cup olive oil

1. Put sweet potatoes in a large saucepan with salted water to cover. Bring to a boil and cook until just tender, about 30 minutes. Drain and rinse under cold running water to cool slightly; drain well. Cut sweet potatoes lengthwise into ½-inch-thick slices and arrange in a single layer, overlapping slightly if necessary, in a large baking dish.

2. In a small bowl, mix together soy sauce, vinegar, ginger, garlic, and oil. Pour over sweet potatoes. Marinate at room temperature for 30 minutes or longer, turning slices once.

3. Prepare a hot fire. Place sweet potato slices on an oiled grill set 4 to 6 inches from coals. Cook 1 minute, then rotate slices 90 degrees and grill for 1 minute longer, to form a cross-hatch pattern. Brush generously with reserved marinade and turn slices over. Repeat process, brushing again with marinade and cooking for an additional 2 minutes, until slices are browned and glossy.

201 ROASTED RED AND YELLOW PEPPERS

Prep: 5 minutes   Cook: 10 minutes   Serves: 8

3 red bell peppers
3 yellow bell peppers

Extra-virgin olive oil

1. Prepare a hot fire. Grill whole peppers, turning frequently, until skin is black all over, about 10 minutes. Remove from grill and enclose in 1 or 2 plastic bags. Set aside for 5 to 10 minutes, until cool enough to handle.

2. Remove peppers from bags and peel off blackened skin under cold running water. Discard stems and seeds. Slice peppers into ½-inch-wide strips.

3. Arrange pepper strips on platter and drizzle lightly with olive oil. Serve at room temperature.

202   MUSHROOM CAPS, GRILLED AND FILLED
Prep: 5 minutes   Cook: 6 to 10 minutes   Serves: 4 to 6

These are a delicious accompaniment to grilled meats.

12   very large fresh mushrooms,
 stems removed
¼   cup Garlic Oil (page 180) or
 olive oil

¼   cup Pesto (page 182) or your
 favorite brand

1. Prepare a hot fire. In a medium bowl, toss mushrooms with oil to coat well.

2. Place mushroom caps, stem side down, on an oiled grill set 4 to 6 inches from coals. Grill until edges are lightly browned, about 3 to 5 minutes. Turn and place 1 teaspoon pesto in the cavity of each mushroom cap. Continue grilling until bottoms of mushrooms are golden brown, about 3 to 5 minutes longer.

203   QUICK GRILLED EGGPLANT
Prep: 15 minutes   Cook: 10 minutes   Serves: 4

1   large eggplant, about 1½
 pounds
¼   cup extra-virgin olive oil
2   garlic cloves, crushed
1½   teaspoons coarse (kosher)
 salt

¼   teaspoon freshly ground
 pepper
 Lemon wedges

1. Prepare a hot fire or use an existing fire. Peel eggplant and cut into 1½-inch cubes. In a medium bowl, toss with olive oil, garlic, salt, and pepper. Thread eggplant onto 4 skewers.

2. Set skewers of eggplant on an oiled grill 4 to 6 inches from coals. Grill, turning frequently and basting with any oil left in bowl, until eggplant is lightly browned and tender, about 10 minutes. Remove from skewers and serve with lemon wedges.

204   GRILLED EGGPLANT SLICES
Prep: 5 minutes   Cook: 10 to 15 minutes   Serves: 6

If the eggplants are larger than 3½ inches in diameter, you may wish to cut each slice in half.

2   medium eggplants
1   teaspoon salt

½   cup olive oil

1. Prepare a hot fire. Cut eggplants crosswise into ½-inch-thick slices and arrange in a single layer in a large pan or on a baking sheet. Sprinkle with salt and drizzle with olive oil, coating both sides well.

2. Grill eggplant slices, turning once or twice, until golden brown outside and tender inside when pierced with tip of a knife, 10 to 15 minutes.

---

205 BLACK PATENT EGGPLANT
Prep: 5 minutes   Cook: 40 to 50 minutes   Serves: 4

Eggplant grilled in this manner has a wonderful smoky flavor and shiny "black patent" skin.

2 small to medium eggplants, ¾ to 1 pound each Extra-virgin olive oil	Salt and freshly ground pepper

1. Prepare a medium-hot fire. Pierce eggplants 2 or 3 times with a sharp knife or 2-tined fork to allow steam to escape and prevent bursting.

2. Set eggplants directly on grill and cook, turning occasionally, until skin is charred and blackened all over and eggplant is puffed out and very tender throughout when pierced with a knife, about 40 to 50 minutes.

3. To serve, cut eggplants lengthwise in half. Eat like a baked potato, letting each guest mash eggplant in skin with olive oil, salt, and pepper.

---

206 GRILLED JAPANESE EGGPLANT WITH PESTO
Prep: 5 minutes   Cook: 10 minutes   Serves: 6

If you have trouble finding the long, slender Asian variety of eggplant, use the smallest ones you can find and adjust the cooking time accordingly.

6 small, narrow Asian eggplants, cut in half lengthwise (about 2 pounds total)	⅓ cup Pesto (page 182) or your favorite brand 3 tablespoons olive oil

1. Using a small sharp knife, score a uniform crisscross pattern ¼ to ½ inch deep in each eggplant half, taking care not to break through skin. With a small spoon, force pesto into cuts.

2. Prepare a hot fire. Lightly brush cut sides of eggplant with oil and grill cut sides down, turning once, until eggplant is tender, about 5 minutes per side.

207   BRUSSELS SPROUTS EN BROCHETTE
Prep: 5 minutes   Cook: 10 minutes   Serves: 4

Skewered Brussels sprouts are fun to eat! Toss them with butter, with olive oil and a tablespoon of lemon juice, or with a few tablespoons of freshly grated Parmesan cheese.

1   **pound Brussels sprouts,**   **Salt and freshly ground**
     trimmed   **pepper**
2   **tablespoons olive oil**

1. Prepare a hot fire. If using bamboo skewers, soak in water at least 30 minutes to prevent burning.

2. Bring a large pot of salted water to a boil. Add Brussels sprouts and cook until just crisp-tender, about 5 minutes. Drain, rinse under cold running water, and drain well. Toss with olive oil to coat. Season with salt and pepper. Thread Brussels sprouts onto skewers.

3. Place Brussels sprouts brochettes on an oiled grill set 4 to 6 inches from coals. Grill, turning occasionally, until lightly browned, about 5 minutes.

208   GRILLED CHILIES WITH CHEESE
Prep: 15 minutes   Cook: 15 to 20 minutes   Serves: 4

8   **Anaheim or 4 fresh poblano**   1½   **tablespoons olive oil**
     chilies
8   **½-inch slices Brie or**
     Monterey Jack cheese,
     about 4 ounces total

1. Prepare a hot fire or use an existing fire. Set chilies on grill 4 to 6 inches from coals and cook, turning, until skin is charred all over, 10 to 15 minutes. Seal in a plastic bag for 10 minutes.

2. Rub chilies under cold running water to remove charred skin, but do not tear them open. Cut stem end off top and carefully pull out as many seeds as possible. Stuff chilies with cheese.

3. Brush olive oil all over chilies. Return to grill and cook, turning, until chilies are lightly browned and cheese is just melted, about 5 minutes. Serve hot.

209 GRILLED RATATOUILLE
Prep: 45 minutes   Cook: 30 minutes   Serves: 6 to 8

The smoky flavor of charcoal brings added dimension to this classic summer vegetable stew. Serve hot off the grill, or refrigerate and serve later at room temperature.

1 pound sweet bell peppers, preferably a mixture of red, green, and yellow	4 whole heads garlic
¾ cup extra-virgin olive oil	1 teaspoon balsamic or red wine vinegar
1 medium eggplant, about 1¼ pounds	½ cup minced parsley
2 pounds ripe tomatoes	1½ teaspoons chopped fresh thyme leaves, or ½ teaspoon dried
1 pound zucchini	Salt and freshly ground pepper
1 pound small yellow onions	

1. Prepare a hot fire. Set whole peppers on an oiled grill and cook, turning frequently, until charred all over, 10 to 15 minutes. Immediately remove from grill and enclose in a plastic bag until cool enough to handle, 5 to 10 minutes. Rub off charred skin under cold running water and discard stem and seeds; slice peppers into 1-inch-wide strips.

2. Meanwhile, set aside ¼ cup olive oil. Cut eggplant lengthwise into ½-inch-thick slices and brush with some of remaining olive oil. Grill, turning once or twice, until nicely browned outside and tender when pierced with a knife, about 10 to 15 minutes.

3. Halve and seed tomatoes, brush lightly with oil, and grill until slightly charred, 3 to 5 minutes. Cut zucchini in half lengthwise and brush lightly with olive oil. Grill, turning occasionally, until browned and crisp-tender, about 5 to 7 minutes.

4. Cut onions in half, leaving skins on. Brush with olive oil and grill until browned outside and tender inside, about 8 to 10 minutes. Remove a slice from stem end of each garlic head to expose tops of cloves. Coat papery outer skin with oil and grill, turning frequently, until garlic cloves are tender when pierced with a knife, about 30 minutes. As vegetables are cooked, transfer them to a rimmed baking sheet and let cool.

5. Cut eggplant into 1-inch dice and place in a large bowl. Coarsely chop tomatoes and cut zucchini into 1-inch lengths; add to eggplant. Remove and discard onion skins; gently break onions into rings. Add to other vegetables in bowl, along with any juices remaining in baking sheet. Squeeze garlic cloves from their skins and add to other vegetables.

6. Gently stir in remaining ¼ cup olive oil, vinegar, parsley, and thyme. Season with salt and pepper. Serve immediately, or refrigerate and serve later at room temperature.

210   PASTA WITH GRILLED RED SAUCE
Prep: 10 minutes   Cook: 15 to 20 minutes   Serves: 4

Here is an unusual pasta with grilled vegetables that makes a delightful accompaniment to almost any grilled meat or fish.

2 red bell peppers	1 garlic clove, crushed
1 medium onion, halved	¼ to ½ teaspoon crushed hot
2½ pounds tomatoes	red pepper flakes
⅓ cup extra-virgin olive oil	¾ teaspoon salt
1 tablespoon balsamic or red	⅛ teaspoon freshly ground
wine vinegar	pepper
¼ cup chopped fresh basil or	6 ounces rigatoni or rotelle
parsley	Grated Parmesan cheese

1. Prepare a hot fire. Rub peppers, cut side of onion, and tomatoes lightly with about 1 tablespoon olive oil. Set peppers and onion on grill 4 to 6 inches from heat. Grill peppers, turning, until charred and blackened all over, 10 to 15 minutes. Seal in a bag and let stand 10 minutes. Grill onion, turning once or twice, until cut sides are browned and onion is softened, 15 to 20 minutes.

2. While peppers are standing, grill tomatoes, turning, until skin is charred and tomatoes are slightly softened, 3 to 5 minutes.

3. Rub peppers under cold running water to remove charred skin. Discard stems and seeds. Dice peppers and onion. Remove cores and skin from tomatoes and coarsely chop. In a large bowl, combine peppers, onion, and tomatoes. Stir in remaining olive oil, vinegar, basil, garlic, hot pepper flakes, salt, and pepper.

4. In a large pot of boiling salted water, cook pasta until tender but still firm, 10 to 12 minutes. Drain, rinse briefly, and drain well. Add pasta to sauce in bowl and toss. Serve warm or at room temperature, with a bowl of Parmesan cheese on the side.

211   GRILLED GRITS GRUYÈRE
Prep: 10 minutes   Chill: 1 hour   Cook: 5 to 10 minutes   Serves: 8

1 cup quick-cooking grits	1 tablespoon butter
½ cup shredded Gruyère or	⅓ cup olive oil
other Swiss cheese	

1. Cook grits according to package directions. Stir in cheese and butter until melted. Transfer mixture to a buttered 8½ x 4½ x 2½-inch loaf pan. Let cool, then cover and refrigerate until firm, 1 hour or longer.

2. Prepare a medium-hot fire. Remove grits from pan by inverting onto a cutting board. Cut into slices ½ inch thick. Brush both sides with olive oil and grill until browned and crisp, carefully turning once, about 5 to 10 minutes.

212 GRILLED POLENTA
Prep: 5 minutes   Cook: 50 to 55 minutes   Chill: 1 hour   Serves: 8

This coarsely ground yellow cornmeal often takes the place of bread or pasta in Northern Italy.

4 cups water	4 tablespoons butter, cut into
1 teaspoon salt	pieces
1 cup polenta	⅓ cup extra-virgin olive oil

1. Butter an 8½ x 4½ x 2½-inch loaf pan and set aside. In a 2½-quart sauce-pan set over medium-high heat, bring water to a boil. Add salt and very gradually pour in polenta, stirring constantly until thickened. Transfer mixture to a double boiler and reduce heat to medium. Continue cooking, stirring frequently, until mixture is creamy and holds together, leaving a crust on sides of pan, about 45 minutes.

2. Stir in butter until well blended. Transfer mixture to prepared pan, spreading evenly. Let cool, then cover and refrigerate until firm, 1 hour or longer.

3. Prepare a medium-hot fire or use an existing fire. Remove polenta from pan by inverting onto a cutting board. Cut into ½-inch-thick slices. Brush both sides with olive oil and place on an oiled grill set 4 to 6 inches from coals. Grill, brushing with oil and carefully turning once, until browned and crisp, about 5 to 10 minutes.

213 GRILLED POLENTA WITH CHEESE
Prep: 5 minutes   Cook: 50 to 55 minutes   Chill: 1 hour   Serves: 8

4 cups water	½ cup grated cheese, such as
1 teaspoon salt	Parmesan, Pecorino,
1 cup polenta	Fontina, or Gorgonzola
4 tablespoons butter, cut into	⅓ cup extra-virgin olive oil
pieces	

1. Butter an 8½ x 4½ x 2½-inch loaf pan and set aside. In a 2½-quart sauce-pan set over medium-high heat, bring water to a boil. Add salt and very gradually pour in polenta, stirring constantly until thickened. Transfer mixture to a double boiler and reduce heat to medium. Continue cooking, stirring frequently, until mixture is creamy and holds together, leaving a crust on sides of pan, about 45 minutes.

2. Stir in butter and cheese until well blended. Transfer mixture to prepared pan. Let cool, then cover and refrigerate until firm, 1 hour or longer.

3. Prepare a medium-hot fire or use an existing fire. Remove polenta from pan by inverting onto a cutting board. Cut into ½-inch-thick slices. Brush both sides with olive oil and place on an oiled grill set 4 to 6 inches from coals. Grill, brushing with oil and carefully turning once, until browned and crisp, about 5 to 10 minutes.

214 GRILLED POLENTA WITH SMOKY TOMATO SAUCE

Prep: 10 minutes   Cook: 50 to 55 minutes   Chill: 1 hour   Serves: 8

4 cups water
1 teaspoon salt
1 cup polenta
4 tablespoons butter, cut into pieces

⅓ cup extra-virgin olive oil
Smoky Tomato Sauce (recipe follows)

1. Butter an 8½ x 4½ x 2½-inch loaf pan and set aside. In a 2½-quart saucepan set over medium-high heat, bring water to a boil. Add salt and very gradually pour in polenta, stirring constantly until thickened. Transfer mixture to a double boiler and reduce heat to medium. Continue cooking, stirring frequently, until mixture is creamy and holds together, leaving a crust on sides of pan, about 45 minutes.

2. Stir in butter until well blended. Transfer mixture to prepared pan. Let cool, then cover and refrigerate until firm, 1 hour or longer.

3. Prepare a medium-hot fire or use an existing fire. Remove polenta from pan by inverting onto a cutting board. Cut into ½-inch-thick slices. Brush both sides with olive oil and place on an oiled grill set 4 to 6 inches from coals. Grill until browned and crisp, brushing with oil and carefully turning once, about 5 to 10 minutes. Meanwhile, reheat tomato sauce. Pour over slices of grilled polenta.

215 SMOKY TOMATO SAUCE

Prep: 10 minutes   Cook: 40 minutes   Makes: about 1 cup

Here's a recipe for the end of summer, when tomatoes are ripe and plentiful. Grilling the vegetables first gives this sauce a unique smoky flavor.

6 medium tomatoes
1 medium onion, halved
1 garlic clove, unpeeled
2 tablespoons olive oil
½ teaspoon salt

⅛ teaspoon freshly ground pepper
2 tablespoons chopped fresh basil, or 1 teaspoon dried
1 tablespoon chopped parsley

1. Prepare a medium-hot fire or use an existing fire. Set tomatoes, onion, and garlic on grill. Grill tomatoes, turning, until skin is charred and tomatoes are slightly softened, about 3 to 5 minutes. Grill onion, turning once or twice, until browned outside, about 10 minutes; onion will still be firm. Grill garlic, turning, until lightly browned, about 5 to 10 minutes. Peel and chop tomatoes, onion, and garlic separately.

2. Heat olive oil in a large skillet or flameproof casserole. Add onion and cook over medium heat until translucent, about 3 minutes. Add garlic and cook, stirring, for 30 seconds. Add tomatoes, salt, and pepper. Reduce heat to medium-low and simmer until sauce is reduced to a thick purée, about 30 minutes. Stir in basil and parsley.

216 TERIYAKI RICE WEDGES

Prep: 30 minutes   Chill: 2 hours   Cook: 10 minutes   Serves: 8

5 cups water	⅓ cup (packed) brown sugar
1 teaspoon salt	1 teaspoon Asian sesame oil
2½ cups long-grain white rice	1 tablespoon peanut oil
⅓ cup soy sauce	

1. Bring water and salt to a boil in a 2½-quart saucepan. Add rice. When water returns to a boil, cover, reduce heat to low, and simmer until all liquid is absorbed, about 25 minutes. Remove lid and let cool for about 10 minutes but do not stir.

2. Line a 9-inch round cake pan with foil or plastic wrap so that a surplus extends well beyond the edges. Spread warm rice evenly in pan, packing down well with back of a spoon. Cover with another large piece of plastic wrap.

3. Using bottom of an 8-inch cake pan (or bottom of a saucepan), press rice down firmly until a compact "cake" is formed between the 2 sheets of plastic wrap in cake pan. Let cool to room temperature and then remove empty pan. Refrigerate rice until firm and cold, 2 hours or overnight.

4. Remove and discard top layer of plastic wrap and invert rice cake onto a cutting board. Peel off and discard foil or plastic lining. Using a large sharp knife, cut rice cake into 8 pie-shaped wedges.

5. In a small bowl, mix soy sauce with brown sugar until dissolved. Stir in sesame oil and peanut oil.

6. Prepare a medium-hot fire. Brush rice wedges with soy mixture. Place on an oiled grill and cook, turning once and brushing with marinade every 2 to 3 minutes, until edges are brown and crisp, about 5 minutes per side.

Chapter 7

Smoke-Touched Salads

Barbecuing adds that extra something special to almost all foods, and heightened tastes are a help when food is served chilled. Zesty marinades also add extra flavor and sometimes double as dressings.

Some, like the Grilled Salad Niçoise or the Grilled Chicken and Zucchini Salad with Mint, make perfect luncheon or light supper dishes. Others, such as the Grilled Asparagus Salad with Caper Vinaigrette, Grilled Potato Salad, and Grilled Pear Salad with Parmesan Cheese, were designed as first courses and accompaniments.

Since all these salads are served either cool or at room temperature, the grilled portions of each can be prepared at the end or on the edge of an established fire a day or two ahead of time. So while each has that delightful kiss of summer smoke, they can all be prepared ahead of time at your leisure.

---

217 GRILLED CORN SALAD
Prep: 30 minutes   Cook: 8 to 13 minutes   Serves: 6

6 ears fresh corn, husked	2 teaspoons minced fresh chives
2 tablespoons corn oil	2 shallots or white of scallion, minced
1 red bell pepper, diced	1 teaspoon sugar
⅔ cup diced red onion	½ teaspoon salt
¼ cup red wine vinegar	¼ teaspoon freshly ground pepper
1 tablespoon minced fresh thyme leaves, or 1 teaspoon dried	½ cup olive oil

1. Prepare a hot fire. Cook corn in a large pot of boiling salted water until just barely tender, about 3 minutes. Drain and rub corn with corn oil. Place corn on grill set 4 to 6 inches from coals. Grill, turning, until lightly browned all over, about 5 to 10 minutes.

2. Cut kernels off cob and place corn in a medium bowl. Add bell pepper and red onion and toss to mix. In a small bowl, mix together vinegar, thyme, chives, shallots, sugar, salt, and pepper. Gradually whisk in olive oil. Pour dressing over grilled corn salad and toss.

218   GRILLED RADICCHIO WITH GORGONZOLA AND PROSCIUTTO

Prep: 5 minutes   Cook: 2 minutes   Serves: 8

Radicchio, a bitter red chicory native to Italy, is becoming increasingly available throughout the U.S. Serve with crunchy Italian breadsticks as an unusual first course.

2 large heads radicchio, about ½ pound each	8 paper-thin slices of prosciutto
½ cup olive oil Freshly ground pepper	2 lemons, cut into 4 wedges each
½ pound Gorgonzola or other blue cheese, crumbled	

1. Cut both radicchio in half from top to bottom; then cut each half again lengthwise to form a total of 8 wedges, each held together by the white central core at base of vegetable.

2. Prepare a medium-hot fire. Brush radicchio wedges lightly with olive oil and grill, turning, until leaves begin to wilt and turn dark, about 1 minute per side.

3. Place a wedge of warm radicchio on an individual serving plate and drizzle with a bit of remaining olive oil. Immediately season with pepper and scatter cheese over top. Loosely drape prosciutto slices next to radicchio. Garnish with lemon wedges.

219   GRILLED ASIAN PORK AND APRICOT SALAD

Prep: 15 minutes   Marinate: 1 hour   Cook: 8 to 10 minutes
Serves: 4 to 6

This colorful salad is a wonderful combination of flavors and textures.

1½ cups coarsely chopped walnuts (about 6 ounces)	½ cup peanut oil
½ cup soy sauce	1½ pounds boneless center-cut pork chops
⅓ cup honey	6 cups finely shredded Napa cabbage or iceberg lettuce
3 tablespoons red wine vinegar	1½ pounds fresh apricots, pitted and quartered, or
3 tablespoons lemon juice	2 pounds canned apricot halves in light syrup, drained
1½ teaspoons minced garlic	
1½ teaspoons minced fresh ginger	

1. Preheat oven to 375°. Place walnuts on a baking sheet and toast in oven until golden brown and fragrant, 8 to 10 minutes, or toast in a foil packet on the grill.

2. In a medium bowl, mix together soy sauce, honey, vinegar, lemon juice, garlic, and ginger. Whisk in oil. Pour half of soy dressing over pork chops and marinate for 1 hour at room temperature; reserve other half for salad dressing.

3. Prepare a hot fire. Drain pork, reserving marinade. Place meat on an oiled grill set 4 to 6 inches from coals. Cook, turning often and brushing with reserved marinade, until chops are browned outside and white throughout but still juicy inside, about 8 to 10 minutes. Cut pork chops crosswise into thin slices.

4. Place cabbage or lettuce in a salad bowl. Top with pork, walnuts, and apricots and toss with reserved soy dressing.

---

220 GRILLED CHICKEN AND ZUCCHINI SALAD WITH MINT

Prep: 45 minutes   Marinate: 2 hours   Cook: 8 to 10 minutes
Serves: 4

This salad is best when served at room temperature. It looks lovely on a bed of lettuce, garnished with sprigs of mint.

¼ cup fresh lime juice
1 tablespoon chopped fresh mint, or 1 teaspoon dried
¼ teaspoon salt
⅛ teaspoon freshly ground pepper
¼ cup olive oil
2 medium zucchini, cut diagonally into ¼-inch slices
4 skinless, boneless chicken breast halves

1½ cups cooked wild rice, or 3 cups cooked white rice
3 medium tomatoes, peeled, seeded, and diced
1 red or yellow bell pepper, seeded and diced
2 tablespoons finely chopped red onion
Mint Vinaigrette (page 181)

1. In a small bowl, mix together lime juice, mint, salt, pepper, and olive oil. Use about 3 tablespoons of this mixture to marinate zucchini. Toss remainder with chicken and marinate 2 hours at room temperature, or overnight in refrigerator.

2. Prepare a hot fire. Remove zucchini and chicken from marinade and grill, turning, until tender, 3 to 5 minutes for zucchini, 8 to 10 minutes for chicken. Slice chicken crosswise on a diagonal into bite-size pieces.

3. In a large mixing bowl, gently toss rice with chicken, zucchini, tomatoes, bell pepper, and red onion.

4. Pour on about half of Mint Vinaigrette and toss again; add remaining vinaigrette to taste. Season with additional salt and pepper, if necessary.

221 GRILLED MUSHROOM SALAD WITH BACON

Prep: 10 minutes   Cook: 15 to 20 minutes   Marinate: 1 hour
Serves: 6

1 pound large mushrooms	⅛ teaspoon freshly ground
⅔ cup olive oil	pepper
¼ cup fresh lemon juice	4 scallions, thinly sliced
1 teaspoon Dijon mustard	Lettuce leaves
½ teaspoon Worcestershire	½ pound bacon, cooked and
sauce	crumbled
½ teaspoon salt	

1. Prepare a hot fire. Cut off mushroom stems flush with caps. Brush mushrooms lightly with olive oil. Place on grill set 4 to 6 inches over coals. Grill, turning and basting with olive oil occasionally, until browned and slightly softened but still firm, about 15 to 20 minutes.

2. In a medium bowl, combine lemon juice, mustard, Worcestershire, salt, and pepper. Whisk in remaining olive oil until sauce is well blended.

3. Thinly slice mushrooms. Add mushrooms and scallions to sauce and toss. Cover and marinate, tossing occasionally, 1 to 2 hours at room temperature or up to 6 hours in refrigerator.

4. To serve, use a slotted spoon to transfer mushrooms and scallions to a lettuce-lined platter. Top with bacon.

222 GRILLED PEAR SALAD WITH PARMESAN CHEESE

Prep: 25 minutes   Cook: 3 to 5 minutes   Serves: 4

This fruit and cheese course is a perfect intermezzo before dessert, and is an excellent way to make use of still-glowing coals after a rich entrée, such as duck, has come off the grill.

⅓ cup walnut halves and	Salt and freshly ground
pieces	pepper
1 tablespoon fresh lemon	2 large firm ripe pears, such as
juice or white wine	Bartlett, Anjou, or Bosc
vinegar	4 cups mixed tender lettuces
1½ tablespoons honey	and/or watercress
1 tablespoon Dijon mustard	2-ounce piece Parmesan
3 tablespoons peanut oil	cheese, preferably
1 tablespoons walnut oil, or	imported
use 1 more tablespoon	
peanut oil	

1. Preheat oven to 350°. Place walnuts in a small baking dish and toast in oven until golden and fragrant, about 10 to 15 minutes, or toast in foil packets on grill.

2. Make vinaigrette in a small bowl by combining lemon juice, honey, and mustard. Whisk in peanut and walnut oils, and season with salt and pepper.

3. Halve and core unpeeled pears. Lightly brush cut surfaces with vinaigrette. Grill pears, turning and basting with a bit more vinaigrette, until just tender, about 3 to 5 minutes. Transfer pears to cutting board, round side up, and make 4 or more equally spaced vertical cuts down the length of each pear half without cutting all the way through. Gently flatten each half so that slices curve to one side, fanning out, and pears lie almost flat.

4. Arrange lettuce on 4 large salad plates. Use a wide metal spatula to transfer 1 pear half to the center of each plate. Using a swivel-bladed vegetable peeler, shave Parmesan cheese into slices and scatter over each salad. Drizzle remaining vinaigrette over salads and top with toasted walnuts.

---

223 GRILLED ITALIAN SUMMER BREAD SALAD

Prep: 30 minutes   Marinate: 20 minutes   Cook: 3 to 5 minutes
Serves: 8

This economical salad is traditionally made from stale Italian bread. Starting with grilled bread brings an exciting new flavor to this classic. Use the edge or end of an existing fire for the few minutes of grilling this requires. If fresh basil is not available, arugula, fresh mint, or flat-leaf parsley makes an acceptable substitute.

½ cup red wine vinegar
½ teaspoon salt
⅛ teaspoon freshly ground pepper
1 cup extra-virgin olive oil
4 large ripe tomatoes, seeded and diced
1 cup shredded or coarsely chopped fresh basil leaves

1 1-pound loaf day-old Italian bread, cut into ½-inch-thick slices
¼ cup Garlic Oil (page 180)
1 large cucumber, seeded and thinly sliced
1 large red onion, peeled and thinly sliced

1. Prepare a hot fire. In a large salad bowl, combine vinegar, salt, pepper, and olive oil. Stir in tomatoes and basil and set aside.

1. Toast bread slices over hot coals, turning until both sides are golden brown, 3 to 5 minutes. Brush one side of each slice with Garlic Oil and set aside, uncovered, to cool to room temperature.

3. Using your hands, break or tear bread slices into pieces about ¾ inch square.

4. Toss bread cubes, cucumber, and red onion with tomato-basil mixture. Cover with plastic wrap and marinate at room temperature at least 20 minutes, or as long as 4 hours. Bread will soften as it absorbs flavors in salad.

224 GRILLED EGGPLANT SALAD
Prep: 10 minutes   Cook: 40 minutes   Serves: 4 to 6

2 large tomatoes
3 fresh Anaheim chilies, or 1
  can chopped green chilies
1 large eggplant (about 1½
  pounds), pierced twice
  with a fork
1 garlic clove, crushed

1 teaspoon ground cumin
1 teaspoon salt
¼ teaspoon cayenne
3 tablespoons red wine
  vinegar
⅓ cup extra-virgin olive oil
½ cup chopped red onion

1. Prepare a hot fire. Set whole tomatoes, fresh chilies, and eggplant on grill. Cook tomatoes, turning frequently, until skin is slightly charred, about 2 minutes. Let cool, then peel off skin, Coarsely chop tomatoes.

2. Grill Anaheim chilies, turning, until charred, about 5 minutes. Seal in a plastic bag and let stand 5 to 10 minutes. Remove charred skin under cold running water; discard stems and seeds. Chop chilies.

3. Grill eggplant, turning, until skin is blackened and eggplant is soft throughout, about 30 minutes. Let cool, then remove skin by rubbing with damp paper towels. Finely chop eggplant.

4. In a medium bowl, combine garlic, cumin, salt, cayenne, and vinegar. Whisk in olive oil. Add chopped eggplant, tomatoes, chilies, and red onion. Stir gently to mix.

225 GRILLED TOMATO AND MOZZARELLA SALAD
Prep: 5 minutes   Cook: 4 minutes   Serves: 4

This salad is best made with ripe summer tomatoes.

2 large beefsteak tomatoes,
  thickly sliced
  Salt and freshly ground
  pepper
3 tablespoons extra-virgin
  olive oil

¼ pound mozzarella cheese,
  thinly sliced
¼ cup finely chopped fresh
  basil or parsley

1. Prepare a medium-hot fire. Season tomatoes with salt and pepper. Brush 1 side of each slice with olive oil. Set tomatoes oiled side down on an oiled grill and cook without turning for about 2 minutes, until very lightly browned. Brush lightly with olive oil and turn carefully with a wide metal spatula. Place a piece of mozzarella on top of each tomato slice and grill, covered, until cheese just begins to melt and tomatoes are softened but still hold their shape, about 2 minutes longer.

2. Transfer cheese-topped tomato slices to a platter. Sprinkle basil over tomatoes and drizzle on remaining olive oil.

226 GRILLED ASPARAGUS SALAD WITH CAPER VINAIGRETTE

Prep: 20 minutes   Cook: 5 minutes   Serves: 4

If edible nasturtiums are plentiful in your garden, they make a stunning garnish for this unusual springtime appetizer salad.

4 small eggs, or 8 quail eggs
16 large asparagus spears, tough ends removed (about 1½ pounds)

Olive oil
Caper Vinaigrette (page 180)

1. Place eggs in a small saucepan and cover with cold water. Bring to a boil over medium heat. Immediately cover pot and remove from heat. Let small eggs stand for 15 minutes, quail eggs for 10 minutes. Drain and rinse under cold water to cool; peel eggs immediately. Store in a bowl of cold water for up to 2 days in refrigerator.

2. Prepare a hot fire. Brush asparagus spears with olive oil and place diagonally across an oiled grill 4 to 6 inches from coals. Grill, turning frequently, until lightly browned and tender, about 5 minutes. Point of a knife should easily pierce stem end.

3. Drain and dry eggs. Cut eggs in half lengthwise with a sharp knife. Arrange 4 asparagus spears on each of 4 salad plates and garnish with hard-cooked egg halves. Spoon Caper Vinaigrette over asparagus and eggs.

227 GRILLED SWEET-AND-SOUR CARROT SALAD

Prep: 15 minutes   Cook: 20 minutes   Marinate: 2 hours
Serves: 8 to 12

2 pounds medium carrots, peeled and trimmed
½ cup olive oil
1 quart tomato juice
1 red onion, thinly sliced
1 green bell pepper, thinly sliced
1 cup sugar

½ teaspoon freshly ground pepper
2 tablespoons prepared white horseradish
¾ cup red wine vinegar
¼ teaspoon hot pepper sauce
1 teaspoon Dijon mustard
½ teaspoon salt

1. Prepare a hot fire. Brush carrots lightly with olive oil and grill, turning every 5 to 7 minutes and brushing with more oil, until lightly browned and crisp-tender, about 20 minutes. As soon as carrots are cool enough to handle, slice them and place in a medium bowl.

2. Add all remaining ingredients to carrots and toss to mix. Cover and marinate at room temperature at least 2 hours, tossing occasionally, or refrigerate overnight or as long as 3 days. Remove carrots and other vegetables with a slotted spoon before serving.

228 GRILLED AND CHILLED STEAK SALAD
Prep: 20 minutes   Marinate: 1 hour   Serves: 6 to 8

This is perfectly delicious picnic fare. Remember to bring along a loaf of good crusty bread.

2 pounds lean charcoal-grilled steak, such as top round or sirloin, chilled and cut into thin diagonal slices
1 red bell pepper, grilled and sliced into long strips about ¼ inch wide
1 yellow bell pepper, grilled and sliced into long strips about ¼ inch wide
1 pound cherry tomatoes, halved if large

1 small red onion, thinly sliced
¼ cup drained capers
1 tablespoon Dijon mustard
¼ teaspoon salt
⅛ teaspoon freshly ground pepper
¼ cup red wine vinegar
¾ cup olive oil
3 bunches fresh watercress, stems removed

1. In a medium bowl, gently toss together steak, red and yellow pepper strips, tomatoes, red onion, and capers. In a small bowl, mix mustard, salt, pepper, and vinegar together. Whisk in olive oil and toss with steak mixture. Cover and marinate 1 to 2 hours at room temperature, or as long as 8 hours refrigerated.

2. Lift steak mixture from marinade with a slotted spoon and place on watercress leaves. Pass remaining marinade as a salad dressing, if desired.

229 MAKE-AHEAD GRILLED SALAD
Prep: 15 minutes   Cook: 10 minutes   Marinate: 8 hours
Serves: 6 to 8

4 yellow squash, sliced lengthwise in half
4 zucchini, sliced lengthwise in half
1 large onion, sliced in half through root end

2 tablespoons vegetable oil
1 cup bottled Italian salad dressing
1 teaspoon salt
½ teaspoon freshly ground pepper

1. Prepare a hot fire. Brush yellow squash, zucchini, and onion with oil. Grill 6 inches from coals, turning occasionally, until vegetables are slightly browned and softened. Remove from heat and let cool. Slice vegetables.

2. In a large bowl, combine grilled vegetables, salad dressing, salt, and pepper. Cover and refrigerate 8 hours or overnight. Drain vegetables and arrange on serving platter.

230 GRILLED ZUCCHINI SALAD WITH MARJORAM

Prep: 10 minutes   Cook: 5 to 7 minutes   Serves: 6 to 8

Nothing says summer like zucchini from the garden!

6 **medium zucchini**	2 **tablespoons balsamic**
1½ **teaspoons salt**	**vinegar**
½ **teaspoon freshly ground**	2 **tablespoons chopped fresh**
pepper	**marjoram leaves, or 1**
⅓ **cup olive oil**	**teaspoon dried**

1. Prepare a hot fire. Slice zucchini crosswise on the diagonal into long slices about ⅜ inch thick and place in a large bowl. Toss with salt, pepper, and olive oil. Grill zucchini, turning once, until browned and tender, about 5 to 7 minutes. Return zucchini to bowl and let cool to room temperature.

2. Gently toss zucchini with vinegar. Season with additional salt and pepper. Transfer to a serving platter and sprinkle with chopped marjoram before serving. (This can be made up to a day in advance and refrigerated, but should be served at room temperature.)

231 GRILLED POTATO SALAD

Prep: 10 minutes   Cook: 15 to 20 minutes   Serves: 6

Since this salad contains no mayonnaise, it can stand safely at room temperature for several hours.

2 **pounds small red or white**	2 **tablespoons white wine**
new potatoes, cut in half	**vinegar**
if larger than 2 inches in	½ **teaspoon salt**
diameter	¼ **teaspoon freshly ground**
½ **cup extra-virgin olive oil**	**pepper**
2 **teaspoons Dijon mustard**	3 **scallions, minced**

1. Prepare a medium-hot fire or use an existing fire. In a medium bowl, toss potatoes with 2 tablespoons olive oil and place on an oiled grill 4 to 6 inches from coals. Cook, turning and moving occasionally until potatoes are lightly browned and just tender when pierced with a fork, about 15 to 20 minutes.

2. In a small bowl, mix together mustard, vinegar, salt, and pepper. Gradually whisk in remaining olive oil until well blended. Pour dressing over potatoes, add scallions, and toss.

232 GRILLED SALAD NIÇOISE
Prep: 45 minutes   Cook: 10 to 12 minutes   Serves: 4

The many components of this salad can be prepared a day in advance and assembled shortly before serving.

8 to 12 tiny new potatoes, or
    4 small red potatoes,
    halved
    Caper Vinaigrette (page 180)
¾ pound green beans,
    trimmed
2 7-ounce tuna steaks, cut
    about 1 inch thick
1 tablespoon olive oil
¼ teaspoon salt
⅛ teaspoon freshly ground
    pepper

1 large head leafy lettuce,
    such as Boston or red leaf,
    well washed and drained
12 cherry tomatoes, halved if
    large
1 small red onion, thinly
    sliced
4 hard-cooked eggs, halved
1 2-ounce can flat anchovy
    fillets, drained
¼ cup tiny black Niçoise
    olives, or ½ cup oil-cured
    olives

1. Steam potatoes until tender, 20 to 30 minutes. While still warm, cut in half lengthwise and toss with 3 tablespoons Caper Vinaigrette; set aside to cool completely.

2. In a large saucepan of salted water, boil green beans until just crisp-tender, 3 to 5 minutes. Drain and rinse under cold running water; drain well.

3. Prepare a hot fire. Brush tuna with olive oil and season with salt and pepper. Place on an oiled grill set 4 to 6 inches over ashen coals. Grill, turning once or twice, until tuna is just cooked through, 10 to 12 minutes. Remove from grill and let cool to room temperature.

4. Line a large platter with lettuce leaves. Use 2 forks to coarsely break tuna into bite-size chunks and place in center of platter. Arrange potatoes, green beans, tomatoes, red onion, and eggs decoratively around tuna. Crisscross anchovy fillets over top and scatter olives over all. Drizzle ¼ cup Caper Vinaigrette over salad. Pass remaining vinaigrette at table.

Chapter 8

Foiled Again!

Here's one of our favorite ways of grilling—it's clean, it's neat, it's easy. Foods are wrapped in foil and steamed on the grill with an imaginative array of seasonings and spices. Entire meals can come off the fire at one time. All the flavor and juices are sealed inside. And there's no cleanup when you're through.

For this type of grilling, we recommend heavy-duty aluminum foil because it will not burn, it forms a more secure packet, and it won't leak.

Most foiled foods are cooked over a medium fire. Depending on whether you are grilling an appetizer, main course, or side dish, either prepare a hot fire and let it burn down or use an existing fire that has cooled.

---

233 NACHOS ON FIRE
Prep: 5 minutes   Cook: 10 to 15 minutes   Serves: 6

Warm these on the side of the grill while your entrée is cooking. If it is important to you that cheese melt smoothly, substitute processed cheese for the natural cheese called for in the recipe.

6 cups tortilla chips
3 cups grated mild Cheddar or Monterey Jack cheese (or a combination of both)

¼ to ⅓ cup chopped or sliced jalapeño peppers, fresh, pickled, or canned, well drained

1. Prepare a medium fire or use an existing fire. Fold a 30-inch-long sheet of heavy-duty aluminum foil in half to create a double thickness. Place tortilla chips in center, no more than 2 chips deep. Scatter cheese over chips and top with chilies.

2. Fold up edges of foil to create a tented package. Using tines of a fork, puncture top of package about 6 times to allow steam to escape so chips will not become soggy. Place package on grill and heat without turning until cheese has melted, about 10 to 15 minutes.

234   WHOLE SALMON IN FOIL
Prep: 10 minutes   Cook: 30 minutes   Serves: 8 to 10

1   5- to 8-pound salmon,
    cleaned and trimmed
1   teaspoon salt
¼   teaspoon freshly ground
    pepper

1   small onion, thinly sliced
1   lemon, sliced
2   tablespoons chopped fresh
    dill, or 1½ teaspoons
    dried

1. Prepare a medium-hot fire. Rinse fish with cold water and pat dry. Season inside of fish with salt and pepper and fill with onion, lemon, and dill. Oil a double thickness of heavy-duty aluminum foil and wrap fish tight, crimping edges to seal.

2. Grill foil-wrapped fish, turning every 10 minutes or so, until fish is opaque in center, about 30 minutes.

235   SCALLOPS IN TARRAGON BUTTER
Prep: 10 minutes   Cook: 15 to 20 minutes   Serves: 4

1   pound sea scallops
1   tablespoon minced fresh
    tarragon, or 1 teaspoon
    dried

2   teaspoons lemon juice
½   teaspoon salt
    Dash of cayenne
4   tablespoons butter

1. Prepare a medium fire. Arrange scallops in a single layer on an 18-inch rectangle of heavy-duty aluminum foil. Season with tarragon, lemon juice, salt, and cayenne. Dot with butter. Fold edges of foil together, pinching to make a secure package.

2. Set package on grill and cook, turning occasionally, until scallops are opaque throughout, about 15 to 20 minutes.

236   FASHIONABLY FAST FOILED FLOUNDER
Prep: 10 minutes   Cook: 20 minutes   Serves 6

2   teaspoons grated lemon
    peel, yellow part only
1   tablespoon chopped parsley
1   teaspoon salt
½   teaspoon freshly ground
    pepper

6   flounder fillets (about 4
    ounces each)
¼   cup dry vermouth
1   tablespoon lemon juice

1. Prepare a medium fire. Combine lemon peel, parsley, salt, and pepper. Rub both sides of fillets with lemon mixture. Roll up each fillet jelly-roll fashion. Place seam side down on an 18-inch rectangle of heavy-duty aluminum foil.

2. Combine vermouth and lemon juice; drizzle over flounder rolls. Cover with another 18-inch rectangle of foil; fold and crimp edges to seal well. Place package on grill 6 inches from coals. Cook, turning occasionally, for about 20 minutes, or until fish is opaque throughout.

---

237 LINDA'S GRILLED TOMATOES
Prep: 10 minutes   Cook: 20 minutes   Serves: 4

These cheesy tomatoes are great with grilled beef.

4 firm ripe tomatoes	¼ cup shredded sharp process
½ teaspoon salt	American cheese
Freshly ground pepper	1 tablespoon butter, melted
¼ cup fresh bread crumbs	1 tablespoon chopped parsley

1. Prepare a medium-hot fire. Cut a ¼- to ½-inch slice from top of each tomato. Sprinkle with salt and pepper.

2. In a small bowl, combine bread crumbs, cheese, and melted butter; toss to mix well. Sprinkle bread crumb mixture over tomatoes and top with parsley. Wrap tomatoes individually in oiled squares of aluminum foil. Fold edges to seal.

3. Place packages on grill set 4 to 6 inches over coals. Grill without turning until tomatoes are heated through and cheese is melted, about 20 minutes.

---

238 ROASTED GARLIC
Prep: 10 minutes   Cook: 45 minutes to 1 hour   Serves: 4

Garlic slowly roasted in this fashion becomes surprisingly sweet. Serve a whole head to each guest. Cloves can be squeezed out and spread on bread or eaten as a vegetable.

4 large whole heads garlic	1 tablespoon chopped fresh
¼ cup olive oil	thyme leaves, or 1
½ teaspoon salt	teaspoon dried
⅛ teaspoon freshly ground	
pepper	

1. Prepare a medium fire. Cut ¼ to ½ inch off top of each head of garlic to expose some cloves. Peel away some of outer papery husk. Place each head on a piece of aluminum foil. Drizzle 1 tablespoon olive oil over each head of garlic and season with salt, pepper, and thyme. Fold up edges of foil to wrap securely.

2. Place foil packets on grill set 4 to 6 inches from coals. Grill, turning once or twice, until garlic is very tender when pierced with a fork, 45 minutes to 1 hour.

239   ITALIAN EGGPLANT PACKETS
Prep: 10 minutes   Cook: 30 minutes   Serves: 6

These packets can be arranged several hours in advance and grilled just before serving.

⅓ cup olive oil
1 medium eggplant, cut into
   12 slices about ½ inch
   thick
2 garlic cloves, minced
2 medium tomatoes, cut into
   ¼-inch-thick slices

1 teaspoon salt
¼ teaspoon freshly ground
   pepper
2 tablespoons chopped fresh
   basil, or 1½ teaspoons
   dried

1. Prepare a medium fire. Cut 6 pieces of heavy-duty aluminum foil at least 12 inches long. Brush one side of each piece lightly with oil.

2. Place an eggplant slice on each piece of foil and generously brush with oil. Sprinkle garlic over eggplant. Top with a tomato slice and season with salt, pepper, and basil. Top with another eggplant slice and drizzle with any remaining oil. Fold edges over to create a secure package. Crimp edges to seal.

3. Place foil packets on grill and cook, turning frequently, until eggplant is tender, about 30 minutes.

240   GARLIC MUSHROOM RAGOUT
Prep: 10 minutes   Cook: 15 to 20 minutes   Serves: 6

Be sure to unwrap this package at the table so everyone can enjoy the heavenly aromas.

1 pound fresh mushrooms,
   sliced
6 shallots or white part of
   scallions, thinly sliced
2 garlic cloves, minced
2 tablespoons minced parsley
2 tablespoons fresh lemon
   juice

½ teaspoon salt
¼ teaspoon freshly ground
   pepper
4 tablespoons butter, cut into
   small bits

1. Prepare a medium fire. In a large bowl, mix mushrooms with shallots, garlic, parsley, lemon juice, salt, and pepper. Place mixture on a double thickness of 18-inch square heavy-duty aluminum foil and dot with butter. Wrap foil packet securely, crimping edges to seal.

2. Place packet on a grill set 4 to 6 inches from coals. Cook, turning 2 or 3 times, until mushrooms are tender, about 15 to 20 minutes.

241 HONEY ONIONS
Prep: 10 minutes   Cook: 30 minutes   Serves: 6

12 small white boiling onions,
    about 1½ inches in
    diameter
2 tablespoons dry sherry

2 tablespoons honey
1 tablespoon butter, melted
1 teaspoon soy sauce
¼ teaspoon allspice

1. Prepare a medium fire. Place onions on 12-inch rectangle of heavy-duty aluminum foil. In a small bowl, combine sherry, honey, melted butter, soy sauce, and allspice, mixing well. Drizzle over onions, then cover package with another rectangle of foil, folding and crimping to seal well.

2. Place package on grill set 6 inches from coals and cook for about 25 to 30 minutes, turning occasionally, until onions are tender.

242 LOUISE'S HERBED CORN
Prep: 10 minutes   Cook: 15 minutes   Serves: 8

8 tablespoons (1 stick) butter,
    softened
2 tablespoons chopped
    parsley

2 tablespoons chopped chives
½ teaspoon salt
Dash of cayenne
8 ears of corn, husked

1. Prepare a medium fire. Blend butter with parsley, chives, salt, and cayenne. Spread 1 heaping tablespoon herb butter over each ear of corn. Wrap corn individually in heavy-duty aluminum foil.

2. Grill 4 to 6 inches over glowing coals, turning occasionally, until tender, about 15 to 20 minutes.

243 GRILLED VEGETABLE MEDLEY
Prep: 10 minutes   Cook: 25 to 30 minutes   Serves: 6

4 medium tomatoes,
    quartered
4 yellow squash, sliced
1 medium onion, thinly sliced
1 tablespoon chopped fresh
    basil, or ¾ teaspoon dried

1 teaspoon salt
¼ teaspoon freshly ground
    pepper

1. Prepare a medium fire. Place vegetables on an 18-inch square of heavy-duty aluminum foil. Season with basil, salt, and pepper. Fold edges over to create a secure package.

2. Place package on grill set 4 to 6 inches from coals. Grill, turning once or twice, until vegetables are tender, about 25 to 30 minutes.

244   SILVER SPUDS
Prep: 30 minutes   Cook: 1 hour   Serves: 8

Save time by leaving skins on the potatoes and slicing them in a food processor.

3 tablespoons vegetable oil
5 pounds potatoes, scrubbed
  and thinly sliced
3 onions, thinly sliced
8 tablespoons (1 stick) butter,
  cut into small pieces

2 teaspoons salt
½ teaspoon freshly ground
  pepper

1. Prepare a medium fire. Fold 2 24-inch-long sheets of heavy-duty aluminum foil in half. Place 1 sheet crosswise over the other. Coat generously with oil. Combine potatoes, onions, and butter in center of foil. Season with salt and pepper. Wrap foil tight, forming a large secure packet.

2. When gray ash has formed on coals, lay foil packet directly on coals. Cook, turning and moving packet every 10 minutes, about 1 hour, or until potato slices are tender when pierced with a fork.

3. To serve, slit packet in center. Use a large spoon to loosen potato slices clinging to foil. Make sure each serving contains some crusty brown slices as well as soft and tender potatoes from center.

245   HERB-SMOKED POTATOES
Prep: 2 minutes   Cook: 30 to 40 minutes   Serves: 1

These can be assembled and left at room temperature several hours before cooking. Make one packet of potatoes for each guest. The herb sprig adds a lovely perfume.

3 to 4 small red potatoes,
  about 2 inches in
  diameter
1 tablespoon olive oil
  Salt and freshly ground
  pepper

1 large sprig of fresh herb,
  such as rosemary or
  thyme

1. Prepare a medium fire. Place potatoes on a 6-inch piece of heavy-duty aluminum foil. Spoon oil over and rotate potatoes to coat. Season with salt and pepper and top with an herb sprig. Fold up edges to create a secure package.

2. Cook package directly on the coals, turning once or twice, until potatoes are tender when pierced with a knife, about 30 to 40 minutes.

246 GRILL-BAKED SWEET POTATO
Prep: 5 minutes   Cook: 45 minutes   Serves: 1

Grill as many sweet potatoes as you have places at the table. Serve with butter, or if you like your sweet potatoes even sweeter, with Honey Butter (page 188).

1 large sweet potato, 6 to 8
ounces

1. Prepare a medium fire or use an existing fire. Wrap sweet potato in heavy-duty aluminum foil. (If you cook more than one potato, wrap each one individually.) Pierce potato several times through foil with tines of a fork or tip of a knife.

2. Place sweet potato on grill set 4 to 6 inches from coals. Grill, turning frequently, until potato is very soft, about 45 minutes.

247 SILVER MINE POTATOES
Prep: 2 minutes   Cook: 45 minutes   Serves: 4

4 Russet baking potatoes,
well scrubbed

Prepare a medium fire. Wrap each potato individually in heavy-duty aluminum foil and bury directly in the coals. Grill, turning once or twice, until potatoes are tender when pierced with a knife, about 45 minutes.

248 GRANDLY GLAZED CARROTS
Prep: 10 minutes   Cook: 30 to 40 minutes   Serves: 6

2 pounds carrots, peeled and
    trimmed
½ teaspoon salt
    Freshly ground pepper
1 tablespoon brown sugar

¼ cup orange liqueur, such as
    Grand Marnier
2 tablespoons butter, chilled
    and cut into bits

1. Prepare a medium fire. Cut carrots into diagonal slices about ¼ inch thick and divide among 6 10-inch sheets of heavy-duty aluminum foil. Season each portion of carrots with salt and pepper; then sprinkle with equal amounts of brown sugar, orange liqueur, and bits of butter. Fold edges of foil over to seal.

2. Cook packets on grill, turning occasionally, until carrots are crisp-tender, 30 to 40 minutes.

249 SCALLION AND CHEDDAR LOAF
Prep: 15 minutes   Cook: 10 to 15 minutes   Makes: 1 loaf

1 1-pound loaf French or
  Italian bread
½ cup chopped scallions
½ pound Cheddar cheese,
  grated (about 2 cups)

8 tablespoons (1 stick) butter,
  softened
½ teaspoon Worcestershire
  sauce
⅛ teaspoon cayenne

1. Prepare a medium fire or use an existing fire. Using a long serrated knife, cut bread into 1-inch slices without slicing completely through bottom crust.

2. Combine scallions, cheese, butter, Worcestershire, and cayenne; blend well. Spread butter mixture over both sides of bread slices. Wrap securely in foil and toast on edge of grill, turning occasionally, until bread is heated through and cheese is melted, about 10 to 15 minutes.

250 GARLIC BREAD
Prep: 10 minutes   Cook: 10 to 15 minutes   Makes: 1 loaf

1 1-pound loaf French or
  Italian bread
8 tablespoons (1 stick) butter,
  softened

1 or 2 garlic cloves, crushed
  Paprika

1. Prepare a medium fire or use an existing fire. Using a long serrated knife, cut bread into 1-inch slices without slicing completely through bottom crust.

2. Combine butter and garlic; mix well until blended. Spread garlic butter over both sides of bread slices. Sprinkle lightly with paprika and wrap securely in foil. Toast on edge of grill, turning occasionally, until heated through, about 10 to 15 minutes.

251 BRANDIED BLUE CHEESE LOAF
Prep: 10 minutes   Cook: 10 to 15 minutes   Makes: 1 loaf

This is wonderful with grilled beef.

1 1-pound loaf French or
  Italian bread
8 tablespoons (1 stick) butter,
  softened

2 ounces blue cheese
1 tablespoon brandy
1 tablespoon minced chives
  Dash of cayenne

1. Prepare a medium fire or use an existing fire. Using a long serrated knife, cut bread into 1-inch slices without slicing completely through bottom crust.

2. Combine butter, blue cheese, brandy, chives, and cayenne; mix to blend well. Spread butter mixture over both sides of bread slices. Wrap securely in foil and toast on edge of grill, turning occasionally, until bread is heated through and cheese is melted, about 10 to 15 minutes.

---

252 CREAMY PESTO BREAD
Prep: 10 minutes   Cook: 10 to 15 minutes   Makes: 1 loaf

1 1-pound loaf French or
   Italian bread
8 tablespoons (1 stick) butter,
   softened
½ cup mayonnaise
2 or 3 garlic cloves, crushed

2 tablespoons grated
   Parmesan cheese
3 tablespoons Pesto (page 182)
   or your favorite brand

1. Prepare a medium fire or use an existing fire. Using a long serrated knife, cut bread into 1-inch slices without slicing completely through the bottom crust.

2. Combine butter, mayonnaise, garlic, Parmesan cheese, and pesto; mix to blend well. Spread pesto butter over both sides of bread slices. Wrap securely in foil and toast on edge of grill, turning occasionally, until heated through, about 10 to 15 minutes.

---

253 PARMESAN LOAF ITALIANO
Prep: 10 minutes   Cook: 10 to 15 minutes   Makes: 1 loaf

1 1-pound loaf French or
   Italian bread
8 tablespoons (1 stick) butter,
   softened
1 tablespoon chopped fresh
   marjoram, or 1 teaspoon
   dried

1 tablespoon ketchup
1 small garlic clove, crushed
½ cup grated Parmesan cheese

1. Prepare a medium fire or use an existing fire. Using a long serrated knife, cut bread into 1-inch slices without completely slicing through the bottom crust.

2. Combine butter, marjoram, ketchup, and garlic until well blended. Spread butter mixture over both sides of bread slices. Sprinkle Parmesan cheese over top of loaf. Wrap securely in foil and toast on edge of grill, turning occasionally, until the bread is heated through and cheese is melted, about 10 to 15 minutes.

254 PARMESAN GARLIC BREAD
Prep: 10 minutes   Cook: 10 to 15 minutes   Makes: 1 loaf

1 1-pound loaf French or
   Italian bread
8 tablespoons (1 stick) butter,
   softened

1 or 2 garlic cloves, crushed
¼ cup grated Parmesan cheese
   Paprika

1. Prepare a medium fire or use an existing fire. Using a long serrated knife, cut bread into 1-inch slices without slicing completely through bottom crust.

2. Combine butter, garlic, and cheese; mix until well blended. Spread butter mixture over both sides of bread slices. Sprinkle lightly with paprika and wrap securely in foil. Toast on edge of grill, turning occasionally, until bread is heated through and cheese is melted, about 10 to 15 minutes.

255 CREAMY GARLIC BREAD
Prep: 10 minutes   Cook: 10 to 15 minutes   Makes: 1 loaf

The flavor is worth every glorious calorie.

1 1-pound loaf French or
   Italian bread
8 tablespoons (1 stick) butter,
   softened

½ cup mayonnaise
2 or 3 garlic cloves, crushed
¼ cup grated Parmesan cheese

1. Prepare a medium fire or use an existing fire. Using a long serrated knife, cut bread into 1-inch slices without slicing completely through the bottom crust.

2. Combine butter, mayonnaise, garlic, and Parmesan; mix to blend well. Spread butter mixture over both sides of bread slices. Wrap securely in foil and toast on edge of grill, turning occasionally, until heated through, about 10 to 15 minutes.

256 GRILLED SQUASH WITH ONIONS
Prep: 10 minutes   Cook: 30 minutes   Serves: 6

This fragrant side dish is wonderful with any grilled meat or seafood.

6 medium yellow squash, cut
   into ½-inch slices
3 medium onions, cut into ½-
   inch slices
¼ teaspoon garlic salt

¼ teaspoon salt
⅛ teaspoon freshly ground
   pepper
2 tablespoons butter, cut into
   8 pieces

1. Prepare a medium fire. Alternate squash and onion slices in rows on a large sheet of heavy-duty aluminum foil. Sprinkle vegetables with garlic salt, salt, and pepper. Dot with butter. Fold foil securely to seal.

2. Place foil package on grill set 4 to 6 inches from coals. Cook without turning until vegetables are crisp-tender when pierced with a fork, about 15 to 20 minutes.

---

257 SWEET AND SAGE ROASTED ONIONS
Prep: 10 minutes   Cook: 30 to 40 minutes   Serves: 8

Vegetable oil
4 large onions, peeled and halved
1 teaspoon salt
¼ teaspoon freshly ground pepper

2 tablespoons honey
2 tablespoons chopped fresh sage, or 2 teaspoons dried

1. Prepare a medium fire. Cut heavy-duty aluminum foil into 6-inch squares and brush with oil. Place an onion half on each. In a small bowl, combine salt, pepper, honey, and sage. Brush mixture over top of each onion half. Wrap tightly in foil.

2. Grill onions, turning occasionally, until soft when pierced with a fork or skewer, about 30 to 40 minutes.

---

258 CRAZY LEGS HERSH
Prep: 15 minutes   Cook: 30 to 40 minutes   Serves: 6 to 8

There are great fun to bring along to a picnic, so wrap them ahead and store in a cooler until ready to grill. If wrapped tightly in foil, the drumsticks will brown rather than steam on the grill.

16 chicken drumsticks
1 cup barbecue sauce, bottled or homemade

Vegetable oil

1. Rinse chicken with cold water and pat dry. Place sauce in shallow dish and rotate drumsticks in sauce to coat each with about 1 tablespoon. Lightly spray or brush inside of 16 6-inch foil sheets with oil and tightly wrap up individual legs, squeezing and pressing out any air pockets. (If made in advance, refrigerate at this point for up to 24 hours.)

2. Prepare a hot fire and set grill 4 to 6 inches from coals. Grill foil-wrapped chicken legs, turning often, until juices run clear when pierced with a fork, about 30 to 40 minutes.

Chapter 9

Grilling Go-Withs: Savory Side Dishes to Make Your Barbecue Complete

Here is everything you need to make your best barbecue complete. For easy entertaining as well as family dining, you won't be able to resist the delectable assortment of do-ahead casseroles, baked beans, potato salads, vegetable salads, pasta salads, bean salads, and quick breads.

These recipes are made in the kitchen hours, or even days, before your barbecue begins. While the foods hot off the grill provide the star attraction, these tasty accompaniments are the supporting players that turn the party into a great performance.

As an added attraction, the chapter ends with the three essentials needed for a classic barbecue buffet—baked beans, potato salad, and coleslaw—all prepared in amounts that will feed twenty-five to fifty hearty eaters.

---

259 CHEESY CHILI RICE
Prep: 10 minutes   Cook: 55 minutes   Serves: 6

1 cup long-grain converted white rice
2 cups sour cream (1 pint)
1 7-ounce can diced green chilies

½ pound Monterey Jack cheese, grated (about 2 cups)
½ cup grated sharp Cheddar cheese

1. Preheat oven to 350°. Cook rice according to package directions.

2. In a small bowl, mix sour cream and chilies. In a buttered 1½- to 2-quart baking dish, alternate layers of cooked rice, Jack cheese, and sour cream mixture. Sprinkle Cheddar cheese evenly over top.

3. Bake, uncovered, until mixture is bubbly and cheese on top begins to brown, about 35 minutes.

260 WHITE BEAN SALAD

Prep: 15 minutes   Cook: 5 minutes   Marinate: 1 hour
Serves: 8 to 10

4 15-ounce cans cannellini
  beans (white kidney
  beans)
½ pound pancetta* or bacon,
  finely diced
2 tablespoons chopped fresh
  sage, or 2 teaspoons
  dried, crumbled
2 tablespoons chopped
  parsley

1 tablespoon fresh lemon
  juice
⅔ cup extra-virgin olive oil
2 garlic cloves, minced
¼ teaspoon freshly ground
  pepper
Salt

1. Place cannellini beans in a large colander and rinse thoroughly under cold running water. Drain well.

2. In a large skillet, cook pancetta or bacon over medium heat until crisp, about 5 minutes. Remove with a slotted spoon and drain on paper towels.

3. In a large salad bowl, gently toss beans with pancetta or bacon, sage, parsley, lemon juice, olive oil, garlic, and pepper. Taste to determine whether salt is necessary. Cover and marinate 1 hour at room temperature or as long as 2 days in refrigerator. Serve at room temperature.

* *Unsmoked bacon that is available at Italian markets and specialty food shops.*

---

261 SPICY BLACK BEAN SALAD

Prep: 30 minutes   Cook: none   Serves: 8

Shiny black beans make a wonderful and unusual salad. A dollop of sour cream is a delicious topping.

3 15-ounce cans black beans
  (frijoles negros)
1 red onion, minced
2 large ripe tomatoes, seeded
  and chopped
½ cup chopped fresh cilantro
  or flat-leaf parsley
3 jalapeño peppers, seeded
  and minced

3 garlic cloves, minced
2 tablespoons lime or lemon
  juice
1½ teaspoons ground cumin
1 tablespoon red wine vinegar
½ cup olive oil
1 teaspoon salt
¼ teaspoon freshly ground
  pepper

1. Place beans in a large colander and rinse well under cold running water. Drain thoroughly.

2. In a large mixing bowl, combine beans with remaining ingredients and toss gently until mixed. If made in advance, cover and refrigerate for up to 2 days. Taste again before serving and season with salt and pepper.

262 DILLED GREEN BEAN SALAD

Prep: 20 minutes   Cook: 2 to 3 minutes   Marinate: 8 hours
Serves: 4 to 6

1 pound fresh green beans,
   trimmed and cut into
   1½-inch lengths
1 tablespoon sugar
⅓ cup warm water
½ cup tarragon or other white
   wine vinegar
1 garlic clove, minced

1½ teaspoons minced fresh dill,
   or ½ teaspoon dried
½ teaspoon salt
½ cup olive oil
  Optional: Bottled sweet
   roasted peppers, cut into
   ⅛-inch strips

1. Bring a large pot of salted water to a boil and add beans. When water returns to a rolling boil, cook for 2 to 3 minutes, or until beans are crisp-tender. Drain beans into a colander and rinse under cold running water; drain well. Transfer beans to a medium bowl.

2. In a small bowl, dissolve sugar in water. Stir in vinegar, garlic, dill, salt, and olive oil. Pour dressing over green beans and toss gently. Cover with plastic wrap and refrigerate, tossing occasionally, 8 hours or overnight. Before serving, garnish with slices of roasted red pepper, if desired.

263 SWEET-AND-SOUR BEAN BAKE WITH BACON

Prep: 20 minutes   Cook: 1½ hours   Serves: 8 to 10

½ pound bacon, coarsely
   chopped
1 large onion, chopped
1 15-ounce can lima beans,
   drained
1 15-ounce can red kidney
   beans, drained
1 15-ounce can butter beans,
   drained

1 15-ounce can pork and
   beans with sauce
1 cup (packed) brown sugar
¼ cup ketchup
¼ cup cider vinegar
⅛ teaspoon cinnamon

1. Preheat oven to 325°. In a 5-quart flameproof casserole, cook bacon over medium heat until browned, 5 to 7 minutes. Remove bacon with slotted spoon and drain on paper towels. Discard all but 1 tablespoon of fat left in pan. Cook onion in bacon fat over medium heat until softened and slightly browned, about 5 to 10 minutes.

2. Add bacon, lima beans, kidney beans, butter beans, pork and beans, brown sugar, ketchup, vinegar, and cinnamon to casserole with onion. Cover and bake for 1 hour. Remove cover and bake for 15 minutes longer.

264   MOIRA'S BROCCOLI CASSEROLE
Prep: 10 minutes   Cook: 45 minutes   Serves: 4 to 6

If you have a microwave to thaw frozen vegetables, this is an instant dish for unexpected guests.

    2   9-ounce packages frozen   ¼   cup chopped onion
        chopped broccoli, thawed   1   5-ounce package frozen
    1   8-ounce jar pasteurized   French-fried onion rings
        process cheese spread

1. Preheat oven to 350°. Grease a 1½-quart baking dish. Drain broccoli in a colander, squeezing out as much water as possible.

2. In a double boiler, heat cheese spread until melted and smooth. Stir in onion and broccoli until well blended. Turn into prepared casserole and bake, uncovered, for 25 minutes, or until hot and bubbly.

3. Arrange frozen onion rings over top of casserole and bake until golden brown at temperature and time directed on the package, about 20 minutes longer.

265   OKLAHOMA "CAVIAR"
Prep: 15 minutes   Cook: 15 minutes   Marinate: 8 hours
Serves: 6 to 8

    1   10-ounce package frozen   1   bay leaf
        black-eyed peas   1   teaspoon salt
    ¾   cup chicken broth or water   ¼   teaspoon freshly ground
    ¼   cup dry white wine   pepper
    ¼   cup red wine vinegar   ½   teaspoon hot pepper sauce
    ¼   cup brown sugar   ½   cup diced celery
    2   tablespoons chili sauce or   ¾   cup diced bell pepper (red,
        ketchup   yellow, or green)
    ½   cup chopped red onion   ½   cup chopped parsley
    1   large garlic clove, minced

1. Cook black-eyed peas according to package directions and drain. Meanwhile, in a medium nonreactive saucepan, combine chicken broth, wine, vinegar, brown sugar, chili sauce, red onion, garlic, bay leaf, salt, pepper, and hot sauce. Bring to a rolling boil over medium-hot heat, stirring to dissolve sugar. Remove from heat.

2. In a medium bowl, combine warm, drained black-eyed peas with warm marinade. Stir in celery and bell pepper. Let stand, tossing occasionally, then refrigerate 8 hours, or overnight, to develop flavors.

3. Before serving, remove vegetables from marinade with a slotted spoon; reserve marinade to store any leftovers. Discard bay leaf and stir in parsley. Serve chilled or at room temperature.

266 BLACK-EYED PEAS WITH SPICY SAUSAGE AND RICE

Prep: 30 minutes   Cook: 7 to 10 minutes   Serves: 8 to 10

This hot and spicy side dish can be made up to a day ahead and reheated in a covered casserole.

1 pound andouille or other spicy sausage, coarsely chopped
2 tablespoons olive oil
1 bunch scallions, chopped
2 medium red bell peppers, chopped
3 large garlic cloves, minced
3 cups cooked long-grain converted white rice

4 cups cooked or canned black-eyed peas, rinsed and drained
2 tablespoons chopped fresh thyme leaves, or 2 teaspoons dried
1 teaspoon salt
1 tablespoon coarsely ground pepper

1. In a large skillet, cook sausage in olive oil over medium heat until lightly browned, 5 to 7 minutes. Add scallions, bell peppers, and garlic and cook until peppers are softened but still brightly colored, about 3 minutes.

2. In a large bowl, mix cooked rice and black-eyed peas. Add sausage and vegetables along with any fat left in skillet. Toss to mix well. Season with thyme, salt, and pepper.

267 MAKE-AHEAD MASHED POTATOES

Prep: 20 minutes   Cook: 1 hour   Serves: 8

8 to 10 medium Russet baking potatoes (about 3½ pounds total)
1 8-ounce package cream cheese, at room temperature

¼ cup sour cream
Salt and freshly ground pepper
2 tablespoons butter, melted
Paprika

1. Boil potatoes in salted water until tender, 25 to 30 minutes. Drain, then peel when cool enough to handle.

2. Using an electric mixer set at medium speed, beat cream cheese with sour cream until blended. Gradually add drained hot potatoes, beating until smooth and soft. Season with salt and pepper.

3. Spoon whipped potatoes into a buttered 2-quart ovenproof casserole and brush surface with melted butter. If made only a few hours before serving, refrigeration is unnecessary; leave in a cool spot at room temperature.

4. Preheat oven to 350°. Bake mashed potatoes until heated through, about 30 minutes, or longer if refrigerated. Sprinkle lightly with paprika before serving.

268 HERBED MOZZARELLA WITH PEPPERS
Prep: 35 minutes   Cook: about 12 minutes   Serves: 8

This colorful salad is a welcome addition to any buffet.

3 garlic cloves, minced
1 onion, thinly sliced
2 tablespoons extra-virgin olive oil
4 large bell peppers (red, yellow, and/or green), cut into ¼-inch strips
2 tablespoons sherry wine vinegar or balsamic vinegar
3 large ripe tomatoes, peeled, seeded, and coarsely chopped
½ teaspoon salt

⅛ teaspoon freshly ground pepper
1 pound mozzarella cheese, preferably fresh, cut into ½-inch dice
½ teaspoon crushed hot red pepper flakes
2 tablespoons minced fresh marjoram, or 1 teaspoon dried
2 tablespoons chopped parsley
2 tablespoons drained capers

1. In a large nonreactive skillet or flameproof casserole, cook garlic and onion in olive oil over medium heat until fragrant and softened but not browned, about 3 minutes. Add bell peppers and cook, stirring often, until softened but still brightly colored, 3 to 4 minutes.

2. Add vinegar, cover, and cook for 3 minutes. Add tomatoes and cook, uncovered, until juices thicken. Season with salt and pepper. Transfer to a large bowl and let cool to room temperature. Add cheese, hot pepper flakes, marjoram, parsley, and capers. Toss to mix well. Serve at room temperature.

269 SPICED FRUIT CASSEROLE
Prep: 10 minutes   Cook: 30 minutes   Serves: 8 to 10

3 cups sliced peaches, or 2 16-ounce cans, drained
3 cups sliced pears, or 2 16-ounce cans, drained
3 cups pineapple chunks, or 1 20-ounce can, drained
3 firm ripe bananas, sliced

6 tablespoons butter
¾ cup (packed) light brown sugar
1 tablespoon fresh lemon juice
1½ teaspoons ground cinnamon
½ teaspoon ground ginger

1. Preheat oven to 325°. In a large bowl, gently toss peaches, pears, pineapple chunks, and bananas. Transfer fruit to a buttered 2½-quart casserole.

2. In a small saucepan, heat butter with brown sugar, lemon juice, cinnamon, and ginger over medium heat until butter melts, about 2 minutes. Pour over fruit and bake until hot and bubbly, about 30 minutes.

270   BAKED PINEAPPLE CASSEROLE
Prep: 15 minutes   Cook: 1 hour   Serves: 8

6 eggs
½ cup sugar
⅓ cup flour
4 cups finely chopped fresh
   pineapple with its juice,
   or 2 1-pound 4-ounce cans
   unsweetened crushed
   pineapple

8 thick slices French or Italian
   bread, crusts removed,
   bread cut into ½-inch
   cubes
½ pound (2 sticks) butter,
   melted

1. Preheat oven to 325°. In a large bowl, whisk eggs with sugar and flour until well blended. Stir in pineapple and its juice and pour into a buttered 9 × 13-inch baking dish.

2. In a medium bowl, toss bread cubes in melted butter and sprinkle bread, along with any butter remaining in bowl, over top of pineapple mixture. (The dish can be covered with plastic wrap at this point and refrigerated for up to 3 hours.)

3. Bake pineapple casserole, uncovered, until custard has set, about 1 hour, or slightly longer if refrigerated.

271   HUMMUS
Prep: 5 minutes   Cook: none   Makes: about 1½ cups

This versatile Middle Eastern specialty can be a dipping sauce, a spread, a filling for pita bread, or a sandwich topping. And be sure to try it with grilled lamb.

1 15-ounce can chick-peas
   (garbanzo beans)
¼ cup tahini (Middle Eastern
   sesame seed paste)*
1 garlic clove, chopped
3 tablespoons extra-virgin
   olive oil

2 tablespoons fresh lemon
   juice
½ teaspoon salt
   Dash of cayenne
   Chopped parsley, as garnish

1. Rinse chick-peas in a colander or sieve under cold running water. Drain well.

2. Combine all ingredients in a food processor or blender and purée until smooth. Cover and refrigerate until chilled. Top with chopped fresh parsley before serving.

* Available in jars at health food stores and Middle Eastern markets, as well as many super-markets.

272 LAYERED OVERNIGHT SALAD
Prep: 30 minutes   Cook: none   Serves: 10 to 12

This salad is great for potlucks or home entertaining, because while you can serve it immediately, it can stand overnight without wilting.

1 pound fresh spinach, washed, dried, and coarsely shredded
1 head iceberg lettuce, coarsely shredded
1 10-ounce package frozen tiny peas, thawed and well drained
2 cups grated Swiss or Cheddar cheese (about ½ pound)
1 cup chopped scallions
1 pound bacon, cooked until crisp and crumbled
6 hard-cooked eggs, coarsely chopped
Salt and freshly ground pepper
1¼ cups mayonnaise
1¼ cups sour cream
¼ cup chopped fresh chives or parsley

1. In a large bowl (preferably somewhat shallow and made of clear glass), layer ingredients in order listed—spinach, lettuce, peas, cheese, scallions, bacon, and eggs. Season eggs with salt and pepper.

2. In a small bowl, mix mayonnaise with sour cream until well blended. Spread over the top of salad, taking care to cover edges to seal in crispness. Sprinkle chives over top and cover tightly with plastic wrap. Refrigerate overnight. Toss just before serving.

273 TOMATO CHEESE PIE
Prep: 25 minutes   Cook: 55 to 60 minutes   Serves: 6 to 8

1 unbaked 9-inch pie crust, well chilled
5 medium tomatoes, sliced
Salt and freshly ground pepper
1 tablespoon chopped fresh basil, or 1 teaspoon dried
1 cup chopped scallions
2 cups grated sharp Cheddar cheese
1 cup mayonnaise
1 teaspoon Dijon mustard
½ cup grated Parmesan cheese

1. Preheat oven to 400°. Prick pie crust all over and bake for 10 to 15 minutes, until lightly browned at edges. Remove from oven.

2. Reduce oven temperature to 325°. Cover bottom of pie crust with a layer of tomato slices. Season lightly with salt and pepper, a bit of basil, and some chopped scallions. Repeat layers once or twice until all tomatoes have been used.

3. Mix Cheddar cheese with mayonnaise and mustard; spread over pie. Top with grated Parmesan cheese. Bake until pie is heated through and top is golden brown, about 45 minutes. Serve warm or at room temperature.

274 SWEET-AND-SOUR BROCCOLI SALAD
Prep: 25 minutes   Cook: 7 to 8 minutes   Serves: 6 to 8

1 pound bacon, coarsely
   chopped
2 bunches fresh broccoli,
   washed and trimmed into
   bite-size florets (about 4
   cups)

1 cup mayonnaise
½ cup sugar
2 tablespoons cider vinegar
4 scallions, chopped
½ cup currants or raisins

1. In a large skillet, cook bacon over medium heat until crisp, about 5 minutes. Drain well.

2. Bring a large pot of salted water to a rolling boil. Add broccoli and cook until crisp-tender, 2 to 3 minutes. Drain broccoli in a colander and rinse under cold running water. Drain well.

3. In a large bowl, combine mayonnaise, sugar, and vinegar. Stir to dissolve sugar. Add broccoli, bacon, scallions, and currants. Toss to coat with dressing. Cover and refrigerate until serving time.

275 WASHINGTON WATERCRESS SALAD
Prep: 15 minutes   Cook: none   Serves: 8

This is a welcome salad for fall. Sliced fresh mushrooms or ½ cup coarsely chopped fresh cranberries make a nice addition.

3 bunches watercress, washed
   and dried
   Apple-Walnut Vinaigrette
   (recipe follows)

2 large Golden Delicious
   apples, cored and diced
½ cup coarsely chopped
   toasted walnuts

1. Trim coarse stems from watercress and place watercress in a large salad bowl. Toss with ¼ cup Apple-Walnut Vinaigrette just to coat leaves.

2. Add apples and walnuts and toss again with ¼ cup dressing. Serve immediately.

APPLE-WALNUT VINAIGRETTE

1 teaspoon Dijon mustard
2 shallots, minced
¼ cup apple juice
¼ cup fresh lemon juice
¼ teaspoon salt

⅛ teaspoon freshly ground
   pepper
1 cup light olive oil
½ cup walnut oil

In a medium bowl, combine mustard, shallots, apple juice, lemon juice, salt, and pepper. Whisk in olive oil and walnut oil. After use, store remaining dressing in covered jar in refrigerator for up to 5 days.

276 FRUITED ROMAINE SALAD WITH WALNUT DRESSING

Prep: 20 minutes   Cook: none   Serves: 6

- 1 head romaine lettuce
- 3 kiwi fruit
- 2 navel oranges
- 2 tablespoons cider vinegar
- 1 teaspoon fresh lemon juice
- ¼ teaspoon salt
- ⅛ teaspoon freshly ground pepper

- ¼ cup light olive oil or vegetable oil
- 3 tablespoons walnut oil
- 1 small red onion, sliced into thin rings
- ⅓ cup coarsely chopped walnuts

1. Wash lettuce and chop or tear into bite-size pieces. Peel and slice kiwis and oranges.

2. In a small bowl, combine vinegar, lemon juice, salt, and pepper. Whisk in olive oil and walnut oil until blended. Set walnut dressing aside.

3. Place lettuce in a bed on a serving platter. Arrange sliced fruits and onion rings over lettuce and drizzle dressing over salad. Sprinkle walnuts on top and serve.

277 SHREDDED CARROT SALAD

Prep: 10 minutes   Cook: none   Serves: 4 to 6

- 3 cups shredded carrots
- 3 scallions, thinly sliced
- 3 tablespoons fresh lemon juice

- 2 tablespoons olive oil
- ¼ cup chopped parsley
- ½ teaspoon salt
  Freshly ground pepper

In a medium bowl, toss together carrots, scallions, lemon juice, olive oil, parsley, salt, and pepper. Cover and refrigerate up to 24 hours before serving.

278 QUICK BOSTON BAKED BEANS

Prep: 15 minutes   Cook: 1 hour   Serves: 6

- 2 1-pound cans New England-style pork and beans
- ½ cup maple syrup
- 1 teaspoon Dijon mustard

- 1 small onion, chopped
- 1 tablespoon ketchup
- 6 bacon slices, cut into ½-inch pieces

1. Preheat oven to 325°. Combine all ingredients and place in a bean pot or other 1½-quart baking dish with a lid.

2. Cover and bake for 45 minutes. Remove cover and bake beans for 15 minutes longer.

279 RED-EYE PORK AND BEANS
Prep: 10 minutes   Cook: 2¼ hours   Serves: 8

4 thick slices of bacon
1 large onion, chopped
1 small green bell pepper, chopped
3 1-pound cans pork and beans

1 cup brewed black coffee
1 teaspoon Dijon mustard
½ cup (packed) brown sugar
1 15½-ounce can tomato sauce
Optional: 2 tablespoons bourbon

1. Preheat oven to 275°. In a large skillet, cook bacon over medium heat until crisp, 5 to 10 minutes. Remove bacon with tongs and drain on paper towels. Pour off all but 2 tablespoons fat from skillet. Crumble bacon coarsely.

2. Add onions and green pepper to bacon fat in skillet and cook over medium heat until onion is softened but not browned, 3 to 5 minutes. Remove with a slotted spoon.

3. In a large ovenproof casserole, combine bacon, onion, green pepper, pork and beans, coffee, mustard, brown sugar, tomato sauce, and bourbon. Stir gently to mix well. Bake, uncovered, for 2 hours, checking periodically to be sure liquid has not completely evaporated. (If it has, add more coffee, bourbon, or water, ½ cup at a time.)

---

280 PASTA SALAD PRIMAVERA
Prep: 10 minutes   Cook: 10 to 12 minutes   Serves: 8 to 10

1 pound pasta shells
1 10-ounce package frozen tiny peas, thawed and well drained
2 tablespoons diced drained pimiento
2 tablespoons drained capers
2 tablespoons chopped parsley

2 medium carrots, shredded
2 medium zucchini, shredded
2 medium yellow crookneck squash, shredded
Creamy Vinaigrette (page 166) or your favorite bottled brand

1. Bring a large pot of salted water to a boil over high heat. Add pasta and cook until tender but still firm, 10 to 12 minutes. Drain into a colander and rinse well under cold running water. Drain thoroughly.

2. In a large bowl, gently toss pasta with peas, pimiento, capers, parsley, carrots, zucchini, and crookneck squash. Moisten with enough Creamy Vinaigrette, about 1 cup, to lightly coat pasta and vegetables. If made in advance, cover and refrigerate for up to 2 days. Before serving, toss again, adding more vinaigrette to moisten, if necessary.

281 PACIFIC RIM SALAD
Prep: 30 minutes   Cook: 8 to 10 minutes   Serves: 8

This salad can be made several hours in advance and refrigerated until serving time.

½ cup slivered almonds
1 pound fresh bean sprouts
1 cup thinly sliced celery
½ cup thinly sliced scallions
1 8-ounce can sliced water chestnuts, well rinsed and drained
½ pound cooked bay shrimp

2 tablespoons currants or raisins
½ cup mayonnaise
¼ cup sour cream
1½ teaspoons curry powder
1 teaspoon soy sauce
½ teaspoon honey

1. Preheat oven to 350°. Place almonds in a single layer on a cookie sheet. Bake, stirring occasionally, until lightly browned, 8 to 10 minutes.

2. In a large bowl, toss bean sprouts with celery, scallions, water chestnuts, shrimp, and currants.

3. In a small bowl, mix mayonnaise, sour cream, curry powder, soy sauce, and honey. Toss with salad to coat well. Just before serving, top with toasted almonds.

282 GREEN BEANS WITH GARLIC VINAIGRETTE
Prep: 15 minutes   Cook: 2 to 3 minutes   Serves: 8

Beans will retain their bright green color if tossed with the dressing just before serving.

2 pounds fresh green beans
2 shallots or white part of scallions, minced
2 garlic cloves, crushed
2 tablespoons white wine vinegar

½ cup olive oil
¼ teaspoon salt
⅛ teaspoon freshly ground pepper

1. Bring a large pot of salted water to a boil and add beans. When water returns to a rolling boil, cook for 2 to 3 minutes, or until beans are crisp-tender. Drain beans into a colander and rinse under cold running water. Drain well.

2. Just before serving, combine shallots, garlic, and vinegar in a large salad bowl. Whisk in olive oil and season with salt and pepper. Add beans, toss until well coated, and serve.

283 ORZO AND BROCCOLI SALAD WITH BASIL VINAIGRETTE
Prep: 10 minutes   Cook: 7 to 9 minutes   Serves: 10

1 pound orzo (rice-shaped
  pasta)
2 bunches fresh broccoli, cut
  into bite-size pieces
1 red bell pepper, diced
½ cup pine nuts, toasted

1 2¼-ounce can sliced black
  olives, drained
Basil Vinaigrette (page 181)
Salt and freshly ground
  pepper

1. In a large pot of boiling salted water, cook pasta until tender but still firm, 5 to 7 minutes. Drain and rinse under cold running water. Drain well.

2. In another large pot of boiling salted water, cook broccoli for about 2 minutes, until crisp-tender and still bright green. Drain in a colander and rinse under cold running water. Drain well.

3. In a large bowl, gently combine pasta and broccoli. Add bell pepper, pine nuts, and olives and toss lightly. Pour in about ½ cup Basil Vinaigrette and toss again. Season with salt and pepper and remaining vinaigrette.

284 SALSA FRESCA
Prep: 15 minutes   Cook: none   Makes: 1 to 1¼ cups

Serve this zesty sauce with quesadillas or as a dip or as a condiment for grilled fish or meats. Although best when freshly made, salsa can be made in advance and refrigerated for up to 2 days.

2 large ripe tomatoes
4 jalapeño or other small
  green chili peppers,
  seeded and quartered
2 bunches scallions (10 to 12),
  trimmed and quartered

⅓ cup chopped fresh cilantro
  or parsley
2 tablespoons fresh lime juice
½ teaspoon salt

1. Cut tomatoes in half and gently squeeze to remove seeds. Coarsely chop tomatoes.

2. In a food processor, chop jalapeño peppers. Add scallions and cilantro or parsley. Process, turning machine quickly on and off, until scallions and cilantro are chopped and jalapeños are minced.

3. In a medium bowl, combine tomatoes, scallions, cilantro, jalapeños, lime juice, and salt. Stir gently to blend.

NOTE: If ripe summer tomatoes are unavailable, substitute 1 28-ounce can peeled whole tomatoes, coarsely chopped and well drained.

285 TOM'S TOMATO CHUTNEY

Prep: 20 minutes   Cook: 1¼ hours   Makes: 3 cups

2 pounds ripe red tomatoes, peeled, seeded, and quartered
8 to 10 large garlic cloves, minced
1 2-inch piece fresh ginger, peeled and grated
1 red bell pepper, chopped

1 tart green apple, peeled, cored, and diced
1 large onion, chopped
1 cup cider vinegar
¾ cup sugar
1 teaspoon salt
¼ teaspoon cayenne
½ cup raisins

Mix all ingredients in a large nonreactive saucepan or flameproof casserole. Bring to a boil over medium heat. Cook, stirring occasionally, until color darkens and mixture thickens, about 1¼ hours. Let cool to room temperature. Cover and refrigerate. Serve chilled or at room temperature.

286 CREAMY SPINACH CASSEROLE

Prep: 10 minutes   Cook: 30 minutes   Serves: 6

2 10-ounce packages frozen chopped spinach, thawed
1 package (1.25-ounce or 1.8-ounce envelope) dry onion soup mix

1 cup sour cream
½ cup grated sharp Cheddar cheese

1. Preheat oven to 350°. Butter a 1-quart baking dish. Drain spinach well in a colander. Squeeze out as much moisture as possible with your hands.

2. Combine spinach with dry soup mix and sour cream and blend well. Transfer to baking dish. Top with cheese and bake, uncovered, 30 minutes, or until hot and bubbly.

287 GREEN AND GOLD ZUCCHINI CASSEROLE

Prep: 15 minutes   Cook: 1 hour   Serves: 6

1 pound medium zucchini
1 cup cracker crumbs
1 cup grated sharp Cheddar cheese
2 eggs, lightly beaten

¼ cup chopped onion
1 tablespoon chopped fresh oregano, or 1 teaspoon dried

1. Preheat oven to 350°. Grate zucchini on large holes of a hand grater or in a food processor.

2. In a large bowl, combine zucchini, cracker crumbs, Cheddar cheese, eggs, onion, and oregano. Mix to blend well. Pour into buttered casserole and bake for 1 hour, or until top is lightly browned.

288 PASTA SALAD PICANTE
Prep: 25 minutes   Cook: 10 minutes   Serves: 6

¾ pound corkscrew or other
  shaped pasta
¼ cup extra-virgin olive oil
¾ cup bottled Mexican picante
  sauce or salsa
1 garlic clove, minced
¾ teaspoon salt
¼ pound feta cheese,
  crumbled

⅓ cup chopped cilantro or
  parsley
½ cup chopped scallions
1 4-ounce can diced mild
  green chilies
1 2¼-ounce can sliced ripe
  olives, drained
2 large tomatoes, chopped

1. Boil pasta in a large pot of salted water until tender but still firm, about 10 minutes. Drain and rinse under cold water. Drain well.

2. In a large mixing bowl, gently toss pasta with olive oil, picante sauce, garlic, salt, feta cheese, cilantro, scallions, chilies, olives, and tomatoes. If not serving immediately, set aside at room temperature for up to 2 hours, or cover and refrigerate for up to 2 days. Serve at room temperature.

289 TABBOULEH
Prep: 10 minutes   Cook: 2 minutes   Marinate: 1 hour   Serves: 6

This refreshing salad of Middle Eastern origin is excellent with grilled lamb. Bulgur is available in health food stores and in many supermarkets.

1 cup cracked bulgur wheat
2 cups boiling water
2 cups chopped parsley
3 medium tomatoes, chopped
½ cup chopped scallions
2 tablespoons chopped fresh
  mint

¾ cup extra-virgin olive oil
⅓ cup fresh lemon juice
2 teaspoons salt
½ teaspoon freshly ground
  pepper

1. Place bulgur in a medium heatproof bowl. Bring 2 cups water to a boil and pour over wheat. Let stand for at least 1 hour or as long as overnight to plump grains. Drain, then squeeze dry in a kitchen towel.

2. In a large bowl, combine bulgur with parsley, tomatoes, scallions, mint, olive oil, and lemon juice. Toss to mix well. Season with salt and pepper.

290 MUSHROOMS AND ARTICHOKE HEARTS VINAIGRETTE

Prep: 20 minutes   Cook: none   Serves: 6

2 6-ounce jars marinated
   artichoke hearts
2 7½ to 8-ounce cans sliced
   water chestnuts, drained
1 pound fresh mushrooms,
   thinly sliced

1 bunch scallions, chopped
2 tablespoons extra-virgin
   olive oil
1½ tablespoons red wine
   vinegar
½ teaspoon salt
   Dash of hot pepper sauce

1. Drain artichokes, reserving marinade from jars. Place artichokes in a medium bowl. Add water chestnuts, mushrooms, and scallions.

2. Add olive oil, vinegar, salt, and hot sauce to reserved artichoke marinade. Whisk well to blend. Pour over vegetables and toss. Serve immediately or cover and marinate in refrigerator for up to 3 days.

291 SOUTHERN SWEET POTATO SALAD

Prep: 10 minutes   Cook: 5 to 7 minutes   Serves: 6 to 8

6 medium sweet potatoes
   (about 3 pounds), peeled
   and cut into ½-inch cubes
1½ cups chopped celery
3 scallions, chopped
1 cup raisins
1 20-ounce can crushed
   pineapple, drained

1 cup chopped pecans
1 cup mayonnaise
1 cup sour cream
2 tablespoons cider vinegar
1 tablespoon honey
½ teaspoon salt
⅛ teaspoon freshly ground
   pepper

1. Bring a large pot of salted water to a boil. Add sweet potato cubes and boil until just tender but still firm enough to hold their shape, 5 to 7 minutes. Drain into a colander and rinse under cold water. Drain well.

2. In a large bowl, gently toss sweet potatoes with celery, scallions, raisins, pineapple, and pecans. In a medium bowl, mix together mayonnaise, sour cream, vinegar, honey, salt, and pepper. Gently toss with sweet potato mixture. Cover and refrigerate until serving time.

292 MARY ANN'S BUTTERMILK-CHEESE LOAF
Prep: 10 to 15 minutes   Cook: 50 minutes   Makes: 1 loaf

2 cups all-purpose flour
2 teaspoons dry mustard
1½ teaspoons baking powder
½ teaspoon baking soda
1 teaspoon salt
 Dash of cayenne

1 cup buttermilk
¼ cup vegetable oil
2 eggs, lightly beaten
6 ounces sharp Cheddar cheese, grated (about 1¼ cups)

1. Preheat oven to 375°. Butter an 8½ × 4½ × 2½-inch loaf pan. In a large bowl, combine flour, mustard, baking powder, baking soda, salt, and cayenne.

2. In a small bowl, mix buttermilk, oil, and eggs until well blended. Add all at once to flour mixture. Mix just until dry ingredients are moistened, then stir in cheese.

3. Pour batter into buttered metal loaf pan and bake until a cake tester inserted in center comes out clean, about 50 minutes. Let cool in pan for about 10 minutes before inverting onto a wire rack to cool completely.

293 CARMELA'S CRUNCHY PEA SALAD
Prep: 15 minutes   Cook: 5 minutes   Serves: 6 to 8

1 10-ounce package frozen peas, thawed and drained
½ cup chopped celery
½ cup chopped scallions
⅔ cup sour cream
8 slices of bacon, coarsely chopped

1 cup coarsely chopped cashews
 Salt and freshly ground pepper

1. In a medium bowl, combine peas with celery, scallions, and sour cream. Toss gently to mix. (If made in advance, cover and refrigerate.)

2. In a large skillet, cook bacon pieces over medium heat until crisp, about 5 minutes. Remove with a slotted spoon and drain well on paper towels.

3. Just before serving, stir cashews and bacon into salad. Season with salt and pepper.

294 SUMMER TORTELLINI SALAD
Prep: 5 minutes   Cook: 12 minutes   Serves: 8

To keep the colors fresh, it is best to assemble this salad right before serving. All the various components, however, can be prepared several days in advance.

¾ pound frozen tortellini (either meat- or cheese-filled)

½ pound fresh green beans, trimmed and cut into thirds

½ pound cherry tomatoes, halved if large

Creamy Vinaigrette (recipe follows) or salad dressing of choice

1. Cook tortellini according to package directions until just tender. Drain in a colander and rinse under cold running water; drain well.

2. Drop green beans into a large pot of rapidly boiling water. When water returns to a full boil, cook for 2 to 3 minutes, or until beans are crisp-tender. Drain and rinse under cold running water; drain well.

3. Gently toss tortellini with beans, tomatoes, and just enough Creamy Vinaigrette to moisten, about ½ cup.

CREAMY VINAIGRETTE

Besides being a terrific all-purpose salad dressing, this tangy vinaigrette is an excellent marinade for chicken and turkey.

¼ cup white wine vinegar

3 tablespoons fresh lemon juice

2 tablespoons plain yogurt

1 teaspoon Dijon mustard

2 large garlic cloves, crushed

½ teaspoon sugar

½ teaspoon salt

½ teaspoon freshly ground pepper

⅛ teaspoon hot pepper sauce

2 tablespoons extra-virgin olive oil

½ cup flavorless vegetable oil

In a jar with a lid, mix vinegar, lemon juice, yogurt, mustard, garlic, sugar, salt, pepper, and hot sauce. Add olive oil and vegetable oil, cover tightly, and shake until blended. After use, store any remaining vinaigrette in refrigerator for up to 5 days.

295 SPINACH SALAD WITH MUSHROOMS AND BACON

Prep: 25 minutes   *Cook: none*   *Serves: 6 to 8*

2 pounds fresh spinach, stemmed, well washed, and dried
½ pound mushrooms, thinly sliced
½ pound bacon, cooked and crumbled
3 hard-cooked eggs, sliced
½ pound cherry tomatoes, halved if large

1½ tablespoons white wine vinegar
1 teaspoon Dijon mustard
⅛ teaspoon salt
⅛ teaspoon freshly ground pepper
¼ cup light olive oil

1. In a salad bowl, combine spinach, mushrooms, bacon, eggs, and tomatoes.

2. In a small bowl, combine vinegar, mustard, salt, and pepper. Whisk in olive oil until well blended. Pour dressing over salad and toss to coat.

296 MARGARET'S MACARONI SALAD

Prep: 25 minutes   *Cook: 10 minutes*   *Chill: 2 hours*   *Serves: 6*

½ pound elbow macaroni
½ cup mayonnaise
½ cup sour cream
2 tablespoons white wine vinegar
2 teaspoons Dijon mustard
1½ teaspoons salt

⅛ teaspoon cayenne
1½ cups chopped celery
½ cup chopped scallions
½ cup chopped parsley
¼ cup chopped black olives
2 tablespoons chopped pimiento

1. Cook macaroni in a large pot of rapidly boiling salted water until tender but still firm, about 10 minutes. Drain in a colander and rinse under cold running water. Drain well.

2. In a large bowl, mix together mayonnaise, sour cream, vinegar, mustard, salt, and cayenne until well blended. Add macaroni and toss to coat. Gently fold in celery, scallions, parsley, olives, and pimiento. For best flavor, cover and refrigerate at least 2 hours before serving.

297   ROQUEFORT TOMATOES
Prep: 10 minutes   Cook: none   Serves: 6 to 8

This is a delicious accompaniment to grilled beef.

6   large ripe tomatoes
    Salt and freshly ground
    pepper
1   small red onion, peeled
2   tablespoons chopped
    parsley

¼   pound Roquefort or other
    blue cheese, crumbled
    (about 1 cup)
3   tablespoons extra-virgin
    olive oil

1. Slice tomatoes about ⅜ inch thick and arrange slightly overlapping on a large serving platter. Season with salt and pepper.

2. Slice onion into thin rings and scatter over tomatoes. Sprinkle parsley and cheese on top. Drizzle olive oil over salad. (Salad can be assembled up to 3 hours ahead and set aside, loosely covered, at room temperature.)

---

298   SARAH'S HUSH PUPPY MUFFINS
Prep: 10 minutes   Cook: 15 to 20 minutes   Makes: 12 muffins

1   cup yellow cornmeal
1   cup flour
1   tablespoon baking powder
1   teaspoon salt
1   teaspoon sugar

⅛   teaspoon cayenne
½   cup finely chopped onion
1   large egg, beaten
⅓   cup milk
2   tablespoons vegetable oil

1. Preheat oven to 425°. Grease 12 muffin cups or line with paper baking cups. In a medium bowl, blend cornmeal, flour, baking powder, salt, sugar, and cayenne. Stir in onion.

2. In a small bowl, beat egg, milk, and oil. Add to cornmeal mixture and as quickly and as lightly as possible, blend ingredients just to moisten. (Do not try for a uniform batter; there will be some lumps.) Spoon into muffin cups and bake until golden brown, 15 to 20 minutes.

---

299   CHEESY MILWAUKEE MUFFINS
Prep: 3 minutes   Cook: 15 to 20 minutes   Makes: 12 muffins

3   cups packaged biscuit and
    baking mix
1   cup grated sharp Cheddar
    cheese

1½   tablespoons sugar
⅛   teaspoon cayenne
1½   cups beer

1. Preheat oven to 400°. Grease 12 muffin cups or line with paper baking cups.

2. In a large bowl, combine baking mix, cheese, sugar, and cayenne. Form a well in center and pour in beer. As quickly and lightly as possible, blend ingredients just to moisten. (Do not try for a uniform batter; there will be some lumps.)

3. Spoon batter into muffin cups and bake until cooked through, 15 to 20 minutes.

---

300   VERY CORNY MUFFINS

Prep: 5 minutes   Cook: 15 to 20 minutes   Makes: 9 muffins

Serve these warm from the oven with Honey Butter (page 188).

1   8½-ounce package corn
   muffin mix
1   egg

⅓   cup milk
1   8½-ounce can cream-style
   corn

1. Preheat oven to 400°. Grease 9 muffin tins or line with paper baking cups. Pour muffin mix into a medium bowl; create a well in center.

2. In a smaller bowl, mix egg with milk. Stir in corn. Pour corn mixture into well in muffin mix. As quickly and lightly as possible, blend ingredients just to moisten. (Do not try for a uniform batter; there will be some lumps.) Spoon batter into muffin cups and bake until cooked through, 15 to 20 minutes.

FOR A REALLY BIG BARBECUE

---

301   LONNIE'S MISSOURI COLESLAW

Prep: 30 minutes   Cook: 5 to 7 minutes   Marinate: 1 hour
Serves: 50

This salad remains crisp in your refrigerator for days, making it ideal for very large gatherings.

5   large cabbages (about 12
   pounds), shredded
3   green bell peppers, chopped
3   red bell peppers, chopped
5   large onions, minced

2½   cups vegetable oil
3¾   cups white wine vinegar
3¾   cups sugar
2½   tablespoons salt
2½   teaspoons celery seed

1. Combine cabbage, peppers, and onions in one or more large bowls. In a large saucepan, combine oil, vinegar, sugar, salt, and celery seed. Cook over medium heat, stirring, until sugar dissolves and mixture boils, 5 to 7 minutes. Pour over cabbage and let stand without stirring for 1 hour.

2. Toss cabbage with dressing and refrigerate for up to 1 week before serving.

302   POTATO SALAD O'DOHERTY

Prep: 25 minutes   Cook: 30 minutes   Marinate: 1 hour   Serves: 50

Maggie Doherty comes from County Donegal, where they eat potatoes —skins and all! Here's a piquant salad suitable for the gathering of an Irish clan.

10 pounds boiling potatoes, such as White Rose	8 cups chopped celery (about 2 bunches)
¾ cup bottled Italian salad dressing	1 cup chopped scallions (about 1 bunch)
3 tablespoons salt	6 cups mayonnaise
1 tablespoon freshly ground pepper	⅓ cup Dijon mustard
10 hard-cooked eggs, coarsely chopped	Paprika

1. In one or more large pots, boil potatoes in salted water over medium-high heat until tender, about 30 minutes. Drain and set aside until just cool enough to handle, about 5 minutes. Potatoes can be peeled if you wish, but it's not necessary.

2. Cut still warm potatoes into ¾-inch chunks and place in one or more large bowls. Toss with salad dressing, salt, and pepper. Cover loosely with plastic wrap and marinate at room temperature for at least 1 hour, or as long as 4 hours.

3. Add eggs, celery, and scallions to potatoes. In a medium bowl, mix mayonnaise and mustard until well blended. Fold into potato salad. Taste for seasoning, adding more salt and pepper, if necessary. Cover tightly and refrigerate for at least 4 hours or up to 3 days. Garnish top of potato salad with paprika before serving.

---

303   ERNESTINE'S SONOMA RANCH BEANS

Prep: 5 minutes   Cook: 2½ hours   Serves: 25

It wouldn't be a barbecue at the Raffo Ranch without a big pot of Ernie's beans. People are amazed at how simply they are made, and everyone loves to eat them.

6 16-ounce (1 pound) cans pork and beans	1 cup molasses
1 cup (packed) brown sugar	3 or 4 bacon slices

1. Preheat oven to 350°. Mix beans with brown sugar and molasses in a large roasting pan.

2. Cut each bacon slice into 3 pieces and arrange on top of beans. Bake, uncovered, for 1½ hours. Turn off heat and leave beans in oven without opening door for 1 hour longer.

Chapter 10

Barbecue Sauces, Marinades, and Glazes

In the world of grilling, little things mean a lot. It's that special marinade, that flavorful oil, or that applause-provoking barbecue sauce that can transform an ordinary cook into a backyard chef.

Marinades contain three basic components: acid, to tenderize and add zip; oil, to add moisture, carry flavor, and promote browning; and herbs and/or spices to provide extra taste. Spending that extra few minutes to add your signature touch to grilled foods will be rewarding to you, your family, and your lucky guests.

When using a marinade as a basting sauce, for food safety either bring the marinade to a boil before brushing over food or use marinade early enough in the cooking process to allow it to become thoroughly cooked before the meat or fish is removed from the grill.

Saucing Secrets

- Because the acid used in some marinades and sauces may react with certain metallic materials, it is best to marinate food in glass or ceramic dishes. Or use heavy-duty plastic bags.

- If meat is not covered by marinade, turn or toss occasionally to ensure even flavoring.

- Be sure to let sauce cool to room temperature before using as a marinade.

- Marinating in the refrigerator is safer than at room temperature.

- Where a range of marinating times is given, the shorter time may be used for convenience, but the longer marinating time produces greater flavor.

- Fish is not ordinarily marinated for longer than 30 minutes because the acid will begin to "cook" the fish.

- Glazes have a high sugar content, which caramelizes under heat to give them their gloss. They must be applied only during the last few minutes of grilling, however, or they will burn.

304 3-ALARM BBQ SAUCE
Prep: 5 minutes   Cook: none   Makes: about 1 cup

You can make this easy sauce as hot as you dare.

1 cup ketchup
3 tablespoons maple syrup or
    honey

1 tablespoon minced garlic
¼ to 1 teaspoon cayenne

Combine ketchup, maple syrup, garlic, and ¼ teaspoon cayenne in a bowl and blend well. Taste and stir in more cayenne, ⅛ teaspoon at a time, until sauce is sufficiently hot to sound 3 alarms! Store sauce in a covered jar in refrigerator for up to 7 days.

305 FIRE AND BRIMSTONE SAUCE
Prep: 10 minutes   Cook: 15 minutes   Makes: about 2½ cups

This all-purpose sauce is suitable for any grilled meats, poultry, or seafood.

1 cup chili sauce
1 cup ketchup
1 cup red wine vinegar
1 medium onion, finely
    chopped
2 tablespoons brown sugar
1 tablespoon Worcestershire
    sauce
2 large garlic cloves, minced

1 teaspoon crushed hot red
    pepper flakes
½ teaspoon salt
½ teaspoon freshly ground
    pepper
½ teaspoon ground cumin
¼ teaspoon cayenne
    Optional: ½ teaspoon liquid
    smoke flavoring

Combine all ingredients in a medium nonreactive saucepan. Simmer, uncovered, over medium heat until onion has softened and sauce is slightly thickened, about 15 minutes. Let sauce cool before using to marinate. Store in a covered jar in refrigerator for up to 7 days.

306 DRUNKEN BARBECUE SAUCE
Prep: 2 minutes   Cook: none   Makes: about 2 cups

This sauce proves that not all barbecue has to be hot.

¾ cup ketchup
½ cup maple syrup
¼ cup vegetable oil

¼ cup bourbon
2 tablespoons cider vinegar
2 tablespoons Dijon mustard

In a medium bowl, combine all ingredients. Whisk to blend well. Store in a covered jar in refrigerator for up to 2 months.

307   FIRECRACKER BARBECUE SAUCE
Prep: 10 minutes   Cook: 15 minutes   Makes: about 1 quart

Make the most out of ingredients already on hand in your kitchen.

2 tablespoons vegetable oil
1 large onion, chopped
1½ cups ketchup
2 tablespoons red wine vinegar
1½ cups water

2 tablespoons Worcestershire sauce
1 tablespoon chili powder
2 teaspoons paprika
1 teaspoon cayenne

In a medium nonreactive saucepan, combine all ingredients. Simmer over low heat for 15 minutes. Let cool to room temperature. Store any leftover sauce in a covered jar in refrigerator for up to 2 weeks.

308   BEER-B-Q SAUCE
Prep: 2 minutes   Cook: 8 to 10 minutes   Makes: about 2½ cups

1 cup beer
1 cup chili sauce
¼ cup cider vinegar

¼ cup molasses
⅛ teaspoon freshly ground pepper

In a medium nonreactive saucepan, combine all ingredients. Bring to a boil over medium heat. Reduce heat and simmer, stirring occasionally, until slightly thickened, 8 to 10 minutes. Let cool before using as a marinade. Store in a covered jar in refrigerator for up to 3 months.

309   1-2-3 ARTILLERY BARBECUE SAUCE
Prep: 5 minutes   Cook: 7 minutes   Makes: about 2 cups

Use this for basting chicken or ribs.

1 10-ounce jar hot red pepper jelly
1 cup ketchup

1 tablespoon Worcestershire sauce

1. In a medium saucepan, warm jelly over medium heat, stirring until melted, about 2 minutes.

2. Sir in ketchup and Worcestershire and cook until sauce is warmed through and flavors are blended, about 5 minutes. Let sauce cool before using to marinate. Store sauce in a covered jar in refrigerator for up to 7 days.

310   FIERY APRICOT BARBECUE SAUCE
Prep: 5 minutes   Cook: 7 minutes   Makes: about 2¼ cups

Here's a perfect balance of hot and sweet for basting pork or poultry.

1   10¾-ounce jar apricot jam
1   cup ketchup
¼   cup cider vinegar
1   tablespoon soy sauce

1   teaspoon minced fresh
      ginger
1   garlic clove, minced
½   teaspoon cayenne

1. In a medium nonreactive saucepan, warm jam over medium heat, stirring until melted, about 2 minutes.

2. Stir in remaining ingredients and simmer, stirring frequently, 5 minutes. Let sauce cool before using to marinate. Store sauce in a covered jar in refrigerator for up to 7 days.

311   BLUE MOUNTAIN BARBECUE SAUCE
Prep: 5 minutes   Cook: 5 to 10 minutes   Makes: about 3 cups

1½   cups ketchup
1   cup strong black coffee
¼   cup brown sugar
¼   cup cider vinegar

2   tablespoons Worcestershire
      sauce
2   tablespoons vegetable oil
½   teaspoon cayenne

In a medium nonreactive saucepan, combine all ingredients. Bring to a boil over medium heat, stirring to dissolve brown sugar. Reduce heat and simmer, stirring occasionally, until slightly thickened, 5 to 10 minutes. Let cool before using as a marinade. Store in a covered jar in refrigerator for up to 3 months.

312   RAGIN' CAJUN SAUCE
Prep: 5 minutes   Cook: 10 minutes   Makes: about 1¼ cups

1   10¾-ounce can condensed
      tomato soup
¼   cup chopped onion
1   tablespoon brown sugar

1   tablespoon Cajun Spice
      Blend (page 185)
1   tablespoon cider vinegar
¼   teaspoon hot pepper sauce

Combine all ingredients in a small saucepan. Bring to a simmer over medium heat. Reduce heat to low, partially cover, and simmer until onion has softened and flavors have blended, about 10 minutes. Let sauce cool before using to marinate. Store sauce in a covered jar in refrigerator for up to 7 days.

313 HONG KONG BBQ SAUCE
Prep: 5 minutes   Cook: 10 minutes   Makes: about 1½ cups

This simple sauce with Asian overtones is perfect for chicken, ribs, or other grilled pork.

1 cup chili sauce	½ teaspoon grated fresh ginger
½ cup hoisin sauce	1 large garlic clove, minced
⅓ cup (packed) brown sugar	

In a medium nonreactive saucepan, combine all ingredients. Bring to a simmer over medium heat and cook, stirring, until brown sugar dissolves and sauce is warmed through, about 10 minutes. Let sauce cool before using to marinate. Store sauce in a covered jar in refrigerator for up to 7 days.

314 SOUP-ER BBQ SAUCE
Prep: 5 minutes   Cook: 10 minutes   Makes: about 1¼ cups

This versatile sauce works well for basting pork, poultry, or beef.

1 10¾-ounce can condensed tomato soup	1 tablespoon red wine vinegar
¼ cup chopped onion	2 teaspoons prepared white horseradish
1 tablespoon brown sugar	

Combine all ingredients in a small saucepan. Bring to a simmer over medium heat. Reduce heat to low, partially cover, and simmer until onion has softened and flavors have blended, about 10 minutes. Let sauce cool if using to marinate. Store sauce in a covered jar in refrigerator for up to 7 days.

315 EAST ASIAN BBQ SAUCE
Prep: 5 minutes   Cook: 10 minutes   Makes: about 1¼ cups

1 10¾-ounce can condensed tomato soup	2 tablespoons soy sauce
3 tablespoons cider vinegar	2 garlic cloves, minced
2 tablespoons honey	1 teaspoon minced fresh ginger

Combine all ingredients in small saucepan. Bring to a simmer over medium heat. Reduce heat to low, partially cover, and simmer until onion has softened and flavors have blended, about 10 minutes. Let sauce cool before using to marinate. Store sauce in a covered jar in refrigerator for up to 7 days.

316   BLAZING VINEYARD BBQ SAUCE
Prep: 5 minutes   Cook: 7 minutes   Makes: 2 cups

This piquant sauce is particularly good slathered on grilled hamburgers.

½ cup grape jelly
1 tablespoon fresh lemon
   juice

1½ cups chili sauce
1 teaspoon chili powder

1. In a medium saucepan, warm jelly over medium heat, stirring until melted, about 2 minutes.

2. Stir in lemon juice, chili sauce, and chili powder. Cook, stirring frequently, until warmed through, about 5 minutes. Let sauce cool before using to marinate. Store sauce in a covered jar in refrigerator for up to 7 days.

317   WILDFIRE BBQ SAUCE
Prep: 10 minutes   Cook: 5 minutes   Makes: about 2 cups

Adding your personal touch to commercial barbecue sauce will give it a noticeable lift.

1 14-ounce bottle barbecue
   sauce
2 tablespoons prepared white
   horseradish
½ medium onion, chopped, or
   1½ teaspoons dehydrated
   minced onion

2 large garlic cloves, minced
1 tablespoon fresh lemon
   juice or vinegar
1 teaspoon brown sugar
½ teaspoon hot pepper sauce

In a medium nonreactive saucepan, combine all ingredients. Bring to a boil over medium heat. Remove from heat and allow to cool. Store extra sauce in a covered jar in refrigerator.

318   KENTUCKY MARINADE
Prep: 5 minutes   Cook: none   Makes: enough for 2 pounds beef, lamb, pork, or chicken

1 bunch scallions
⅓ cup Dijon mustard
¼ cup flavorless vegetable oil

¼ cup (packed) brown sugar
¼ cup bourbon whiskey

Process all ingredients in a food processor or blender until thoroughly combined. Marinade can be stored in a covered jar in refrigerator for 3 days.

319 CALIFORNIA HERB MARINADE

Prep: 5 minutes   Cook: none   Makes: enough for 2 pounds beef or lamb or 3 pounds chicken

Use red wine for beef or lamb, white wine for chicken.

1½ tablespoons All-Purpose
    Herb Blend (page 183)
2 tablespoons fresh lemon
    juice

½ cup dry red or white wine
¼ cup extra-virgin olive oil
1 garlic clove, crushed

In a food processor or blender, combine all ingredients and process until well blended. Marinade can be stored in a covered jar in refrigerator for up to 3 days before using.

320 CHINESE-STYLE MARINADE

Prep: 5 minutes   Cook: none   Makes: about ⅔ cup; enough for 2 pounds of meat

This is always a favorite for meat, fish, or fowl.

⅓ cup soy sauce
¼ cup brown sugar
3 tablespoons dry sherry
2 large garlic cloves, minced

1 tablespoon peanut or
    vegetable oil
1 teaspoon Asian sesame oil

In a small bowl, combine all ingredients. Stir to dissolve brown sugar. Pour over meat in a shallow pan or in a heavy-duty plastic bag; turn to coat well.

321 LEMON PEPPER MARINADE

Prep: 5 minutes   Cook: none   Makes: enough for 3 pounds beef, lamb, pork, or chicken

⅔ cup dry white wine
⅓ cup olive oil
    Grated zest of 2 lemons
    Juice of 2 lemons

1 large garlic clove
1 tablespoon whole black
    peppercorns, crushed

Process all ingredients in a food processor or blender until thoroughly combined. Marinade can be stored in a covered jar in refrigerator for 3 days.

322 MEXICAN MARINADE WITH TEQUILA AND LIME

Prep: 10 minutes   Marinate: 2 hours   Cook: none   Makes: enough for 3 pounds chicken or fish

10 ancho chilies*
1 garlic clove, chopped
½ teaspoon salt

2 tablespoons tequila
2 tablespoons fresh lime juice
½ cup olive oil

1. Place chilies in a heatproof bowl and cover with boiling water. Weight chilies down with a plate so they are fully submerged; let stand 2 hours to soften.

2. Remove and discard stems and seeds from chilies. In a food processor, purée chilies with garlic, salt, tequila, and lime juice. With machine on, slowly pour olive oil through feed tube. Marinade can be stored in a covered jar in the refrigerator for 3 days.

* Dried mild ancho chilies are available in cellophane bags at Mexican markets, many supermarkets, and specialty food shops.

323 PORT WINE MARINADE

Prep: 5 minutes   Cook: none   Makes: enough for 3 pounds of meat

This spicy rendition lends itself to dark meat poultry, such as duck or chicken legs and thighs.

½ cup port wine
¼ cup vegetable oil
1 tablespoon red wine vinegar

½ teaspoon ground allspice
¼ teaspoon ground ginger
⅛ teaspoon ground cloves

Process all ingredients in a food processor or blender until thoroughly combined. Marinade can be stored indefinitely in a covered jar in refrigerator.

324 ROSEMARY MARINADE

Prep: 10 minutes   Cook: none   Makes: enough for 4 pounds meat

2 tablespoons chopped fresh rosemary, or 2 teaspoons dried
½ cup dry white wine

½ cup extra-virgin olive oil
1 garlic clove
½ teaspoon salt

Process all ingredients in a food processor or blender until thoroughly combined. Marinade can be stored in a covered jar in refrigerator for 3 days.

325   SANGRITA MARINADE

Prep: 5 minutes   Cook: none   Makes: enough for 3 pounds beef, lamb, pork, or chicken

1 cup orange juice	2 tablespoons tequila
½ cup tomato juice	½ teaspoon salt
1 small onion, coarsely chopped	¼ teaspoon hot pepper sauce

Process all ingredients in a food processor or blender until thoroughly combined. Marinade can be stored in a covered jar in refrigerator for 3 days.

326   SANTA FE MARINADE

Prep: 10 minutes   Cook: none   Makes: enough for 3 pounds beef, lamb, pork, or poultry

1½ cups beer	¼ cup fresh lime juice
½ cup chopped cilantro	1 tablespoon chili powder
2 large garlic cloves	1½ teaspoons ground cumin

Process all ingredients in a food processor or blender until thoroughly combined. Marinade can be stored in a covered jar in refrigerator for 2 days.

327   TROPICAL MARINADE

Prep: 5 minutes   Cook: none   Makes: enough for 2 pounds beef, lamb, pork, or poultry

⅔ cup pineapple juice	3 tablespoons cider vinegar
2 garlic cloves	1 teaspoon ground ginger
3 tablespoons brown sugar	¼ teaspoon cayenne

Process all ingredients in a food processor or blender until thoroughly combined. Marinade can be stored in a covered jar in refrigerator for 3 days.

328   GARLIC OIL
Prep: 10 minutes   Marinate: 2 hours   Cook: none   Makes: 1 cup

Brush on mushrooms, chicken, shrimp, or vegetables while they are grilling or use in place of olive oil in marinades and basting sauces.

10 to 12 large garlic cloves   **1 cup olive or vegetable oil**

1. Crush garlic cloves with the side of a cleaver or a knife and remove papery skin. Put garlic in a clean glass jar or a bottle with a narrow neck and pour in olive oil. Cover with a tight-fitting lid or cork.

2. Let oil and garlic stand for 2 hours at room temperature, then refrigerate. Use within two weeks.

329   HERB OIL
Prep: 5 minutes   Marinate: 48 hours   Cook: none   Makes: 2 cups

Here's a good way to use herb trimmings from your garden and make a uniquely flavored oil for your kitchen.

2 cups olive or vegetable oil   **1 sprig fresh thyme, or ½**
1 sprig fresh tarragon, or   **teaspoon dried**
   ½ teaspoon dried   **1 small dried hot red pepper**
1 sprig fresh oregano, or
   1 teaspoon dried

1. Combine all ingredients in a clean glass jar or bottle with a narrow neck and a tight-fitting lid or cork.

2. Let oil, herbs, and hot pepper stand for at least 48 hours at room temperature before using. Store in a cool place.

330   CAPER VINAIGRETTE
Prep: 5 minutes   Cook: none   Makes: about 1¼ cups

Capers make this a piquant dressing that doubles as a fine marinade for fish.

1½ teaspoons Dijon mustard   **¼ cup tarragon or white wine**
1 teaspoon salt   **vinegar**
¼ teaspoon freshly ground   **¾ cup olive oil**
   pepper   **3 tablespoons capers, drained**

Combine mustard, salt, pepper, and vinegar in a small bowl. Whisk in olive oil until well blended. Stir in capers.

331   MINT VINAIGRETTE
Prep: 5 minutes   Cook: none   Makes: about 1¼ cups

Mint is a natural with lamb. This also makes an excellent dressing to sprinkle over grilled plum tomatoes.

½ cup chopped fresh mint, or
   1 tablespoon dried
1 large garlic clove, peeled
2 tablespoons white wine
   vinegar

2 tablespoons fresh lime juice
1 tablespoon Dijon mustard
¾ cup olive oil
   Salt and freshly ground
   pepper

Purée mint and garlic in a food processor or blender. Add vinegar, lime juice, and mustard; blend well. With machine on, gradually pour in oil. Season with salt and pepper.

332   BASIL VINAIGRETTE
Prep: 5 minutes   Cook: none   Makes: about 1 cup

Sherry wine vinegar and fresh basil make this dressing an excellent marinade for hearty meats, like beef and lamb.

1 large bunch fresh basil,*
   leaves only
¼ cup sherry wine vinegar
   or red wine vinegar
2 large garlic cloves, crushed

¼ teaspoon salt
⅛ teaspoon freshly ground
   pepper
¾ cup olive oil

In a food processor or blender, puree basil, vinegar, garlic, salt, and pepper. With machine on, gradually add oil in a thin stream.

* *If fresh basil is unavailable, substitute 1 teaspoon dried basil and ⅓ cup chopped fresh parsley.*

333   MINT PESTO
Prep: 10 minutes   Cook: none   Makes: 1¼ cups

2 cups loosely packed fresh
   mint leaves
½ cup loosely packed chopped
   parsley
2 garlic cloves, peeled
¼ cup extra-virgin olive oil
¼ teaspoon salt

⅛ teaspoon freshly ground
   pepper
½ cup grated Parmesan cheese
¼ cup pine nuts or walnuts
1 tablespoon fresh lemon
   juice

Combine all ingredients in a food processor or blender. Process, turning machine quickly on and off several times and then letting it run, until a coarse paste forms.

334   PESTO
Prep: 15 minutes   Cook: none   Makes: about 2 cups

While most of us know pesto as a sauce for pasta, it pairs beautifully with many grilled foods.

2 cups lightly packed fresh
    basil leaves
3 small garlic cloves, minced
½ cup grated Parmesan cheese
¾ cup extra-virgin olive oil
1 tablespoon pine nuts
    (pignoli) or blanched
    almonds

1½ teaspoons salt
¼ teaspoon freshly ground
    pepper

In a food processor or blender, combine basil, garlic, Parmesan cheese, olive oil, pine nuts, salt, and pepper. Purée until smooth. Use pesto immediately, store in an airtight container in refrigerator for up to 4 days, or freeze.

335   BLACK OLIVE PESTO
Prep: 20 minutes   Cook: none   Makes: 1¼ cups

1 cup calamata or other oil-
    cured black olives, pitted
1 talespoon capers, drained
2 garlic cloves, crushed
1 tablespoon grated Parmesan
    cheese
½ cup Italian flat-leaf parsley
    leaves
1½ teaspoons chopped fresh
    thyme, or ½ teaspoon
    dried

½ cup extra-virgin olive oil
    Dash of cayenne
    Dash of freshly ground
    pepper
1 tablespoon fresh lemon
    juice

In a food processor or blender, combine olives, capers, garlic, Parmesan cheese, parsley, and thyme. Process, turning machine quickly on and off, until ingredients are chopped. Add olive oil and blend to a coarse paste. Season with cayenne, black pepper, and lemon juice.

336 ROSEMARY-ORANGE PESTO
Prep: 10 minutes   Cook: 7 to 10 minutes   Makes: 1¼ cups

¼ cup coarsely chopped
  walnuts
1 cup coarsely chopped
  scallions (about 1 bunch)
½ cup Italian flat-leaf parsley
  leaves
2 tablespoons fresh rosemary,
  or 1 teaspoon dried

1 tablespoon grated orange
  zest
2 garlic cloves, peeled
½ cup extra-virgin olive oil
2 tablespoons grated
  Parmesan cheese
1 tablespoon balsamic vinegar
¼ teaspoon cayenne

1. Preheat oven to 350°. Spread out nuts in a small baking pan and roast, shaking pan once or twice, until fragrant and toasted, 7 to 10 minutes.

2. In a food processor or blender, combine scallions, parsley, rosemary, orange zest, and garlic. Process, turning machine quickly on and off, until ingredients are finely chopped. Add olive oil, Parmesan cheese, vinegar, cayenne, and toasted walnuts. Process to a coarse paste.

337 ALL-PURPOSE HERB BLEND
Prep: 10 minutes   Cook: none   Makes: about ¾ cup

Use as seasoning for grilled hamburgers, chicken, or pork. To create an herb-smoked flavor when grilling, soften ¼ cup herb blend in 1 cup warm water for 15 minutes; then sprinkle wet herbs directly on coals during last 10 minutes of cooking.

¼ cup dried rosemary leaves
¼ cup dried basil leaves
2 tablespoons dried marjoram
  leaves
2 tablespoons garlic powder
2 tablespoons dried thyme
  leaves

1 tablespoon salt
4 bay leaves, crushed
2 teaspoons dried sage leaves
2 teaspoons onion powder
½ teaspoon cayenne

Combine all ingredients by hand or in the bowl of a food processor or blender until well mixed. Store in an airtight container.

338 CURRANT AND MUSTARD GLAZE
Prep: 5 minutes   Cook: 5 minutes   Makes: about 1¼ cups

    1 cup red currant jelly   2 tablespoons Dijon mustard
    2 tablespoons dry red wine

1. Place all ingedients in a small nonreactive saucepan and simmer over medium-low heat, stirring until well blended, 5 minutes.

2. Brush on pork or poultry during the last 5 to 10 minutes of grilling over medium to low heat to impart added flavor and a shiny glaze. Watch carefully, because the high sugar content of this glaze makes it susceptible to burning. Leftover glaze can be stored almost indefinitely in refrigerator.

339 BRANDIED APRICOT GLAZE
Prep: 5 minutes   Cook: 5 minutes   Makes: about 1¼ cups

    1 cup apricot jam   1 tablespoon soy sauce
    3 tablespoons brandy

1. Place all ingredients in a small saucepan. Cook over medium-low heat, stirring to blend well, for 5 minutes.

2. Brush on pork or poultry during last 5 to 10 minutes of grilling over medium to low heat to impart added flavor and a shiny glaze. Watch carefully, because the high sugar content of this glaze makes it susceptible to burning. Leftover glaze can be stored almost indefinitely in refrigerator.

340 GINGERED CRANBERRY GLAZE
Prep: 5 minutes   Cook: 5 minutes   Makes: about 1 cup

    1 cup jellied cranberry sauce   2 teaspoons minced fresh
    2 tablespoons port wine   ginger, or ½ teaspoon
                                       dried

1. Place all ingredients in a small nonreactive saucepan over medium-low heat. Simmer, stirring until well blended, about 5 minutes.

2. Brush on pork or poultry during the last 5 to 10 minutes of grilling over medium to low heat to impart added flavor and a shiny glaze. Watch carefully, because the high sugar content of this glaze makes it susceptible to burning. Leftover glaze can be stored almost indefinitely in refrigerator.

341 ORANGE MAPLE GLAZE
Prep: 5 minutes   Cook: 5 minutes   Makes: about 1¼ cups

1 6-ounce can frozen orange juice concentrate, thawed	½ cup maple syrup 1 tablespoon soy sauce

1. Place all ingredients in a small saucepan over medium-low heat. Simmer, stirring until well blended, about 5 minutes.

2. Brush glaze on pork or poultry during last 5 to 10 minutes of grilling over medium to low heat to impart added flavor and a shiny glaze. Watch carefully, because the high sugar content of this glaze makes it susceptible to burning. Leftover glaze can be stored almost indefinitely in refrigerator.

342 SPICY PLUM SAUCE
Prep: 5 minutes   Cook: 5 minutes   Makes: about 1¼ cups

This sweetly spiced sauce makes a perfect glaze for Cornish hens, duck, and grilled pork. It is also an excellent dipping sauce for satays and other kebabs.

1 10-ounce jar plum jam or preserves 1 tablespoon dry white wine or fresh lemon juice	½ teaspoon cinnamon ¼ teaspoon powdered ginger ⅛ teaspoon ground cloves

1. In a small saucepan, heat jam over medium heat, stirring occasionally, until melted and warm, 2 to 3 minutes.

2. Add remaining ingredients and stir to blend well. Simmer 2 minutes. If using as a glaze, let cool slightly before brushing over meat.

343 CAJUN SPICE BLEND
Prep: 5 minutes   Cook: none   Makes: ⅔ cup

Rub this on food to be grilled, or mix it with a bit of oil and brush over poultry or fish kebabs. It's also great sprinkled on buttered popcorn.

2 tablespoons cayenne 2 tablespoons paprika 2 tablespoons garlic powder 1 tablespoon dried oregano leaves 1 tablespoon dried thyme leaves	1 tablespoon onion powder 1 tablespoon salt ½ teaspoon freshly ground white pepper ½ teaspoon freshly ground black pepper

Combine all ingredients and whisk by hand to blend, or whirl together in food processor or blender. Store in an airtight container.

344 ONION SAUCE
Prep: 5 minutes   Cook: 10 minutes   Makes: 1¼ cups

Here's a zesty condiment that's especially good with beef and pork.

3 tablespoons butter
⅓ cup finely chopped onion
⅓ cup finely chopped green pepper
¾ cup ketchup

2 tablespoons brown sugar
1 teaspoon prepared white horseradish
½ teaspoon salt

1. Melt butter in a large skillet over medium heat. Add onion and green pepper and cook, stirring frequently, until soft but not browned, about 5 minutes.

2. Stir in ketchup, brown sugar, horseradish, and salt. Simmer, stirring frequently, 5 minutes.

Chapter 11

Hot and Sweet

If the fire's still going, why not use your barbecue to prepare dessert? Fruits are especially good on the grill, because their natural sugar caramelizes over the coals.

Here's an assortment of imaginative ideas for everything from apples and bananas to pineapple and strawberries. Turn store-bought poundcake into a toasty sundae, or glaze it with chocolate and a whisper of raspberry.

Enjoy those last embers, just as you did the campfires of your childhood, and if the spirit moves you, get out those sticks and rustle up S'Mores.

345 SCALLOPED APPLES WITH RAISINS
Prep: 10 minutes   Cook: 20 to 30 minutes   Serves: 6 to 8

This is delicious over ice cream or simply served on its own.

2 **20-ounce cans apple slices, drained**	⅛ **teaspoon salt**
¼ **cup raisins**	¼ **teaspoon ground cinnamon**
1 **tablespoon lemon juice**	¼ **teaspoon ground cloves**
¼ **cup (packed) brown sugar**	3 **tablespoons chilled butter, cut into small bits**
2 **tablespoons flour**	**Optional: Vanilla ice cream**

1. Prepare a medium fire. In a large bowl, toss apples with raisins and lemon juice. Place apple slices on a double thickness of 18-inch square heavy-duty aluminum foil. In a small bowl, combine brown sugar, flour, salt, cinnamon, cloves, and butter; sprinkle over apple mixture. Fold edges over and crimp to seal.

2. Place foil package on a grill set 4 to 6 inches from coals. Cook, turning over once or twice, until heated through, about 20 to 30 minutes. Serve over ice cream, if desired.

346 EVE'S DILEMMA
Prep: 5 minutes   Cook: 30 to 40 minutes   Serves: 1

1 tart apple, such as Granny
    Smith or Pippin, cored
1 teaspoon finely chopped
    walnuts or pecans
1 tablespoon brown sugar

1 teaspoon currants or raisins
1 tablespoon unsalted butter,
    plus softened butter or oil
    for foil

1. Prepare a medium fire. Butter or oil an 8-inch piece of heavy-duty aluminum foil. Place apple on center of foil and fill with walnuts, brown sugar, and raisins. Top with butter. Fold edges to make a secure package.

2. Cook foil package on grill, turning occasionally, until apple is tender when pierced with a knife, about 30 to 40 minutes.

347 BANANAS IN BLACK
Prep: 2 minutes   Cook: 45 minutes   Serves: 6

Serve these as you would baked potatoes: make an incision through the skin to season and fluff up the flesh with a bit of butter. They are wonderful as dessert or with grilled dark meat poultry or curried meats.

6 slightly underripe bananas
6 tablespoons Honey Butter
    (recipe follows) or
    unsalted butter

1. Prepare a medium fire or use an existing fire. Place unpeeled bananas on an oiled grill set 4 to 6 inches from coals. Cook, turning frequently, until skin is blackened and bananas are quite tender when pierced with the tip of a knife, about 45 minutes.

2. Make a 3-inch lengthwise slit in each banana and squeeze the ends a bit to expose the fruit within the skin. Top with a pat of Honey Butter.

HONEY BUTTER

8 tablespoons (1 stick)
    unsalted butter, softened

¼ to ⅓ cup honey, to taste

1. In a food processor or blender, combine butter and honey. Process until thoroughly mixed. Pack into crocks, or refrigerate until barely firm and form into 1 or 2 cylinders on plastic wrap; roll up and twist ends to seal.

2. Refrigerate for up to 10 days or freeze for months.

348 CHIQUITA'S REVENGE
Prep: 5 minutes   Cook: 10 to 15 minutes   Serves: 1

This is delicious by itself or celestial when topped with a dab of sweetened whipped cream.

1 medium banana, slightly underripe	Optional: 2 teaspoons dark rum
1½ teaspoons fresh lemon juice	Sweetened whipped cream
1 tablespoon brown sugar	or vanilla ice cream
1 tablespoon chilled butter, cut into bits, plus softened butter or oil for foil	

1. Prepare a medium fire. Butter or oil an 8-inch piece of heavy-duty aluminum foil. Peel banana and cut into ¼-inch diagonal slices; place in center of foil. Sprinkle with lemon juice and brown sugar and dot with butter. Sprinkle with rum, if desired. Fold edges to make a secure package.

2. Place package on grill and cook, turning once or twice, until sugar has carmelized and bananas are tender, about 10 to 15 minutes. Top with sweetened whipped cream or vanilla ice cream.

---

349 BREAKFAST GOES BANANAS
Prep: 10 minutes   Cook: 4 minutes   Serves: 4

Here's the perfect finale to a tropical dinner for dessert-loving friends. Heat commercially made frozen waffles in your toaster to make last-minute assembly a breeze.

¼ cup maple syrup	Vanilla ice cream, whipped
4 small firm ripe bananas	cream, or sour cream
4 tablespoons butter, melted	¼ cup coarsely chopped
4 waffles, heated	macadamia nuts

1. Prepare a medium-hot fire or use an existing fire. Warm maple syrup in a small saucepan set on edge of grill.

2. Peel bananas and cut lengthwise in half. Brush with melted butter and place on an oiled grill set 4 to 6 inches from coals. Grill, brushing with butter and carefully turning once, until bananas are browned outside and just tender, about 4 minutes.

3. To assemble each serving, place 2 grilled banana halves crisscrossed on top of a waffle to form an *X*. Top with a scoop of ice cream (or whipped cream or sour cream), drizzle with warm maple syrup, and sprinkle with macadamia nuts.

350   CHARCOAL-TOASTED POUNDCAKE WITH FRESH FRUIT AND WHIPPED CREAM

Prep: 10 minutes   Cook: 3 to 4 minutes   Serves: 6 to 8

Use those still-glowing embers to toast this dessert after a grilled dinner.

1 poundcake, homemade or
  purchased
4 tablespoons unsalted butter,
  melted

2½ cups fresh fruit slices, such
   as peaches or nectarines
   Sweetened whipped cream

1. Prepare a medium-hot charcoal fire or use an existing fire that has burned a little past white hot. Clean grill with a wire brush to remove any food or ash particles.

2. Cut cake into 8 slices ½ to ¾ inch thick and brush both sides with melted butter. Grill buttered cake slices 4 to 6 inches from coals, turning once, until lightly browned, about 1½ to 2 minutes per side. Transfer to serving plates and garnish with fresh fruit and whipped cream.

351   POUNDCAKE SUNDAE

Prep: 10 minutes   Cook: 3 to 4 minutes   Serves: 6 to 8

½ cup seedless jam, such as
  apricot or strawberry
1 tablespoon liqueur, such as
  amaretto or kirsch
1 poundcake, homemade or
  purchased

4 tablespoons unsalted butter,
  melted
1 pint vanilla ice cream
⅓ cup coarsely chopped
  toasted almonds

1. Prepare a medium-hot charcoal fire or use an existing fire that has burned a little past white hot. Clean grill with a wire brush to remove any food or ash particles. Heat jam and liqueur in a small pan on side of grill, stirring occasionally, until melted and smooth.

2. Cut cake into 8 slices ½ to ¾ inch thick and brush both sides with melted butter. Grill buttered cake slices 4 to 6 inches from coals, turning once, until lightly browned, about 1½ to 2 minutes per side. Transfer to serving plates and top poundcake with a scoop of vanilla ice cream, 1 tablespoon jam sauce, and about 2 teaspoons toasted almonds.

352 SUNSHINE POUNDCAKE
Prep: 5 minutes   Cook: 3 to 4 minutes   Serves: 6 to 8

1 poundcake, homemade or purchased	½ cup lemon curd, purchased or homemade
4 tablespoons unsalted butter, melted	Fresh strawberries

1. Prepare a medium-hot charcoal fire or use an existing fire that has burned a little past white hot. Clean grill with a wire brush to remove any food or ash particles.

2. Cut cake into 8 slices ½ to ¾ inch thick and brush both sides with melted butter. Grill buttered cake slices 4 to 6 inches from coals, turning once, until lightly browned, about 1½ to 2 minutes per side. Transfer to serving plates and spread each slice with 1 tablespoon lemon curd. Garnish with fresh strawberries.

---

353 CHOCOLATE-RASPBERRIED POUNDCAKE
Prep: 10 minutes   Cook: 2 to 4 minutes   Serves: 6 to 8

1 pint fresh raspberries, or 1 10-ounce package unsweetened frozen raspberries, thawed	2 tablespoons unsalted butter, melted
1 to 2 tablespoons sugar	⅓ cup mini chocolate chips
1 poundcake, homemade or purchased	Optional: Fresh raspberries

1. In a food processor or blender, combine raspberries with 1 to 2 tablespoons sugar to taste and purée until smooth. Cover and refrigerate raspberry purée until serving time.

2. Prepare a medium-hot fire or use an existing fire that has burned a little past white-hot. Clean grill with a wire brush to remove any food or ash particles. Shortly before grilling, cover each of 6 to 8 dessert plates with 1 to 2 tablespoons raspberry purée.

3. Cut cake into 8 slices ½ to ¾ inch thick and brush both sides with melted butter. Place on grill set 4 to 6 inches from coals and grill until lightly browned on bottom, about 1 to 2 minutes.

4. Turn cake over and immediately sprinkle about 2 mini chocolate chips over each slice. Use a knife or long metal spatula to gently spread chips over cake as they melt. Grill until second side is lightly browned, about 1 to 2 minutes longer. Set cake on raspberry purée and garnish with fresh raspberries, if desired.

354 TIPSY POUNDCAKE
Prep: 5 minutes   Cook: 3 to 4 minutes   Serves: 6 to 8

1 poundcake, homemade or
   purchased
4 tablespoons unsalted butter,
   melted

⅓ cup cream sherry or other
   sweet wine
Sweetened whipped cream
   or powdered sugar

1. Prepare a medium-hot charcoal fire or use an existing fire that has burned a little past white hot. Clean grill with a wire brush to remove any food or ash particles.

2. Cut cake into 8 slices ½ to ¾ inch thick and brush both sides with melted butter. Grill buttered cake slices 4 to 6 inches from coals, turning once, until lightly browned, about 1½ to 2 minutes per side. Transfer to serving plates and sprinkle each warm poundcake slice with about 2 teaspoons cream sherry. Top with a dollop of sweetened whipped cream or a dusting of powdered sugar.

355 GRILLED FRUIT WITH CREAMY PEANUT SAUCE
Prep: 15 minutes   Cook: 5 minutes   Serves: 6

1 cup low-fat vanilla yogurt
2 tablespoons creamy peanut
   butter
½ cup orange juice
1 tablespoon sugar
1 medium pineapple, peeled
   and cut into 1-inch slices

2 bananas, cut into quarters
2 cups large fresh strawberries
2 tablespoons finely chopped
   peanuts

1. Prepare a medium fire. Combine yogurt and peanut butter, mixing well. In another bowl, combine orange juice and sugar, stirring until sugar is dissolved. Add pineapple slices, bananas, and strawberries to sweetened orange juice and toss gently.

2. Carefully lift fruit from juice and set directly on an oiled grill 6 inches from coals. Grill quickly, taking care when turning fragile fruit, for about 5 minutes, or until fruit is hot and slightly browned.

3. Place grilled fruit into 6 individual serving dishes, spoon yogurt-peanut butter mixture over top, and sprinkle with chopped peanuts.

356 GINGERED NECTARINE ICE CREAM SAUCE
Prep: 10 minutes   Cook: 20 to 25 minutes   Makes: 2 cups

1 pound nectarines
3 tablespoons lemon juice
1½ cups honey

1 tablespoon chopped
  candied ginger

1. Pit and chop nectarines.

2. Prepare a medium fire. In a medium bowl, combine chopped nectarines, lemon juice, honey, and candied ginger. Place nectarine mixture on a double thickness of 18-inch square heavy-duty aluminum foil. Fold edges over and crimp to seal.

3. Place package on a grill set 6 inches from coals. Cook, turning once or twice, until heated through, about 20 to 25 minutes.

357 MAPLE-GLAZED PINEAPPLE
Prep: 10 minutes   Cook: 10 minutes   Serves: 4

1 medium pineapple
4 tablespoons butter

¼ cup maple syrup or honey

1. Prepare a medium fire. Submerge whole pineapple in water for 10 minutes to moisten fronds so they don't burn. In a small pan on side of grill, melt butter and stir in maple syrup. Remove pineapple from water and cut into quarters, slicing off wedge of fibrous core, leaving the fronds on.

2. Place pineapple quarters on an oiled grill and cook, turning and basting with maple butter, until golden brown, about 10 minutes.

358 SPICED PLUM ICE CREAM SAUCE
Prep: 10 minutes   Cook: 20 to 25 minutes   Makes: 2 cups

2 pounds plums
3 tablespoons lemon juice

1½ cups honey
½ teaspoon cinnamon

1. Pit and chop plums.

2. Prepare a medium fire. In a medium bowl, combine chopped plums, lemon juice, honey, and cinnamon. Place plum mixture on a double thickness of 18-inch square heavy-duty aluminum foil. Fold edges over and crimp to seal.

3. Place package on grill set 6 inches from coals. Cook, turning once or twice, until heated through, about 20 to 25 minutes.

359   SNAPPY PEACHES
Prep: 5 minutes   Cook: 5 to 8 minutes   Serves: 6

6 gingersnaps, crushed
1½ teaspoons sugar
¼ teaspoon ground cinnamon
6 canned peach halves

3 tablespoons unsalted butter, melted
6 scoops of vanilla ice cream

1. Prepare a medium fire. Combine gingersnap crumbs, sugar, and cinnamon. Place peach halves on a 12-inch rectangle of heavy-duty aluminum foil. Fill each peach cavity with crumb mixture, then drizzle with butter. Top package with another rectangle of foil; fold and crimp edges to seal well.

2. Place package on grill 6 inches from coals. Grill without turning until thoroughly heated, about 5 to 8 minutes. Remove from heat, place each peach half in a bowl, and top with a scoop of vanilla ice cream.

360   PEACHY KEEN ICE CREAM SAUCE
Prep: 10 minutes   Cook: 20 to 25 minutes   Makes: 2 cups

1 pound ripe peaches
3 tablespoons lemon juice
1½ cups honey

¼ teaspoon ground ginger
¼ teaspoon ground allspice

1. Bring a large saucepan of water to a boil over high heat. Drop in peaches and boil 1 to 2 minutes, until skins loosen. Drain into a colander. Peel and finely chop peaches.

2. Prepare a medium fire. In a medium bowl, combine chopped peaches, lemon juice, honey, ginger, and allspice. Place peach mixture on a double thickness of 18-inch square heavy-duty aluminum foil. Fold edges over and crimp to seal.

3. Place package on a grill set 6 inches from coals. Cook, turning once or twice, until heated through, about 20 to 25 minutes.

361 GLAZED PEACH KEBABS
Prep: 10 minutes   Cook: 10 minutes   Serves: 4

Serve these warm on top of vanilla ice cream.

4 large firm peaches	1 tablespoon peach brandy or
¼ cup fresh lemon juice	orange juice
4 tablespoons butter	Optional: Vanilla ice cream

1. Prepare a medium fire. Peel peaches, cut into 6 wedges, and place in a bowl. Toss with lemon juice. Place butter and peach brandy in a small saucepan and warm on edge of grill. If using bamboo skewers, soak in water at least 30 minutes to prevent burning.

2. Thread peaches on skewers and place on an oiled grill. Cook, turning once and basting until browned outside but not too soft, about 10 minutes. Serve peaches by themselves or with vanilla ice cream.

362 CHILLED GRILLED ORANGES IN MARSALA SYRUP
Prep: 15 minutes   Cook: 17 minutes   Marinate: 2 hours
Serves: 8 to 10

Zest of 1 orange, cut into very thin strips	2½ cups sweet Marsala wine
8 medium navel oranges	⅓ cup orange-flavored liqueur, such as Triple Sec
2 tablespoons butter, melted	2 cinnamon sticks
1 cup sugar	

1. Prepare a hot fire or use an existing fire. In a small saucepan, bring 2 cups water to a boil. Add orange zest and boil for 3 minutes. Drain and rinse under cold running water; drain well. Pat dry on paper towels. Set orange zest aside.

2. Slice off ends from oranges and peel away all skin and white pith. Cut oranges crosswise into ¼-inch-thick rounds. Reserve any juice in a large heatproof bowl. Brush orange slices with butter and place on an oiled grill, turning once, until lightly browned outside, about 3 to 4 minutes. Transfer to the heatproof bowl.

3. In a medium nonreactive saucepan, combine sugar, Marsala, orange liqueur, and cinnamon sticks. Bring to a boil over medium heat and cook until sauce has a slightly syrupy consistency, about 10 minutes. Stir in reserved orange zest.

4. Pour syrup over grilled orange slices. Stir gently to combine with any juice in bowl. Cover and refrigerate 2 hours, until chilled, or up to 3 days. Discard cinnamon sticks before serving.

363 HOT POT CHOCOLATE FONDUE
Prep: 10 minutes   Cook: 5 to 10 minutes   Serves: 8 to 12

Prepare the fruit and cake ahead and put the ingredients for the fondue in the pot. Then enjoy the rest of your dinner and put this on the grill when the fire is almost out.

1 12-ounce bag semisweet chocolate chips
¼ cup heavy cream
1 tablespoon Grand Marnier or Tia Maria
3 cups assorted fruit: orange sections, strawberries, banana chunks, fresh or dried apricot halves, apple or peach wedges

1 cup cubed poundcake, or 8 to 12 ladyfingers

1. Use the end of an existing fire, so the heat is very low. In a fondue pot or a medium enameled or stainless steel heavy saucepan with a heatproof handle, combine chocolate chips and cream. Set on grill and cook, stirring frequently, until chocolate is melted and mixture is smooth, 5 to 10 minutes. Remove from heat and stir in Grand Marnier or Tia Maria.

2. Use long-handled forks or long thin bamboo skewers to dip fruit and cake into chocolate. If fondue cools and thickens, return to fire for a few minutes to rewarm.

364 JUBILEED CHERRIES
Prep: 10 minutes   Cook: 20 minutes   Serves: 4 to 6

1 16-ounce can pitted sweet or sour red cherries and their juice
2 tablespoons sugar

2 tablespoons kirsch
2 tablespoons brandy
1 tablespoon cornstarch
1 pint vanilla ice cream

1. Prepare a medium fire. In a medium bowl, combine cherries and their juice with sugar, kirsch, brandy, and cornstarch. Stir to dissolve sugar and cornstarch. Place mixture on a double thickness of 18-inch square heavy-duty aluminum foil. Fold edges over and crimp to seal.

2. Place foil package on a grill set 4 to 6 inches from coals. Cook, turning once or twice, until heated through, about 20 minutes. Serve over vanilla ice cream.

365 S'MORES
Prep: 5 minutes   Cook: 2 to 3 minutes   Serves: 4

2 1½-ounce plain chocolate candy bars	8 graham cracker squares
	4 large marshmallows

1. Prepare a medium fire or use an existing fire that has burned a little past white hot. Cut or break candy bars in half crosswise and place 1 square of chocolate on top of each of 4 graham crackers.

2. Thread 1 or 2 marshmallows on long metal skewers (or pointed sticks) and toast directly over glowing coals, turning every few seconds, until golden and bubbly, about 2 to 3 minutes. (If marshmallows ignite, simply blow out the flame—it's part of the fun!)

3. Use a fork to slide 1 marshmallow onto each piece of chocolate, then top with remaining graham crackers to form sandwiches. Gently press together so warmth of marshmallow will soften chocolate. Serve immediately.

Index

About the Author

A native of Missouri, Lonnie Gandara has long been a leading California culinary consultant and professional party planner. With an advanced certificate from the Paris Cordon Bleu, she was well known in San Francisco for her sold-out Bay area grilling course. A former caterer, she has barbecued and grilled all over the world, including Europe, Mexico, Hong Kong, and Bangkok.

Gandara is the author of *Fish and Shellfish* and *Ice Cream* (both for the California Culinary Academy), and *The Complete Poultry Cookbook* (HP Books). She is a member of the International Association of Cooking Professionals, the American Institute of Wine and Food, and the San Francisco Professional Food Society.